BONAVENTURE

GREAT MEDIEVAL THINKERS

Series Editor
Brian Davies
Blackfriars, University of Oxford,
and Fordham University

DUNS SCOTUS
Richard Cross

BERNARD OF CLAIRVAUX
Gillian R. Evans

JOHN SCOTTUS ERIUGENA
Deirdre Carabine

ROBERT GROSSETESTE
James McEvoy

BOETHIUS
John Marenbon

PETER LOMBARD
Philipp W. Rosemann

BONAVENTURE

Christopher M. Cullen

OXFORD
UNIVERSITY PRESS
2006

OXFORD
UNIVERSITY PRESS

Oxford University Press, Inc., publishes works that further
Oxford University's objective of excellence
in research, scholarship, and education.

Oxford   New York
Auckland   Cape Town   Dar es Salaam   Hong Kong   Karachi
Kuala Lumpur   Madrid   Melbourne   Mexico City   Nairobi
New Delhi   Shanghai   Taipei   Toronto

With offices in
Argentina   Austria   Brazil   Chile   Czech Republic   France   Greece
Guatemala   Hungary   Italy   Japan   Poland   Portugal   Singapore
South Korea   Switzerland   Thailand   Turkey   Ukraine   Vietnam

Copyright © 2006 by Oxford University Press, Inc.

Published by Oxford University Press, Inc.
198 Madison Avenue, New York, New York 10016

www.oup.com

Oxford is a registered trademark of Oxford University Press

Library of Congress Cataloging-in-Publication Data
Cullen, Christopher M.
Bonaventure / Christopher M. Cullen.
p. cm.—(Great medieval thinkers)
Includes bibliographical references and index.
ISBN-13: 978-0-19-514925-8; 978-0-19-514926-5 (pbk.)

1. Bonaventure, Saint, Cardinal, ca. 1217–1274.   2. Philosophy,
Medieval.   3. Theology—History—Middle Ages, 600–1500.   I. Title.   II. Series.
B765.B74C85   2006
189'.4—dc22   2005012591

Printed in the United States of America
on acid-free paper

Matri patrique
parentibus optimis

Series Foreword

Many people would be surprised to be told that there *were* any great medieval thinkers. If a *great* thinker is one from whom we can learn today, and if "medieval" serves as an adjective for describing anything which existed from (roughly) the years 600 to 1500 A.D., then, so it is often supposed, medieval thinkers cannot be called "great."

Why not? One answer often given appeals to ways in which medieval authors with a taste for argument and speculation tend to invoke "authorities," especially religious ones. Such invocation of authority is not the stuff of which great thought is made—so it is commonly said today. It is also sometimes said that greatness is not to be found in the thinking of those who lived before the rise of modern science, not to mention that of modern philosophy and theology. Students of science are nowadays hardly ever referred to literature earlier than the seventeenth century. Contemporary students of philosophy in the twentieth century are often taught nothing about the history of ideas between Aristotle (384–322 B.C.) and Descartes (1596–1650). Modern students of theology have often been frequently encouraged to believe that sound theological thinking is a product of the nineteenth century.

Yet the origins of modern science lie in the conviction that the world is open to rational investigation and is orderly rather than chaotic—a conviction that came fully to birth, and was systematically explored and developed, during the middle ages. And it is in medieval thinking that we find some of the most sophisticated and rigorous philosophical and theological discussions ever offered for human consumption—not surprisingly, perhaps, if we note that medieval philosophers and theologians, like their contemporary counterparts, were mostly university teachers who participated in an ongoing worldwide debate. They were not (like many seventeenth, eighteenth, and even nineteenth century philosophers and theologians) people working in relative isolation from a large community of teachers and students with whom they were regularly involved. As for the question of appeal to authority: it is certainly true that many medieval thinkers believed in authority (especially religious authority) as a serious court of appeal. But as many contemporary philosophers are increasingly reminding us, authority is as much an ingredient in our thinking as it was in that of medieval thinkers. Most of what we take ourselves to know derives from the trust we have reposed in our various teachers, colleagues, and friends. When it comes to reliance on authority, the main difference between us and medieval thinkers lies in the fact that their reliance on authority was often more focused and explicitly acknowledged than is ours. It does not lie in the fact that it was uncritical and naive in a way that our reliance on authority is not.

In recent years, such truths have come to be increasingly recognized at what we might call the "academic" level. No longer disposed to think of the Middle Ages as "dark" (meaning "lacking in intellectual richness"), many university departments (and many publishers of books and journals) now devote a lot of their energy to the study of medieval thinking. And they do so, not simply on the assumption that it is historically important, but also in the light of the increasingly developing insight that it is full of things with which to dialogue and from which to learn. Following a long period in which medieval thinking was thought to be of only antiquarian interest, we are now witnessing its revival as a contemporary voice—one to converse with, one from which we might learn.

The *Great Medieval Thinkers* series reflects and is part of this exciting revival. Written by a distinguished team of experts, it aims to provide substantial introductions to a range of medieval authors. And it does so on the assumption that they are as worth reading today as they were when they wrote. Students of medieval "literature" (e.g. the writings of Chaucer) are currently well supplied (if not over-supplied) with secondary works to aid them when reading the objects of their concern. But those with an interest in medieval philosophy and theology are by no means so fortunate when it comes to reliable and accessible volumes. The *Great Medieval Thinkers* series therefore aspires to remedy that deficiency by concentrating on medieval philosophers and theologians, and by offering solid overviews of their lives and thought coupled with contemporary reflection on what they had to say. Taken individually, volumes in the series provide valuable treatments of single thinkers many of whom are not currently covered by any comparable volumes. Taken together, they constitute a rich and distinguished history and discussion of medieval philosophy and theology considered as a whole. With an eye on college and university students, and with an eye on the general reader, authors of volumes in the series strive to write in a clear and accessible manner so that each of the thinkers they write on can be learned about by those who have no previous knowledge about them. But each contributor to the series also intends to inform, engage, and generally entertain, even those with specialist knowledge in the area of medieval thinking. So, as well as surveying and introducing, volumes in the series seek to advance the state of medieval studies both at the historical and the speculative level.

The subject of the present volume (sometimes referred to as the *Doctor Seraphicus*) is, perhaps, currently one of the best known and most studied of medieval thinkers—along with authors such as Anselm, Aquinas, and Scotus. Working roughly in the middle of the thirteenth century, he taught at the University of Paris and played a major role in the development of the Franciscan Order, founded by Francis of Assisi. Well translated into English and other languages, his writings form part of what we might call the traditional "canon" of medieval philosophical and theological literature. There have, however, been comparatively few attempts on the part of recent scholars to present a study of Bonaventure's thinking in its entirety.

In the present book Christopher Cullen offers us just such a work. Rather than focusing only on select aspects of Bonaventure's writings (though not avoiding attention to details), he invites us to take a bird's-eye view of Bonaventure's writings and invites us to consider them as reflecting or constituting a system of ideas in which parts blend together to form a coherent whole. In particular, and by following Bonaventure's own division of the sciences, he draws our attention to ways in which philosophy and theology come together from Bonaventure's perspective. Though sometimes taken to be a mystic and/or nothing but a theologian, Bonaventure was very much a man of argument and ideas. Whatever else he was, he was also a philosopher who needs to be firmly placed in the scholastic context to which he belonged (something not always properly appreciated). In the pages that follow, Professor Cullen shows us how Bonaventure appears when approached accordingly and with a sense of his ideas as they can be found in writings dating from throughout his career. What does the thought of Bonaventure look like when viewed as a whole? The present volume provides one expert answer to that question.

Brian Davies

Preface

This book is a survey of the thought of Bonaventure. Among the relatively few such surveys, this one attempts something new: to analyze Bonaventure's thought by following his own division of the branches of philosophy and theology. Some might say that Bonaventure only wrote theological texts and any attempt to provide a separate account of his philosophy is doomed to falsify his thought. I disagree with this contention, and believe that considerable weight should be given to Bonaventure's views on the division and methods of the arts and sciences as he presents them in his treatise, *On the Reduction of the Arts to Theology* (*De reductione artium ad theologiam*). In this important text, Bonaventure himself clearly regards philosophy and theology as distinct fields of study, and even though he did not write strictly philosophical texts, he did provide a great many philosophical arguments in the course of his writings, especially in his *Commentary on the Sentences of Peter Lombard*. By "philosophical arguments," I mean those that rely on reason alone and make no use of a premise drawn from revelation in coming to their conclusion.

This is not to say that Bonaventure provides us with a philosophy autonomous from revelation or theology. On the contrary, he attempted what has been called a "Christian philosophy," to borrow a term from the twentieth century's eminent historian of medieval philosophy, Étienne Gilson (1884–1978).[1] Gilson established that medieval thinkers had attempted a philosophy in harmony with Christianity. Of course, it is not easy to say precisely what this means in practice. Such an endeavor stands

or falls on its details, specifically on the relationship between propositions
drawn from what is understood as divine revelation and those drawn from
reason. Bonaventure regards philosophy as dependent on theology (i.e.,
as heteronymous, at least in part), not for its premises, nor even for ac-
complishing its task of attaining wisdom (*pace* many interpreters of Bonaventure), but rather for *fulfilling* its task and bringing it to perfection.
This distinction is perhaps subtle, but absolutely crucial to what he is
trying to accomplish. Bonaventure set a difficult job for himself in thinking that philosophy ought to remain open to theology: for demarcating
the domain of truth (in order to prevent some errors); for prompting the
investigation of questions that would likely otherwise be omitted; and for
leading the mind from a high wisdom that is found in this life in the
practice of theology, to the highest wisdom that is found in the next life
in the beatific vision.

Furthermore, because I follow Bonaventure's ordering of the disciplines
of human knowledge, I believe it would be incorrect to pursue a theological order in the presentation of his philosophy. While it cannot be denied
that he was a theologian and that his writings are theological, Bonaventure nevertheless meticulously outlines the whole range of human knowing, including all the distinct disciplines and the proper order of their
study. This order is not theological, from God to creatures, but philosophical, from creatures to God. Bonaventure's own ordering of the disciplines confirms the validity of Jan Aertsen's recent complaint against
Gilson's adoption of the theological order when explaining medieval philosophy.[2]

Bonaventure's identification of the branches of theology can be found
in his only *summa* of theology, the *Breviloquium*. It is better to follow
Bonaventure's own organization of the discipline of theology in this text
than in his much longer and more comprehensive *Commentary on the
Sentences of Peter Lombard*, wherein Lombard organized the divisions of
theology and therefore considerably bound any commentator.[3]

By utilizing Bonaventure's own division of the branches of philosophy
and theology, I do not follow a chronological order. Besides respecting
the author's own careful division of human knowledge, I agree with Gilson
that there is little, if any, substantial development in Bonaventure's thinking.[4] Bonaventure seems to have thought through the main elements of
his theological system from very early in his career; hence, his *Commentary on the Sentences* should have a priority of place in any accurate reading. This systematic approach is contrary to the developmental approach
advocated by Rufin Silic and subsequently followed by others, but this

book should serve to clarify the substantial unity of Bonaventure's thought across the various stages of his career.[5]

By giving a prominent place to the *Commentary on the Sentences*, I also hope to demystify Bonaventure. Of course, I want to clarify many of his teachings, but I also read Bonaventure, first and foremost, as the Scholastic he was, that is, as a scientific theologian and philosopher, and not as a mystic, or one who regards theological matters to be beyond rational investigation or who relies on intuition rather than argument in matters of theological or philosophical import. Bonaventure the scholastic is found most clearly in his *Commentary*.

My intention here is not to deny that Bonaventure was a mystic or a doctor of the emotions. Bernard McGinn is surely correct in his judgment that "Bernard of Clairvaux and Bonaventure—the *doctor mellifluus* and the *doctor seraphicus*—may be justly described as the two premier mystical teachers of the medieval West."[6] Rather, I wish to show how Bonaventure's mysticism is rooted in his own rigorous and rational investigation of great philosophical and theological issues. Furthermore, while Bonaventure clearly takes seriously the human passions and affections, and like Augustine, views them as having an essential role in human life, his mysticism and "emotionalism" (for lack of a better term) flow from intellectual positions on certain perennial issues, positions that can be subjected to analysis and critique.

There are many stereotypes of Bonaventure. Various authors have presented him as the archvillain in the corruption of the primitive spirit of St. Francis of Assisi (ca. 1182–1226) by institutionalizing Francis's vision, by moderating his understanding of poverty, and by vastly expanding the order's academic orientation. Others have tried to present Bonaventure as purely anti-Aristotelian. Context, however, helps to overcome these stereotypes. For example, while there can be no question that Bonaventure significantly reinforced the intellectual turn that the Franciscan order took in the generation just before him, it is good to keep in mind that it was St. Francis himself who appointed St. Anthony of Padua (1195–1231) the first theologian of the order, and that it was Bonaventure's predecessor as minister general of the Franciscans who accepted into the order the most prominent professor of the day at the University of Paris, Alexander of Hales (ca. 1185–1245). His "anti-Aristotelianism" has to be read in the context of contemporary Averroism. I consistently use such data in an attempt to recontextualize Bonaventure's thought within a complex and dynamic era.

Given that there are so many studies focusing on particular aspects of

Bonaventure's thought, and few that attempt a comprehensive view of either his philosophy or theology, let alone both, this book presents an overview of his synthesis rather than a critical assessment in the light of modern concerns. In attempting to attain this bird's-eye view of Bonaventure's thought, it is not possible, given length constraints, to also provide a running critique. My goal has not been another study of some particular aspect of his thought, nor another critique that compares Bonaventure and Aquinas, or Bonaventure and a modern theologian. Rather, my intention is to offer an intelligent reading that displays something rarely seen, namely, "Bonaventurianism," as a whole, just for itself, and on its own terms—in other words, as an elaborate and sophisticated synthesis, created in a specific historical context.

I first wish to thank Brian Davies, the editor of Oxford University Press's *Great Medieval Thinkers* series for inviting me to write this volume and then encouraging me to complete it. I thank Avery Cardinal Dulles, SJ, for reading part of the manuscript, as well as Joseph Koterski, SJ, for his proofreading of parts and his general encouragement. Especially, I wish to thank Joseph Lienhard, SJ, for meticulously reading parts of this manuscript during its preparation.

Contents

List of Abbreviations

Apol. paup.	Apologia pauperum
Brevil.	Breviloquium
Christus mag.	Sermo Christus unus omnium magister
Comm. Eccl.	Commentarius in librum Ecclesiastes
Comm. Lc.	Commentarius in Evangelium Lucae
Decem praec.	Collationes de decem praeceptis
De donis	Collationes de septem donis Spiritus Sancti
Hexaem.	Collationes in Hexaemeron
Itin.	Itinerarium mentis in Deum
Leg. maj.	Legenda major sancti Francisci
Leg. min.	Legenda minor sancti Francisci
Lign. vit.	Lignum vitae
M. Trin.	Quaestiones disputatae de mysterio Trinitatis
Perf. ev.	Quaestiones disputatae de perfectione evangelica
Red. art.	De reductione atrium ad theologiam
Sc. Chr.	Quaestiones disputatae de scientia Christi
In I, II, II, IV Sent.	Commentarius in I, II, III, IV librum Sententiarum
Solil.	Soliloquium de quatuor mentalibus exercitiis
Trib. qu.	Epistola de tribus quaest.
Triplic. via	De triplici via

I

The Love of Wisdom

Introduction

The Life and Times of Bonaventure

When Bonaventure came to Paris as a young man in his teens, probably in 1234 or 1235, he arrived in a city undergoing extraordinary rebirth. The king of France, Louis IX (r. 1226–1270, canonized in 1297), was transforming Paris—making it the destination for Europe's best and brightest. Artisans were working on completing the Church of Notre Dame in the heart of the city; students were flocking to the city's Left Bank; France's nobles were building townhouses (*hotels*) to be near king and court. This transformation of the capital had begun a generation earlier under Philip II Augustus (r. 1180–1223), the grandfather of Louis IX, when he built a defensive wall around the entire city and paved its streets. Three historic movements—one intellectual, one educational, and one religious—had recently converged on the banks of the Seine when Bonaventure began his new life in Paris.

The first of these movements had put the city in intellectual ferment, the likes of which had not been seen in the West since antiquity: The West had "discovered" Aristotle (384–322 B.C.). It is hard to appreciate the degree to which Aristotle captured the attention of medieval scholars. Although his logical works had been available in translation from late antiquity (thanks to the late Roman translator Boethius [ca. 480–525/6] and others), the major texts of the Aristotelian corpus had begun arriving only in the twelfth century and had continued to be translated in the

3

early decades of the thirteenth century. The explosion of interest in the works of Aristotle seems all the more extraordinary when one considers the relatively lukewarm response that he received in antiquity. Not only had his works come very near to being lost, but even Plotinus (204/5–270), one of the most important thinkers to thoroughly engage Aristotle's ideas, rejected a good many of them. In sharp contrast to this tepid reception in antiquity, Aristotle found generations of enthusiastic readers among the medievals, beginning in the twelfth century. For the first time since the close of classical antiquity, medieval scholars had access to the Greek philosophical heritage.[1] The Greek achievement took their breath away. Indeed, as the thirteenth century wore on, many of them had a tendency to follow the teachings of Aristotle more strictly than those of Christ. It is precisely this latter group of radical Aristotelians, followers of the strict reading of Aristotle by the Arab philosopher Averroes (1126–1198), who dominated the last decade of Bonaventure's life. Indeed, beginning in the 1260s, Bonaventure launched a series of conferences that were blistering attacks on the errors of Aristotle, at least as interpreted by the Averroists. The "anti-Aristotelianism" of these attacks must be carefully situated in their context, so as not lose sight of Bonaventure's extensive debt to Aristotle.

The rediscovery of Aristotle allowed Latin Christianity to renew and vastly expand its appropriation of the Greek philosophical heritage, which found remote warrant in Augustine's (354–430) classic work on education and biblical exegesis, On Christian Doctrine (De doctrina christiana), and built on the proximate foundation laid by twelfth-century schools, especially Hugh of St. Victor's (1096–1141) plan for the reform of education, the Didascalicon. In his influential text, Augustine authorized Christians to take from the philosophers whatever they found true and to make it their own, as the Israelites had despoiled the Egyptians in the Exodus at the command of God. After centuries of interruption, this despoiling, or Christianization, of "the intellectual deposit of the Greco-Roman past" began anew, in the late eleventh-century school of Anselm of Laon (d. 1117), and continued in subsequent generations in the schools of Paris.[2] But Augustine's warrant was limited: The Christian was only to pursue secular subjects to the extent that they contributed to an understanding of scripture.[3] Hugh expanded the warrant: The Christian was to pursue all subjects as a means to restoring the knowledge lost in the Fall.[4] All the arts and sciences are paths to God.[5] The thirteenth-century appropriation of the Aristotelian corpus (and of the Neoplatonic texts that were believed to be a part of this corpus) built on the work of the twelfth-century "renascence" and brought to fruition a new, scientific, and systematic method for practicing philosophy and theology. This scientific method consisted of a dialectical analysis of discordant views through rigorous questioning and examination. Indeed, these new doctrines, examined under this novel method, led to the birth of a new school—Scholasticism. As it has recently been put, Scholasticism's aim was "nothing less than to embrace all knowledge and every kind of activity in a single world-view."[6] The Scholastics found Aristotle to be a kindred spirit in this endeavor; his work constitutes a sort of encyclopedia of knowledge. What is more, the Scholastics found in Aristotle's work the great tool for their endeavor—logic (the title for Aristotle's trilogy of logical works was the "organon" or "tool"). It is difficult to understand the thought of Bonaventure without the larger context of this complex intellectual movement that so shaped the Middle Ages.

The second great movement that Bonaventure encountered in Paris was the recent turn to "universities" for education. For much of the Middle Ages, formal education had primarily taken place in the monastery or in the cathedral school. In fact, the cathedral school at Paris was well known for some of its distinguished teachers, such as William of Champeaux (ca. 1070–1122) and Peter Abelard (1079–1142). In 1200, disputes between students and civil authorities precipitated a crisis. Philip II responded by exempting the masters and students from civil jurisdiction: He granted this community of scholars a charter with special privileges that placed them under the authority of the bishop of Paris and his designated chancellor.[7] This act marks the formation of a semiautonomous corporate body with its own organization and governance, a sort of guild, like the art guilds of the day. "*Universitas*" was the word applied to this body, a word used for any body or association that had an independent juridical status. Another university developed at almost the same time across the English Channel at Oxford, and yet another was to follow not long afterward at Cambridge. Universities eventually arose in towns and cities throughout Europe, ideally having four faculties: arts, law, medicine, and theology. The "central driving force" in the development of these universities was the goal of organizing all knowledge into a systematic and universal account of reality.[8] Bonaventure eventually taught for a time at Paris's university while holding one of the academic chairs there.

The third great movement that Bonaventure encountered in Paris was religious in nature. It began in the spring of 1207, when a young former soldier from the Umbrian town of Assisi heard the painted crucifix in a small church speak to him. This event marked the beginning of a complete conversion of life for Francis Bernardone of Assisi. His father had planned that he would take over the family's cloth business, but Francis instead decided to spend his life imitating Christ as closely as he could. He lived in poverty and chastity and traveled from town to town to preach the Gospel. He quickly attracted followers who also wanted "to walk in Christ's footsteps" (as the earliest rule referred to this way of life), and by 1209, he and his small band of twelve went to Rome in order to obtain the approval of Pope Innocent III. Innocent's approval of their simple rule of life is regarded as the official founding of the Franciscans, or the Order of Friars Minor. Francis inspired a whole movement that was eventually to include three orders: A second order (eventually called the "Poor Clares") began when a friend, Clare of Assisi, asked to embrace his rule of life; and a third order for laypeople, and later clerics, also arose.[9] Francis and his religious orders renewed the whole church.

The Franciscans were part of a larger group of new religious orders that lived in poverty and survived on alms. These "mendicant" orders had an enormous impact on the life of the church, but it was the Friars Minor (as the Franciscans were called to distinguish them from the other mendicant orders, also known as friars)[10] who left an indelible imprint on Catholic Christianity that endures to this day and is felt at every level of the church's life. The Christmas crèche is but one prominent example of Francis's impact on Catholic piety.

The First Order of the Franciscans drew thousands of vocations in its early years. In the spring of 1209, when Pope Innocent III gave official approval to the rule drawn up by Francis, the "poor man" from Assisi had a mere twelve followers. Yet, by the time of a general chapter, held twelve years later in 1221, some three thousand friars attended. By the death of Francis in 1226, it has been calculated that there were some five thousand friars.[11] By 1242, there were more than thirty Franciscan convents in France alone; by 1256, thirty-two years after the arrival of the first Franciscans in England, there were forty-nine convents in England with 1,242 friars.[12] The growth continued throughout the thirteenth century; some estimates put their worldwide numbers by 1300 between thirty and forty thousand.[13] Franciscans gained influence at all levels of society, from the humblest to the highest. The king of France, Louis IX, for example, was a member of the Franciscans' lay fraternity (or "third order") and had himself buried in the robes of a Franciscan.

Unlike monks, the First Order of Franciscans did not commit themselves to stability, that is, living in one place, but moved about as their apostolic work demanded. They often lived in cities, where they preached and administered the sacraments in urban churches. Innocent III and his successor, Honorius III, eventually found in the Franciscans a model of the apostolic life (*vita apostolica*, or the life of the apostles).[14] Thirteenth-century popes relied more and more on the new mendicant orders to revivify Christian life and to enact the pastoral program set down by the most important of all the medieval church councils, Lateran IV, which Innocent himself presided over in 1215. Indeed, the papacy's trust in the Franciscans can be seen in the increasing number of Francis's followers who were promoted to the episcopacy (at least forty in the eighteen years between 1243 and 1261).[15]

Lateran IV set down a vast renewal program for the whole Christian life. Among its more important provisions, it mandated that every Catholic receive communion and go to confession at least once a year: "All the faithful of either sex, after they have reached the age of discernment, should individually confess all their sins in a faithful manner to their own priest at least once a year, and let them take care to do what they can to perform penance imposed on them. Let them reverently receive the sacrament of the eucharist at least at Easter."[16] The mendicant orders provided the papacy with the means of implementing this pastoral program by taking up two fundamental duties: preaching and hearing confessions. Both duties required education, as the council fathers had clearly realized in their renewed call for the establishment of schools in episcopal and monastic centers. And so, the mendicant orders, especially the Dominicans and Franciscans, began to establish a system of schools for training the friars.[17]

Francis had been wary of learning and studies—in his seventh admonition, he warns about the danger of wanting knowledge for the sake of being thought wiser than others[18]—but as the friars became more involved in the Lateran IV reforms, the necessity of acquiring at least a basic knowledge of the Bible and the church fathers became clear. Hence, certain friaries were to have a *lector* (lecturer) responsible for the education of the brethren. The first lector and the first to teach theology in a friary was Anthony of Padua, a Portuguese and one-time Augustinian canon who joined the Franciscans.[19] Anthony would not take up the task of teaching theology until he received Francis's permission. In giving it, however, Francis added the proviso that he "not extinguish the Spirit of prayer and devotion."[20] Anthony's appointment as a teacher of theology in the friary marks the earliest beginning of what would eventually become a network of Franciscan theological centers, consisting both of *studia generalia* (within nearly every province) and convent schools, run by a lector, who lectured to all friars, including those preparing for more advanced studies. (Only a select few, Bonaventure among them, would be sent to study at one of the three principal *studia generalia* for all of Europe, that is, Paris, Oxford, and Cambridge.)[21]

Bonaventure has said that he loved the life of Francis, because it seemed like the early church of the simple fishermen. He saw in the life of the early Franciscans clear evidence of the order being a divine work, rather than a product of human prudence.

For the next four decades, after his arrival in Paris, Bonaventure played a central role in all of these great medieval movements—Aristotelianism and Scholasticism, the university, and Franciscanism.

Yet, for all of the influence that these new movements had on Bonaventure, his thought remained firmly rooted in that intellectual giant from late antiquity who so shaped the whole of medieval life and culture, namely, Augustine of Hippo. Augustine remained the predominant influence, outside the Bible, on Bonaventure's thought, both philosophically and theologically. It was an Augustine read through the eyes of Anselm of Canterbury (1033–1109) and Hugh of St. Victor (1096–1141). Nevertheless, it is precisely this allegiance to Augustine on a number of key points that helps render Bonaventure "the most medieval" of thinkers, as Gilson so aptly proclaimed him in his book on Bonaventure's philosophy.[22]

No contemporary accounts of Bonaventure's life have come down to us. A biography written in the thirteenth century by Zamorra, a Spanish Franciscan, is lost.[23] The earliest biography still extant was written by Mariano of Florence at the end of the fifteenth century, almost two hundred years after Bonaventure's death. An important source of information is an account of him in the Chronicle of the Twenty-four Generals. This work concerns the ministers general of the Franciscans and dates from circa 1369; it incorporates an earlier text written in the thirteenth century by Bernard of Besse (fl. ca. 1283), who was a secretary-companion of Bonaventure for a time.[24]

The lack of biographical materials, however, does not prevent us from reconstructing the main events of his life. He was, after all, minister general of the largest religious order of his day and a widely known doctor of theology who inspired a whole generation of Augustinians. Some specific dates in the life Bonaventure are known with certitude: the date of his election as general of the Franciscan order (1257) and the date of his death while attending the second Council of Lyons (1274). Although other exact dates are subject to dispute, the sequence of major events in Bonaventure's life is generally clear. Since a near-contemporary document tells us that he died at age fifty-three, and we know the year of his death, it has usually been thought that he was born in 1221.[25] Some scholars in recent decades have challenged this traditional date, however, arguing that his birth must be no later than 1217, but there is still solid evidence for it. Those who defend the earlier date of birth point to university statutes that require those teaching theology to be thirty-five years old, and to rules of the Franciscan order that require the minister general to have attained his fortieth year. Since Bonaventure became a master of theology in 1253 and was elected minister general in 1257, these scholars argue that he must have been born by 1217 (*terminus ante quem*) to reach the minimum age for these two events. However, Theodore Crowley has pointed out that the university statute in question dates from 1215 and thus may not have applied thirty-five years later, and the Franciscan rule in question dates from the seventeenth-century *Consitutiones Urbanae* (1628), and may also not apply, even if these constitutions did codify nearly a century of practice.[26] Crowley's chronology defends the traditional date of 1221 for Bonaventure's birth, has him entering the order in 1238 at the young age of seventeen, receiving the license in 1245, and becoming a master in 1248.[27]

Bonaventure was born in a small town in the hills of Lazio, named Bagnoregio.[28] Bagnoregio rises on a towering hill above a sweeping landscape of jagged peaks of white volcanic stone (*tufa*) set against the backdrop of the dark, looming Appenine Mountains on the horizon. These white hills (called *calanchi*) are, in essence, piles of solidified lava formed from a series of volcanic eruptions seven hundred thousand years ago.[29] Sheer cliffs sweep down from Bagnoregio's walls into the deep surrounding valley below, drained by streams and covered with trees and shrubs. These peculiar white hills make the rugged setting of this isolated Lazian hill town look like something from another planet; its piercing beauty is haunting and otherworldly—a truly ethereal setting, fit for the birthplace of one of the great mystics of the medieval world.

Bagnoregio's name derives from *Balneum regis* (bath of the king), which refers to hot springs that were nearby. The Etruscans were among the first to settle in these hills, and the town of *Balneum regis* arose on the basic outlines of the Etruscan village. The Goths, the Byzantines, and the Lombards all occupied the town at one point or another. In the eighth century, this area became part of the Papal States, as it was when Bonaventure was born. Today, a lone, steep donkey trail leads up to the medieval town, which remains largely unchanged except for the parts that have disappeared in earthquakes. Visitors enter through the arched Gate of Santa Maria into narrow, cobblestone streets lined with medieval houses. At the center of town, where the north-south and east-west axis first traced by the Etruscans is found, the streets open onto a piazza, bordered on one side with the town's one-time cathedral of San Donato, on another by the Palazzo del Comune (town hall), and on still another by the palazzi of the nobles. The house where Bonaventure lived was but a few steps from this piazza; it is long since gone, destroyed when it slid into the valley below in a 1695 earthquake. A small stone plaque on the edge of town marks the site.

Bonaventure's father was Giovanni di Fidanza; his mother was Maria di Ritello. Mariano says that Bonaventure's father practiced medicine. At baptism, Bonaventure received his father's name, Giovanni; he apparently received the name "Bonaventure" after entering the Franciscans. Almost nothing is known of Bonaventure's childhood. In writing of his own life with regard to Saint Francis, Bonaventure relates that he suffered from a very grave illness as a child and that it was the intercession of the saint obtained through his mother's prayers that miraculously saved him.[30] It is claimed that Francis himself preached in Bagnoregio and founded its friary, the Convent of San Francesco, which was located in a section of the town now lost.[31] According to testimony for Bonaventure's canonization, he received his early education with the Franciscans in his hometown at their friary.[32]

As mentioned, in 1234–1235 as a teenager, Bonaventure set off for studies in Paris. While at the University of Paris, he encountered a well-known professor, Alexander of Hales (ca. 1185–1245),[33] who became Bonaventure's principal and most influential teacher. We know that Alexander had significant influence on Bonaventure from the latter's own pen: Bonaventure calls him "master and father,"[34] and says that he considers himself a continuator of Alexander's work.[35]

Alexander of Hales is an important and influential figure in the thirteenth century: first, because he made extensive use of philosophy in his theological work in order to engage many speculative questions in the sacred science, and also because he exercised considerable influence upon the early Franciscan school. He flourished at a pivotal time, when the university was in its infancy and when the entire Aristotelian corpus had begun arriving in Latin Europe.

Alexander also studied in Paris and completed his master of arts degree before 1210 and his master of theology before 1220. Throughout most of his academic career he was a secular priest, but in 1236, when he was at least fifty, he joined the recently founded Franciscan order. (The Franciscans had arrived in Paris in 1217.)[36] When he joined the order, he retained (amidst some controversy) his position as regent master (*magister regens*) in the university. Alexander consequently became the first Franciscan to hold a chair at the University of Paris.

Alexander was one of the earliest theologians to engage the thought of Aristotle at the recently founded University of Paris. His effort to engage Aristotle was rigorous; he quotes from all the Stagirite's major texts.[37] In this regard, Alexander was on the cutting edge of the scholarship of his day; yet, he remains fundamentally an Augustinian on a whole range of issues. Indeed, Alexander has long been regarded as the font for what is commonly referred to as "the Augustinian school." It is commonly held that there were four high-medieval schools: Franciscan Augustinianism (divided into three currents), Christian Aristotelianism (Thomism), Averroistic Aristotelianism, and scientifico-physical Augustinianism.[38] Alexander shaped the early Franciscan school and its Augustinian orientation.

At the same time, Alexander's reading of Augustine is nearly always through the eyes of Anselm. Anselm was largely neglected in the twelfth century, but this neglect dissipated in the thirteenth, thanks in no small part to the influence of Alexander, and later to Bonaventure and Aquinas.[39] Particularly significant for the Franciscans is that Alexander will read Aristotle while remaining fundamentally convinced of an Anselmian Augustinianism.

Alexander is not the only Franciscan who influenced Bonaventure in Paris. Jean de la Rochelle (d. 1245), who was Alexander's successor as regent master in the Franciscan chair, also had an influence on Bonaventure, as did Odo Rigaud (d. 1274), Rochelle's successor, and Rigaud's successor, William of Melitona. Bonaventure also came under the influence of the Dominican, Guerric of Saint-Quentin, and the secular master, Guiard of Laon.

The exact date of Bonaventure's entrance into the order is not known. Some have maintained that he entered in 1238, others 1243.[40] If he entered in 1238, it would have been at the very young age of seventeen,[41] and he would have just finished his master of arts degree in that same year. Those scholars who disagree with this dating think that Bonaventure became a master of arts in 1242 and entered the order in 1243. Regardless of the date, he would have done his novitiate in Paris, even though he was a member of the Roman Province.

In 1250, Bonaventure began his *Commentary on the Sentences of Peter Lombard*. He likely received his license to teach theology in 1254. Bonaventure's entrance into the guild of masters of theology was scheduled for 1254, but it was delayed until October 1257 because of a dispute between the secular and the mendicant masters. Bonaventure's inception into the guild of masters came about only as a result of papal intervention. In August 1257, Bonaventure and his colleague, Thomas Aquinas, formally took possession of their chairs in theology at the university. The question of Bonaventure's formal entrance into the university faculty was a moot point by October of that year, however, because in February, a general chapter of the Franciscans had elected him the eighth minister general of the order.

Bonaventure became the leader of a dynamic order, but one that was facing several grave problems. First of all, Bonaventure's predecessor, John Buralli of Parma, faced a heresy trial and resigned the generalship rather than drag the whole order under suspicion. John of Parma had come under the influence of the writings of a twelfth-century monk by the name of Joachim of Fiore (d. 1202), whose writings had become popular around mid-century among many Franciscans. These writings are filled with apocalyptic ideas that led a great many of the Spirituals into believing that the age of the church was giving way to an age of the spirit, inaugurated by the coming of Francis.

When Bonaventure became minister general, the order was somewhat divided, though not nearly as much as it would be in the decades after his death. One group, which would later harden their positions and come to be known as the Spirituals, fought against any mitigations of the rule, especially with regard to property. Another group, later referred to as the Conventuals, constituted the majority of the order and was generally inclined to accept various permissions from the popes that allowed the order the "use" of property. However, these groups did not yet possess the fixed positions that would develop later in the century, and care must be taken not to read back into this period the positions of the Spirituals and Conventuals.

Bonaventure did nothing to abrogate the earlier decision of a general chapter to suspend papal bulls relaxing the observance of poverty on various points.[42] He did, however, try to mitigate the observance of poverty where it interfered with the possibility of learning in houses of study.[43]

We can find the intellectual basis for Bonaventure's moderating approach in a series of early *Disputed Questions on Evangelical Perfection* delivered in 1256 at the beginning of the academic year at Paris. In these, Bonaventure defends mendicant poverty against the vigorous attacks of certain secular priests, led by William of St. Amour (1200–1272). For Francis, poverty was the defining characteristic in his life of imitating Christ; to imitate Christ is, above all, to be poor. It was his central passion, as can be seen in his repeated reference to "Lady Poverty." "So much importance did he attach to the principle of poverty that he made it a particular sign of Christ."[44] In this way, poverty becomes a sort of end in itself.

In his *Disputed Questions*, Bonaventure gently but unambiguously corrects the beloved founder's extreme, if not dangerously enthusiastic, claims for poverty. Bonaventure recontextualizes poverty in the whole Christian life. Poverty is carefully presented, not as an end in itself, but as a particularly effective means to insuring two essential Christian virtues: (1) the fundamental humility that every Christian should have before God, and (2) the charity that is the Christian life. In other words, Bonaventure subordinates poverty to the absolutely foundational virtues of humility and charity.

He does this by arguing that the summary of the whole of Christian perfection consists in humility.[45] This fundamental humility involves the exterior and interior vilification of oneself, that is, the recognition of one's own nothingness as a creature: "Therefore, since all things, which have been made, abide by the one principle and were produced from nothing, that man is truly wise who really recognizes the nothingness (nihilitatem) of himself and of others, and the sublimity of the first principle."[46] This foundational humility is essential to living the Christian life; indeed, it is the truth on which the Christian builds his life. If there is a reason why the Christian renounces temporal goods, it is that he has seen the nothingness of creation.

Furthermore, religious poverty is a means to growth in charity. It is the principium fundamentale, or fundamental principle, precisely because it involves a complete renunciation of cupidity as the great obstacle, and ever-present danger, to love or caritas. Cupidity is so pernicious because it locks people within a cycle of selfish love that prevents them from going out to neighbor and to God. Poverty then becomes the Christian's best defense against cupidity.

Another problem that Bonaventure faced was the sheer shize of the order with thousands of friars divided into thirty-six provinces. Bonaventure's letters from early in his generalship indicate his keen awareness of the problems facing the relatively new order. He did much to keep different groups of Franciscans together, one of the many reasons that have led a majority of Franciscan historians to regard Bonaventure's generalate as a blessing in which his moderation saved the order from chaos.[47] For those who are inclined to doubt this view, it is important to recall that shortly after his death, the order fell into nearly four decades of fractious dispute, which turned deadly in 1318, when four Spirituals were burned at the stake in Marseilles.[48]

At the General Chapter of Paris in 1266, Bonaventure's new biography of Francis was approved, every friary was to have a copy, and all earlier biographies were to be destroyed. Today, we see the extent to which this decree was enacted in that there are more than four hundred surviving manuscripts of the Legenda major.

In 1265, Pope Clement IV wanted to appoint Bonaventure archbishop of York, but Bonaventure declined. On May 23, 1273, however, Pope Gregory X made Bonaventure a cardinal. (In fact, it has become the traditional iconography for Bonaventure to depict him wearing the vestiture of a cardinal, especially the wide-brimmed cardinal's hat known as the *galero*.) In November 1273, Gregory prevailed upon him to become bishop of Albano, and consecrated him in the same month at Lyons. In May 1274, Bonaventure resigned as minister general.

Unlike his contemporary, Thomas Aquinas, who never arrived at the second Council of Lyons, Bonaventure not only attended the council, but made singular contributions that helped with its central purpose, namely, reunification with the Greek Church of the East.[49] This was one of three goals that Pope Gregory X had for the council when he called it; he also wanted to organize military relief for Jerusalem and to bring about various reforms within the church.[50] When the council opened on May 7, 1274, Bonaventure, as one of the cardinal-bishops, sat on the pope's right as the pontiff delivered the opening address.

The Greeks arrived late, including the former archbishop of Constantinople, Germanus, now the archbishop of Nicea, and the chancellor of the Byzantine emperor. In the fourth session of the council, on July 6, the Greeks accepted a profession of faith that included a recognition of papal primacy, the doctrine of purgatory, and the number of sacraments as seven.[51] A mass was celebrated after the union of the Roman and Greek church was secured with an oath. During the mass, the creed was sung in Latin and Greek with the *filioque* clause (lit., "and from the Son" as in the claim that the Spirit "proceeds from the Father and the Son"), and the Greeks were allowed to keep the traditional wording of their creed. Nevertheless, this seemingly happy union was to fall apart for various reasons: The Byzantine emperor had supported it only for political reasons; the Greek bishops would not accept it; and Pope Martin V, who ascended the papal throne in 1281, supported the plans of the king of Naples for a conquest of the East.[52]

Bonaventure died unexpectedly in the early morning hours of July 15, 1274, eight days after the union had been completed. Pope Gregory X himself, the council fathers from both the East and West, and the papal curia were in attendance. Bonaventure was buried in the Franciscan church in Lyons. He was canonized April 14, 1432, by the Franciscan pope, Sixtus IV; on March 14, 1588, Pope Sixtus V made him a doctor of the church with the title, "Seraphic Doctor" (*Doctor Seraphicus*). In the eighteenth century, his tomb was raided and the relics destroyed by a mob of French revolutionaries.

Writings

Just in sheer size, Bonaventure's corpus of writings is impressive (filling nine folio volumes, each around seven hundred pages in length printed in double columns), when we consider that he composed many of these while minister general of the fastest growing religious order of his day. A group of Friars Minor, led by Fidelis a Fanna, from the Collegium S. Bonaventura, located at Quaracchi near Florence, edited and published the works of Bonaventure.[53] The first four folio volumes contain his *Commentary on the Sentences*; volume 5 contains eight short, but important, scholastic treatises; volumes 6 and 7 contain his scriptural commentaries; volume 8 his mystical and ascetical works; and volume 9 his sermons. These writings include theological texts, disputed questions, university conferences, biblical commentaries, letters, and sermons.

While certain writings cannot be accurately dated, Bonaventure's works can be broken down in general into two main periods of his life— those from his time teaching at the University of Paris, that is, his "regency"; and those from the period of his generalate. Among his theological texts, the longest and most important work is the *Commentary on the Sentences of Peter Lombard*. By the time Bonaventure was at the University of Paris, it had become the custom for bachelors seeking the masters in theology (the medieval university's highest degree) to comment on the Lombard. Because this commentary is Bonaventure's most important text, a word needs to be said about the Lombard himself and his famous text. Peter the Lombard was born in Lombardy between 1095 and 1100. He went to Paris for studies in 1136 and became a canon of Notre Dame in 1145. In 1159, he became bishop of Paris, an office he held for only a year, since he died in July 1160.[54] This twelfth-century ecclesiastic exercised considerable influence over Scholasticism, because he developed a textbook of theology that was to shape the way generations of theologians would approach various theological topics; indeed, it remained the standard textbook until Cajetan (1469–1534) began using Aquinas's *Summa Theologiae*, more than three centuries later.[55]

A sentence collection was a systematic compilation and exposition of texts from the Bible and the church fathers. In that it attempted to deal with discordance among authorities, its development is parallel to the work of Gratian in canon law; it moves by the same driving force as the Jurist's *Concordance of Discordant Canons*. Peter did not invent the genre of sentence collection, but he did much to advance it, and in so doing, significantly altered the way theology was done. The method of this genre inclined theology to be systematic. Indeed, sentence collection and systematic theology developed so clearly hand in hand that they may be regarded as two sides of a single invention of the twelfth century.[56] "The *Sentences* constitute the Lombardian *summa* that emerged out of the course of systematic theology that Peter taught for well-nigh two decades."[57] Its contents are the following: "Book I treats of God: the Trinity, God's attributes, providence, predestination, evil; Book II of the creation: the work of the six days, angels, demons, the fall, grace, sin; Book III of the Incarnation, Redemption, the virtues, the ten commandments; Book IV of the sacraments, first in general, then the seven in particular, and the four last things, death, judgment, hell, heaven."[58]

The final edition of the *Sentences* dates from the years 1155–1157, after Peter had read the newly translated *De fide orthodoxa* by John Damascene. "This author gave Peter the tools with which to reformulate his position of Trinitarian theology and Christology and to develop new arguments against views he rejected."[59] The *Sentences* is a complex work. While it has been described as an "Augustinian breviary"[60] because of its large number of quotes from Augustine, the Lombard took a somewhat critical approach to Augustine.

Another important theological text is Bonaventure's *Breviloquium* ("Brief Commentary"). This text is a small summa of theology that aims at treating briefly the whole range of topics in Christian theology. Bonaventure says that he composed it for the sake of fellow Franciscans with the purpose of reaffirming the centrality of the scriptures in the exposition of the faith. The Augustinian character of the *Breviloquium* is apparent. There is no theology apart from the enlightenment of the human mind, found in the infused virtue of faith reflecting on divine revelation in sacred scripture. Reason without faith will fall into error. The text is particularly important in terms of biblical hermeneutics or interpretation. It presents clearly and carefully the four levels of meaning found in a biblical text by most medieval believers. These levels are usually divided into the material, or literal, meaning and the three spiritual meanings: allegorical, anagogical, and tropological. This doctrine is discussed in more detail in the chapter on theology.

In 1259, early in his generalate, Bonaventure withdrew to a mountain retreat called La Verna. On this rugged and heavily wooded mountain in the summer of 1224, Francis had received the stigmata, or marks from the wounds of the crucified Christ. After returning from his mountain retreat, Bonaventure composed his most famous work, *Journey of the Mind to God* (*Itinerarium mentis in Deum*). It is an explanation of how the mind can ascend to God through six steps from the contemplation of sensible things to God himself. It is a text that can be read for many different purposes. It is a theological work that draws extensively on metaphysics; indeed, its depth is really only revealed when read with an eye open to its metaphysical doctrines. Yet, at the same time, it is one of the most popular works in spiritual theology in the entire history of Christian thought.

There are three sets of disputed questions (*quaestiones disputatae*) of particular import from the period of Bonaventure's "regency" or university teaching career: *Disputed Questions on Evangelical Perfection* (*Quaestiones disputatae de perfectione evangelica*), *Disputed Questions on the Knowledge of Christ* (*Quaestiones disputatae de scientia Christi*), and *Disputed Questions on the Mystery of the Trinity* (*Quaestiones disputatae de mysterio trinitatis*). The first of these conferences was given at the request of the king of France, Louis IX, in response to a crisis brought about by a secular master's attack on the mendicants. In 1254, William of Saint-Amour, a secular master at the University of Paris, made a vigorous attack on very idea of a mendicant religious life in a book called *Liber de antichristo*. In 1256, he renewed his attack on the mendicant way of life in his *Tractatus de perculis novissimorum temporum*. William argued the extreme position that poverty was a moral evil. As a result of this controversy, Louis IX asked the university to solemnly decide the question. The first to respond was Thomas Aquinas; the second was the Franciscan, Thomas of York; the third was Bonaventure. On October 5, 1256, Pope Alexander IV condemned William of Saint-Amour's position.

The *Disputed Questions on the Knowledge of Christ* (perhaps 1253–1254) treats the theological problem of what Christ knew in his divine and human natures. However, it also provides an extensive and important discussion of the philosophical problem of how knowledge and certitude are attained. These questions are especially important for understanding Bonaventure's doctrine of illumination; but they cannot be read in isolation from his treatment of knowledge in the *Commentary on the Sentences*, because the disputed questions do not treat his doctrine of the agent intellect and its act of abstraction.

The *Disputed Questions on the Trinity* contain an important discussion of how the existence of God is known, namely, as an analytic truth that is self-evident (at least in itself) and beyond doubt. Regardless of where one begins—whether in the sensible world, the soul's self-awareness, or the idea of God—God's existence is evident to the truly perceptive. Bonaventure also presents in this text "necessary reasons" for the triune nature of God.[61]

Bonaventure gave a number of important series of university conferences or *collationes* over the course of his life. The *collatio* was a monastic custom that the Dominican, Jordan of Saxony, introduced in 1231 into the university context for Sundays and feast days. The audience consisted of masters and students at any level of degree. These conferences were reported or taken down by secretaries, who then showed them to the speaker for correction and approval.

The first set of Bonaventure's conferences that has come down to us is called the *Collations on the Ten Commandments* (*Collationes de decem praeceptis*) and dates from March 1267.[62] In these conferences, Bonaventure attempts to respond to the Averroistic views that the world is eternal and that there is one agent intellect by which all human beings know, a doctrine usually referred to as "monopsychism."

Another set of conferences also addresses the Averroist crisis: the *Collations on the Seven Gifts* (*Collationes de septem donis*), given in Lent of 1268.[63] In this text, Bonaventure particularly attacks Gérard d'Abbeville, who renewed the criticism of the mendicant religious life.

The most important of Bonaventure's conferences is called *Collations on the Six Days* (*Collationes in hexaemeron*), in which he comments on the six days of creation. These have come down to us in two redactions; the second of which was not chosen for inclusion in the Quaracchi edition, and was subsequently edited and published by Ferdinand Delorme.[64] These conferences were the second occasion for Bonaventure to comment on the Genesis text; the first was in his *Sentences* commentary. Bonaventure uses this text to present a stinging attack on the Averroists in the midst of the crisis brought on by their interpretation and unswerving allegiance to Aristotle.

[Bonaventure's approach to dealing with the Averroist crisis contrasts radically with Aquinas's. Whereas Aquinas tried to meet the crisis by rescuing Aristotle, that is, by trying to insure that Aristotle was correctly interpreted, Bonaventure argues that the problem lies much deeper: the Averroists' fundamental error was to use reason to judge the truths of the faith. While Aquinas attacks their interpretation of Aristotle, Bonaventure attacks their fundamental rationalism, which would subject the truths of the faith to the judgment of reason and the criticism of philosophy. In these conferences, Bonaventure finally presents his complete catalogue of errors attributable to Aristotle: (1) the denial of exemplarism (or the theory of forms in a transcendent cause, which Bonaventure explicitly associates with Plato); (2) denial of divine knowledge of world; (3) the necessity of all things (which flows from the second, according to Bonaventure, since if God does not know the world, all things happen either by chance or by absolute necessity; the former is impossible, so the latter must obtain); (4) the denial of eternal life where reward or punishment is found; (5) the eternity of the world; and (6) the existence of a single intellect for all men (a view that Bonaventure is careful to say Averroes attributes to Aristotle).[65]

Bonaventure's biblical commentaries are numerous. His commentary on Saint Luke, which fills an entire folio volume in his *Opera omnia*, is designed to aid preachers in their work. He also produced commentaries on Ecclesiastes, Wisdom, and on the Gospel of Saint John. His commentary on Ecclesiastes presents some of his most central and profound ideas. The world is a sign from God: "Every creature is the divine word, because it speaks of God."[66] To love the world above God is to confuse the sign for its giver. Charity or true love involves recognizing the sign as a sign, and thereby turning one's love to the sign giver.

In 1260, the General Chapter of the Friars Minor, held at Narbonne, commissioned Bonaventure to compose a new biography of Francis. Since the Chapter used the Latin term *legenda* in its decree, Bonaventure's biography is referred to as the *Legenda major* (as opposed to the *Legenda minor*, which he composed as a shorter version for liturgical usage). When the Chapter issued its commission to the minister general, three biographies of Francis already existed, two by Thomas of Celano and one by Julian of Speyer. Some historians have argued that the primary motivation for this new biography was concern that the earlier accounts overemphasized the primitive spirit. Bonaventure's work is understood as an attempt to institutionalize the primitive spirit and to preserve the peace of the order in the face of conflicts over learning and poverty.[67] Bonaventure himself, however, says that his purpose was merely to "gather together" the accounts of Francis's virtues, actions, and words, either forgotten or scattered like so many fragments. He says in the prologue that he visited the sites of the holy man's birth, life, and death. The final product draws extensively on the biographies by Celano and Julian, but Bonaventure follows a different organization, and he interprets the life of Francis in the light of his own spiritual theology.

There are 569 extant complete sermons listed in the *Opera omnia* of Bonaventure. The Quaracchi editors divide them into four categories: *de tempore*, *de sanctis*, *de Beata Maria Virgine*, and *de diversis*. One of the most important of these sermons is his "One Is Your Teacher, Christ" (*Unus est magister vester, Christus*) from 1253 or 1254.[68]

Bonaventure has long been famous for his work in spiritual theology. A concern for spirituality marks the whole of his life's work from his *Commentary on the Sentences* to his *Collationes in hexaemeron*. However, he has a number of works that focus on this area of theology: *On the Threefold Way* (*De triplici via*), *Soliloquies* (*Soliliquium*), the *Tree of Life*

(*Lignum vitae*), *On the Five Feasts of the Child, Jesus* (*De quinque festivitatibus pueri Jesu*), *Treatise on Preparation for Mass* (*Tractatus de praeparatione ad missam*), *On the Rule of the Soul* (*De regimine animae*), *On the Perfection of Life for Sisters* (*De perfectione vitae ad sorores*), and *On the Six Wings of the Seraphim* (*De sex alis seraphim*). Among these, *De triplici via* is particularly important, because it presents the spiritual life in three stages or ways: the purgative, the illuminative, and the unitive. These ways have become classic means of describing the dynamic of the Christian life of grace.

The disputes within thirteenth-century Scholasticism first came to light thanks to the research in the 1880s of Franz Ehrle.[69] It eventually became customary to speak of various "schools" in the late medieval period, for example, the Thomist, the Franciscan, and the Scotist. Gilson contributed significantly to this tendency, because his work disclosed many of the differences among the Scholastics. However, some have criticized this discussion of schools for imposing greater self-consciousness and cohesion to thinkers who shared certain theses. At most, we should speak of certain theological or philosophical stances, rather than of schools. Yet, there remains a certain justification for labeling the thinkers who hold common theses as schools.[70]

Influence

Bonaventure exercised considerable influence both theologically and philosophically among thirteenth-century Franciscans, that is, until the coming of John Duns Scotus (ca. 1266–1308). The Franciscan school, prior to Scotus, bore the imprint of both Bonaventure and his teacher, Alexander of Hales. But after the career of Scotus, Bonaventure's influence waned and was not to enjoy a revival until the sixteenth century, when another family of Franciscans, the Capuchins, adopted him as their principal doctor in both theological and philosophical issues.

Bonaventure is usually described as being one of the most important Augustinians in the thirteenth century. While there is earlier evidence of Augustinianism in the work of William of Auvergne (ca. 1180–1249), Robert Grosseteste (ca. 1175–1253), and in the *Summa fratris Alexandri*, usually attributed to Alexander of Hales,[71] the Augustinians of the second half of the thirteenth century drew much of their inspiration and doctrine from Bonaventure. Among his disciples were John Peckham (ca. 1225–1292), who became an influential archbishop of Canterbury; Walter of Bruges (d. 1307), regent master at Paris (probably 1267–1268); and Walter's successor as regent master (1268–1269), Eustace of Arras (ca. 1255–1291).[72] Among Peckham's students was Matthew of Aquasparta (ca. 1237–1302), whose distinguished career included such offices as minister general of the Franciscans, archbishop, cardinal, and close advisor to Pope Boniface VIII. Matthew wrote extensively in defense of various Bonaventurian doctrines—in particular, divine illumination—and is usually regarded as Scholastic Augustinianism's most vigorous defender. It has become common to speak of an "early Franciscan school," in which Bonaventure is the major figure and Augustine the predominant influence. In this way, this group of "disciples" is distinguished from the later or "new" Franciscan school, which owes more to Duns Scotus, who inspired a considerably different set of disciples.[73]

In the fourteenth century, after Bonaventure's influence began to wane, Alexander of Alexandria (d. 1314), who was also a minister general of the Franciscans, wrote a *Summa quaestionum S. Bonaventurae.* Interest in Bonaventure revived in the century between his canonization in 1482 and his elevation as a doctor of the church in 1588. In 1593, a Capuchin, Pedro Trigoso de Calatayud, attempted a *Summa theologica* based on the seraphic doctor's writings.[74]

It is largely accurate to say that Bonaventure became the leading spokesman for the Augustinian tradition in the thirteenth century. Yet, the story is not so simple. Because his own relation to the thought of Aristotle is not simple, we have to avoid falling into an overly rigid division of the factions into the Augustinians and the Aristotelians.

Bonaventure took up the task of engaging Aristotle in the years immediately after 1250. He studied the philosopher's thought extensively and made considerable use of Aristotle's work in his own writings. He quotes Aristotle 1,015 times, from every one of the philosopher's works except the *Politics*, which was not yet translated.[75] Bonaventure quotes *De anima* the most often (138 times), followed closely by the *Physics* (136 times). The *Topics* (134 times), *Nicomachean Ethics* (131), and *Metaphysics* (125) are next in order of frequency. He quotes from a work that was attributed to Aristotle, the *Liber de Causis*, forty-seven times. (Aquinas was the first to realize that this work is not Aristotle's.) Bonaventure incorporated certain key Aristotelian doctrines into his own thought. For example, he combines a considerable amount of Aristotle's cognitional theory with his own, such as a doctrine of the agent intellect and of abstraction. He repeats a number of times the Aristotelian position that knowledge begins in the senses. By adopting the Aristotelian position of abstraction, he affirms that cognition is a form of being.[76]

So it is clear that Bonaventure does not merely repeat Augustinian theses. A more adequate view of Bonaventure recognizes that he created his own synthesis. Scholasticism was long interpreted simply as the appropriation of Aristotelian philosophy by Christian thinkers; a more adequate interpretation takes account of the tremendous breadth of the Scholastic syntheses.

Bonaventure's synthesis remains, at a profound level, Augustinian. Bonaventure himself testifies to the high regard in which he held Augustine:

> No one has ever described the nature of time and matter in a better way than blessed Augustine in his *Confessions*. No one has ever explained the origin of forms and the manner of propagation of being so well as it may be found in his *Commentary on Genesis*. In like manner his treatise *On the Trinity* bears witness that no one has provided a better solution to the questions concerning the soul. Again, it is evident from his book *On the City of God* that no one has investigated with greater understanding the nature of the creation of the world. To condense it all in a few words, no question has been propounded by the masters whose solution may not be found in the works of this Doctor.[77]

As this letter indicates and as this study will show, Gilson was right to regard Bonaventure's synthesis as the full expression of medieval Augustinianism. It is in this regard that one can see him as the source of the Augustinianism of the 1270s.[78]

Yet, an accurate reading of Bonaventure has to strike a balance: It has to take account of the pervasive influence of Aristotle in his thought, while at the same time recognizing the fundamentally Augustinian character of his mind.

Christian Wisdom

The notion of wisdom (*sapientia*) is so central in the thought of Bonaventure that its pursuit can safely be considered the whole purpose of his life and work. At the beginning of one of his most important works, he exhorts us to be "lovers of wisdom" (*sapientiae amatores*),[1] for apart from wisdom we can know neither the peace nor the happiness that alone satiate the human being. In this regard, Bonaventure's quest for wisdom is always a striving for happiness, which he regards as man's final end. Hence, there is an urgency and passionate intensity evident throughout his writings. The quest for wisdom originates here in this world through the use of reason, but it finds its most fruitful and direct way in the science of God's own revelation, namely, theology. Theology is not a purely speculative science; it is also an eminently practical science, concerned with issues of life-and-death importance to the soul. Bonaventure takes a middle position on the question of whether theology is a speculative or practical science—it is a sapiential habit.[2] Faith resides in the intellect, but its purpose is to move the affections. Contemplation and holiness are inseparable, but to make us good is theology's principal aim. Theology is a whole way of life and its goal is nothing less than union with God. It decides everything, for it is the queen of the sciences. The quest for wisdom may lead through all the arts and sciences, but eventually, these multiform paths ought to lead the lover of wisdom on a journey back to God Himself, for wisdom is one with God. In fact, in the end, wisdom is the most proper name of God.[3]

In order to understand this larger journey to wisdom, it is helpful to begin by examining some of the many different senses in which Bonaventure uses the term "wisdom" (*sapientia*). An examination of this concept reveals his understanding of both theology and philosophy, the relationship between these two disciplines, and finally the foundational unity of all knowledge.[4]

First, it is important to be aware that Bonaventure uses the term "wisdom" in both a subjective and objective sense, that is, he refers to a quality of mind in the human subject and also to an object of the mind that, upon sufficient familiarity, brings about the subjective quality. In the former sense, it is an intellectual virtue; in the latter, it closely refers to "science" or "doctrine" as a body of knowledge.

In writing about the gifts of wisdom, understanding, and knowledge in his *Commentary on the Sentences*, Bonaventure carefully distinguishes different uses of the term "wisdom" (*sapientia*). First, it can be used in a common sense (*communiter*) to refer to a general cognition of things; wisdom in this sense is the cognition of things divine and human, as Augustine would say. He quotes Aristotle's *Metaphysics* to make much the same point, "The wise person is the one who knows all things in compliance with what is fitting."[5] In this general sense, wisdom can be identified with knowing philosophy.

Second, Bonaventure uses this term in a less-common sense (*minus communiter*) to refer to the cognition of the eternal things. In this sense, Bonaventure distinguishes wisdom from science, which is the cognition of created things; his use of the term here is very similar to Aristotle's cognition of the highest causes (except that Bonaventure would include the divine ideas in his account of the highest causes). In this less-general sense, wisdom can be identified with knowing metaphysics, that is, the science of being as being, not as changing, or living, and so forth.

Third, Bonaventure uses the term "wisdom" in a proper sense (*proprie*) to refer to the cognition of God according to piety, in other words, a cognition of God insofar as he is worshiped in faith, hope, and love.[6] In this proper sense, wisdom refers to true religion, that is, a life given to the love and worship of the Triune God, as Augustine calls "true religion" in his text of that name.[7]

Finally, Bonaventure uses "wisdom" in a stricter sense (*magis stricte*) to refer to the mind's ecstatic union with God. In this sense, it refers to the cognition of God by experience (*cognitionem Dei experimentalem*); it is a mystical state that begins in cognition and ends in affection.[8] Wisdom, in this strict sense, is not merely a distant goal for eternity, but is already the goal of human life on earth. Bonaventure thinks that peace accompanies this state, peace that belongs to the mind of the true contemplative who has been filled by the light of heavenly wisdom.[9] It is a knowledge that comes about by tasting, that is, by experience. In a later text, Bonaventure associates this wisdom with one of its principal effects, a peace born of an ecstatic going out of the self into a loving union with God. Hence, he can also call wisdom in this sense an *excessus mentalis*, and indeed, charity itself. The self is forgotten, and all curiosity and striving after knowledge are silenced; he therefore calls this wisdom a certain learned ignorance (*quaedam ignorantia docta*). He will also call this "the Christian wisdom" (*sapientia christiana*), for it is Christ who makes possible this ascent of the mind.[10]

In each of these different senses of "wisdom," Bonaventure is speaking of a certain disposition or quality of the soul—what he, like other Scholastics, would technically call a *habitus*. This disposition leads the mind into certain patterns of thinking that serve to develop its inherent capacities. In this regard, then, wisdom is one of the perfections of which the mind is capable. And because wisdom is not identical with the soul itself, but something acquired—either through our own efforts or as a divine gift—it is also an "accident" or property of the soul.[11]

This general outline of Bonaventure's understanding of the term "wisdom" closely parallels his detailed discussion of the meaning of wisdom found in his work, *Collations on the Six Days of Creation* (*Collationes in hexaemeron*). In the second conference, Bonaventure clearly treats wisdom as an object of learning; this "objective" wisdom is fourfold.[12] First, there is "uniform wisdom" (*sapientia uniformis*), found in the eternal rules that are the basic principles of all knowledge by which we judge, whether about speculative matters or about practical ones. This wisdom is found through the use of reason, that is, of philosophy, specifically in logic and ethics.

Second, there is "omniform wisdom" (*sapientia omniformis*), which comes from knowing the Creator through His creation. This wisdom is accessible to reason, but the philosophers often remain focused on the things themselves rather than rising to the one who made them. This wisdom is only accessible to those who are able to see the things of the world as signs and not merely as things. Bonaventure is drawing on a medieval notion that creation is a book, but he transforms this medieval opinion into a metaphysical theory. Bonaventure develops a semiotic metaphysics to explain how all things are intentional signs (*signa data*) from God: "He who does not allow himself to be illumined by the glory of created things is blind; he who does not awaken to their call is deaf; he who does not praise God for all his works is mute; he who does not discover the First Principle from all these signs is a fool."[13]

As with scripture, the danger is to see only the literal meaning and not the sign-value of things. "We do not find her [wisdom], just as the unlettered layman is not interested in the contents of the book that he holds in his hands. So it is with us. The language of the universe has become like Greek, Hebrew, or some barbarous language; it has become fundamentally unknown."[14]

There is also a "multiform wisdom" (sapientia multiformis), which is found in the understanding of sacred scripture. Only the believer who can penetrate through the veiled meaning of scripture to its spiritual sense can gain this wisdom, which comes through revelation. Finally, there is "formless wisdom" (sapientia nulliformis); those who are contemplative find this wisdom in the interior knowledge of God. In explicating the nature of formless wisdom, Bonaventure draws on the apophatic teachings of Pseudo-Dionysius. He speaks of this wisdom as formless, because the mind is unable to grasp it in any concept or to express it in any proposition. In this way, it is beyond form; it is no-form. This wisdom is ineffable.

This mention of formless wisdom brings us to the last, but by no means, least distinction that Bonaventure makes with regard to the meaning of wisdom, that is, the distinction between created and uncreated wisdom. Behind the whole universe there is uncreated wisdom; wisdom itself stands behind everything that is. The formless wisdom that the mystic glimpses is the uncreated wisdom.[15] Bonaventure also identifies uncreated wisdom with the eternal divine Word and with truth.[16] Hence, the search for wisdom and for truth leads through the multitude of paths in this world to the unity of the Word, which is wisdom and truth.

If the whole purpose of Bonaventure's life was the pursuit of wisdom, it can also be said that much of his vast corpus of writing was a defense of the mind's ability to attain truth. And the truth that the mind can attain is ultimately one; all the multifarious paths of knowledge find their unity in the one truth. Given this view of the metaphysical unity of truth and wisdom, we must be careful in distinguishing between theology and philosophy. It is not just that these disciplines ultimately lead to the same object; it is that Christianity is the true philosophy, for it is the wisdom that draws man to his proper end and goal.

Theology and philosophy are different ways of considering reality; hence, many things that they consider are the same. However, while philosophy examines them under the light of reason, theology examines things under the light of faith. The fundamental conviction for the whole Scholastic endeavor is that faith and reason cannot ultimately contradict each other, for the God who has revealed himself through the faith is the same God who created the world and human reason. The truth is one.

⌈ This view sets up a complex and highly nuanced relationship between faith and reason and between the disciplines of theology and philosophy. And yet, it is in these relationships that we find the distinguishing characteristics of Bonaventure's thought, for the distinctive mark of Bonaventurianism is what has been called "anti-Aristotelianism." This anti-Aristotelianism, however, is really a rejection of a particular reading of Aristotle, such as was found among the contemporary Averrroists, in which reason is closed to revelation and philosophy is utterly independent of theology.[17]

Perhaps the best way to begin to understand this complex relationship is to see Bonaventure's position as a moderate one within two extremes: on the one hand, it is a mean between a thorough rationalism, which would regard philosophy as the highest wisdom, and, on the other hand, a thorough fideism, which would forswear any use of philosophy at all. The former extreme became an increasingly grave threat during Bonaventure's own lifetime with the rise of a radical or "Averroistic" Aristotelianism, which maintained a strict separation between faith and reason and saw religion as the interpretation and mythic presentation of truth for the uneducated masses. Even though the threat of this rationalistic position increasingly occupied the thought of Bonaventure, we cannot understand his position unless we also see its moderation. The tendency has been to focus on him as an anti-Aristotelian (at least, of Averroist Aristotelianism); but it is important to recognize the role he gives to philosophy in attaining wisdom. The contemporary rationalism of the Averroists held that philosophy is the highest wisdom and the doctrines of religion are to be judged by reason. It is precisely this extreme rationalism that Bonaventure regards as a profound error; in a series of works in the 1260s, he condemned it in no uncertain terms. In his eyes, the scholar's task is not to sit in judgment on revelation or to prove or disprove it. Revelation is true because it is from God. The scholar's task is to understand better what God has revealed by clarifying and penetrating the layers of its meaning. ⌉

Although the identification of wisdom with Christianity may be most striking to the modern reader, more noteworthy in the context of medieval thought is Bonaventure's clear affirmation that the intellect can attain wisdom through the exercise of reason. Bonaventure has delineated a path to wisdom that is not wholly identical with Christianity. This development is characteristic of Scholastic thought in general. As the eminent historian of medieval thought, Marie-Dominique Chenu, OP, has shown, the twelfth century attempted a distinction between philosophy and theology.[18] The twelfth-century theologians "made room" for philosophy. Bonaventure belongs in this Scholastic tradition. He argues that there is wisdom to be found in the use of reason: in philosophy in general, and in metaphysics in particular.

A distinction, however, is not the same as a separation. To distinguish in order to ultimately unite is not an easy undertaking. And so, Bonaventure, like other Scholastics, attempts a difficult task: both to defend philosophy as a means to wisdom and also to subordinate it to theology. Philosophy, he argues, is a means to wisdom as long as it is subordinate to the control of revelation. In practice, this seems to have a twofold meaning, one negative, one positive: (a) the philosopher looks to the doctrines of the faith in order to avoid falling into error without actually basing an argument on a premise taken from revelation; and (b) the philosopher remains open to the positive impetus that the doctrines of the faith may provide to philosophical speculation, either on issues that the philosopher would not normally take up or on issues that otherwise may not be pursued with equal thoroughness.

Bonaventure makes a clear distinction between the methods of philosophy and theology. We see this at work in his *Commentary on the Sentences*, where he consistently states whether a particular argument is from reason or not. Theology takes its data from revelation and proceeds from God to His effects; philosophy takes its start from effects and proceeds to the first cause. As Bonaventure quotes Augustine at the beginning of the *Breviloquium*, "What we believe, we owe to authority; what we understand, to reason."[19]

Bonaventure argues that theology gains from the use of reason and philosophy. Indeed, reason provides a threefold benefit to the faith: it confounds the adversaries of the faith; it encourages those weak in faith, and it delights those perfect in faith.[20] At other points, however, Bonaventure seems to regard reason not merely as a beneficial partner to theology, but as an essential companion, without which theology could not carry out its task.

While Bonaventure affirms the value of philosophy as a path to wisdom, he also stresses that any attempt to work out a philosophy independent of the faith is necessarily doomed to fall into errors: "It is necessary that a philosopher fall into some error unless he is helped by the ray of faith."[21] If philosophy is made formally distinct from faith, it becomes a hodgepodge of truths mingled with errors—a jumble rather than an organized whole because it lacks the center of the created order, and it is mingled with errors because it lacks the light of faith.[22] It is faith that keeps philosophy from error. Philosophy cannot reach its own goal without the aid of a higher science.

Bonaventure argues that we see human reason's (and hence philosophy's) proclivity to error in the work of Plato and Aristotle. Plato was focused on the eternal reasons to the exclusion of natural science; Aristotle was focused on the things of the world to the exclusion of the eternal reasons. Only Augustine, with the light of faith, achieved a comprehensive wisdom: He posited the forms as ideas in the divine mind and yet maintained that the things of the world were real.[23]

It is important to note that Bonaventure does not deny that philosophy can attain truth without faith; rather, he says that the truths discovered by such an autonomous philosophy will be mixed with errors.[24] It is important then to make a clear distinction between an autonomous philosophy and a heteronomous one; the latter looks to theology to restrain it from falling into positive error. Bonaventure regards philosophy as capable of achieving certitude using its own proper methods.

⌈Reason, however, also receives a positive contribution from the faith, which is essential for philosophy to be brought to completion. Faith allows one to understand what might not otherwise be understood. According to Bonaventure, the faith is an intrinsic principle to the philosopher that guides him to greater and greater understanding—it is not a merely extrinsic norm that prevents the philosopher from falling into error.⌉

Of course, it must be conceded that the reader finds Bonaventure's philosophical views embedded within his theological work. Yet, it is possible to extract his philosophical views from this context without falsifying them because he consistently distinguishes between arguments based on the authority of the faith (de fide) and those based on reason (de ratione). His philosophical views do not rely on divine revelation, even though they are subject to the negative control of revelation and have benefited from the influence of theological truths.

The delicate balance between philosophy and theology that Bonaventure attempted to maintain is best portrayed in his short treatise now called On the Reduction of the Arts to Theology (De reductione artium ad theologiam). This text is among his most important; the "reduction" to which it refers is a "leading back" of all the arts and sciences to theology, and of all cognition to God. All knowledge leads up to the study of sacred scripture, the study of God's own revelation. The multiform wisdom of God is found above all in sacred scripture, but because wisdom "lies hidden in all knowledge and in all nature," all the disciplines can lead us to God.[25] Granted, the height of wisdom is found in Christ; nevertheless, Christ, as the wisdom of God, is found hidden in all creation. In this sense, creation too is revelation. Bonaventure thus provides an entire Christian paideia or curriculum. In this regard, it is helpful to see this text as belonging to the tradition of education set out by Augustine in *De doctrina christiana*. It is seminal in the history of education, because it justifies the study of disciplines other than scripture and theology. Bonaventure's *De reductione* stands squarely within this tradition, while yet modifying it.

Philosophy plays a crucial role in this *paideia*. It is the height of natural wisdom and understanding; it investigates the threefold truth (*triplex veritas*): the truth of speech, the truth of being, and the truth of morals; it is the seventh of the liberal arts, and the others find their summit in it. Philosophy involves an ascent from being, and its principles, to God; but it leads up to a further ascent made possible by God's own revelation. Philosophy is thus an ancillary discipline to theology. All knowledge, the arts, reflect the font of intelligibility, and therefore the reduction of which Bonaventure speaks is ultimately an ascent of the mind to God in the order of knowledge. *De reductione* is thus a companion piece to the *Itinerarium*, which is the ascent of the mind to God in the order of being. Bonaventure seeks an ultimate ground for all human knowledge and action. All human knowledge and art is grounded in the exemplary ideas of the Word of God. Bonaventure's *De reductione* appears as a reassertion of the Augustinian educational settlement in the midst of a secularizing tendency among certain types of Aristotelianism.

In his work *On the Reduction of the Arts to Theology*, Bonaventure attempts to show how all knowledge and all the arts lead man up to theology. Specifically, he thinks that all knowledge is a form of enlightenment and that all light flows from the fontal source of light, God. He speaks of the four lights of the arts and sciences: an exterior, an inferior, an interior, and a superior light. This parallels the Augustinian method of ascent to God found in the *Confessions*, in which Augustine speaks of returning to himself and then entering into his inward self in order to behold the inner light. Bonaventure considers four lights that are ultimately united in the one light: This fourfold light constitutes the illumination of all human knowledge.

The first of the lights he examines is the exterior light. This is the light of the mechanical arts, which are concerned with external things and with those things intended to supply the needs of the body. This exterior light is divided into the seven mechanical arts: weaving, armor making, agriculture, hunting, navigation, medicine, and drama (*theatrica*). Bonaventure takes this enumeration of the mechanical arts from Hugh of St. Victor. Six of these are useful because they bring comfort and banish need; one is enjoyable, because it brings consolation and banishes sorrow—this is dramatics, which Bonaventure perceives as embracing every form of entertainment.

The second light that Bonaventure treats is the inferior light, which is of sense perception. It illumines with respect to natural forms. This light has five divisions corresponding to the five senses.

Next, Bonaventure treats an interior light, the light of philosophical knowledge. It illumines with respect to intelligible truth. It has three divisions: rational, natural, and moral. The light of natural philosophy concerns the truth of things, and it enlightens the mind to discern the causes of being. It is further divided into metaphysics, physics, and mathematics. Finally, Bonaventure discusses the superior light, which is the light of grace and of sacred scripture. It illumines with respect to the saving truth.

Bonaventure presents a threefold division of philosophy into rational, natural, and moral that ultimately goes back to the Stoics,[26] but he is obviously not endorsing the materialism implicit in the Stoic division of the sciences. Nevertheless, this division might seem to eliminate metaphysics as a separate science since it makes it a branch of natural philosophy. However, on closer inspection, it is obvious that Bonaventure has not eliminated metaphysics; on the contrary, he is clearly giving it a high place in the order of knowledge. Indeed, it is the height of human science; it is concerned with things under a particular aspect, namely, insofar as they exist or are "beings" that are caused. By placing metaphysics within the order of natural philosophy, he does not give it the sort of autonomy that certain readings of Aristotle might, such as that of the Greek commentators or Averroes. He is rejecting the view that some drew from their reading of Aristotle that would make metaphysics the science of God. If its proper object were God, it would follow that metaphysics is the science of God. Even to make its proper object separate substance (rather than common being) is to move in this direction. In this view, metaphysics becomes an autonomous rational theology. Such a division of the sciences, Bonaventure seems to suggest, leads to a rationalism in which all knowledge depends on reason, including knowledge of the divine.

In general, the Scholastics, including Bonaventure, would not deny the vital importance of metaphysics, that is, of a science that investigates the ultimate cause of being, namely, God, insofar as He can be known by reason. Indeed, it is a distinguishing mark of Scholasticism that it sees the great value such a science can be to theology and the faith in general. But Scholasticism is playing with dynamite here, and Bonaventure is keenly aware of the explosive force of this issue. The volatile problem with metaphysics is found in its tendency to "take over" and to become independent. In other words, it becomes difficult to synthesize a supernatural revelation and a theology derived from such revelation with an autonomous science. An autonomous philosophy or, more precisely, metaphysics, tends to render supernatural theology one of three things within the field of human knowledge: either (1) an addendum, (2) a mythic and popular presentation of philosophy (Averroes), or (3) an impossibility (Hegel). In the second and third of these possibilities, metaphysics is not only autonomous; it is the sole, authentic science of God. In other words, in Bonaventure's eyes, philosophy's death lies in becoming a closed system, no longer in need of nor open to a higher science. "Not until the eighteenth century could one suggest with impunity, though not without some hostile reaction, that unhindered reason was the only appropriate means of investigating all phenomena, including revealed religion."[27]

Bonaventure thus carefully outlines a hierarchy of knowledge in which theology is the queen of the sciences. Theology must rule the university or else it will become, at best, one science among many. If Bonaventure makes clear that theology is the queen of the sciences, he is also defending philosophy as the handmaiden. The "handmaiden approach" (as Edward Grant terms it) to relating philosophy and theology goes back to Philo Judaeus (30 B.C.–50 A.D.) and was absorbed into Christianity by Clement of Alexandria (150–215).[28] Philosophy has a rightful and essential place as the organizing discipline that serves as the link between the lower sciences and the higher science of theology. Philosophy discloses what Bonaventure would call the "Metaphysical Center," Christ the divine Word.[29] All knowledge must be "reduced" to the one truth of Christ. Indeed, there can be no truth apart from Christ, the Metaphysical Center.

A book that sets out to discuss the philosophy of Bonaventure needs to include some consideration of the long-term dispute about the very existence of any such philosophy that has taken place in the twentieth century between two prominent scholars in the field of medieval thought—Étienne Gilson and Ferdinand van Steenberghen.

As already mentioned, Gilson argued consistently that there was authentic philosophical thought to be found in the Middle Ages, but that its approach during that time was distinctive, because it was in the context of Christian faith. He called this "Christian philosophy," a term he borrowed from Leo XIII's encyclical, Aeterni Patris (1879). According to Gilson, the Christian philosopher does not prescind from faith, even though he uses a method different from that of the theologian. The theologian proceeds from the authority of revelation; the philosopher proceeds from reason, while still using the data of revelation. The philosopher philosophizes in the light of faith, and this light makes a positive contribution to his philosophizing even though he does not formally appeal to the doctrines of the faith in his arguments.

Gilson found a particularly clear example of Christian philosophy in the thought of Bonaventure. The very title of his book, *The Christian Philosophy of Saint Bonaventure*, suggests his contentious thesis, namely, that Bonaventure's synthesis is truly philosophical. Gilson saw in Bonaventure's thought a distinctly Christian philosophy, that is, "every philosophy which, although keeping the two orders formally distinct, nevertheless considers the Christian revelation as an indispensable auxiliary to reason."[30] Indeed, Gilson presents it as one of the great syntheses of Christian thought and the most "medieval" one at that.[31]

Gilson argues, however, that the thirteenth century provides us with two different understandings of Christian philosophy, and Bonaventure and Aquinas typify these two approaches. In Aquinas's thought, philosophy has a certain relative autonomy. While it has its own proper methods, it accepts the extrinsic control of the faith. As a result, philosophy is formally distinct from theology. In Bonaventure, however, philosophy is heteronomous (especially because it cannot avoid error without theology) and is strengthened by the intrinsic influence of the faith. On this point, we confront a striking difference between Bonaventure and his fellow Scholastics.

Van Steenberghen disagreed vigorously with Gilson about the existence of a philosophy of Bonaventure and maintained that Bonaventure's real contributions are theological. He is, at best, an eclectic philosopher, whose synthesis holds together only on theological positions.[32] "The unity of his thought is certainly not a philosophical unity—on this most important point both M. Gilson and Fr. Mandonnet are in complete agreement."[33] In this way, he cannot be said to have developed a truly philosophical synthesis. Gilson was wrong to present "a mutilated exposition of his theology" as his "philosophy" (mutilated because it ignores the exclusively theological elements).[34]

Van Steenberghen makes a distinction between philosophy as *Weltanschauung* (worldview) and scientific philosophy. In the former sense, philosophy refers to the general worldview of any society or culture. "For the Christian, philosophy, understood as *Weltanschauung*, is necessarily subject to the authority of faith, or, to be more exact, to the authority of divine revelation. . . . This Christian wisdom positively excludes any purely human wisdom which might claim to be the supreme standard for thought and action."[35] Scientific philosophy (or philosophy as a scientific discipline) begins from evident principles, is assisted by a critically defined method, and draws up a systematic interpretation of the order of the universe.[36] Scientific philosophy had a place with theology and the sciences in a complete organization of the intellectual life.

With this definition of philosophy, Van Steenberghen examined the history of Christian thought and concluded that the theological synthesis of St. Augustine did not differentiate philosophy in a scientific way from Christian wisdom. For Augustine, Christianity is the true wisdom, and the true philosophy is a love of this wisdom.

Van Steenberghen argues that philosophy, as a general worldview, was Christian and Augustinian in the Middle Ages. For example, in the twelfth century, from the perspective of scientific philosophy, there was no philosophical Augustinianism for the simple reason that there were no philosophical systems at all. Even though there was considerable interest in dialectics, the twelfth century's knowledge of philosophical problems was fragmentary and its forays into philosophical issues outside of dialectics were eclectic and unsystematic.[37] In the first half of the thirteenth century, all the theologians were primarily influenced by the increasing number of texts from Aristotle. As a result, members of the theology faculty developed various forms of an eclectic Aristotelianism, or what one might call a Neoplatonizing Aristotelianism. But these developments were always in the context of a theological framework; as a result, they remained fundamentally Augustinian in spirit. The Augustinianism of the faculty was theological in character. They often paid scant attention to the formal distinction between philosophy and theology, and, as a result, frequently subordinated the former to the latter. Philosophy was merely an instrument serving the speculative method of theology. Their philosophy then remained eclectic; its unity was based on principles drawn from theological sources. "So the historians who oppose the trend introduced by St. Albert and St. Thomas to the 'traditional Augustinian' trend do not realize that the philosophical-theological movement prior to 1250 is neither traditional nor essentially Augustinian. . . . In short, what is commonly called pre-Thomist Augustinianism is the teaching of the Faculty of Theology, in the state at which it had arrived about 1230 under the influence of philosophy."[38]

Van Steenberghen asks whether Bonaventure's *Sentences* contains a philosophy.[39] He answers unambiguously that it is strictly a theological synthesis, because Bonaventure did not sufficiently think out philosophical problems for their own sakes. "The unity of his thought is certainly not a philosophical unity."[40] Van Steenberghen maintains that Bonaventure's "heteronomous philosophy" is theological speculation; that he is an Augustinian solely in theology; and that in philosophy, he is an eclectic

Aristotelian. "In short, St. Bonaventure's philosophy is an eclectic Aristotelianism with neo-Platonic tendencies, put at the service of an Augustinian theology."[41]

Gilson responds to Van Steenberghen that Bonaventure's thought does have a philosophical unity, but it is found in Christ—understood here as the Word, the perfect, interior expressive likeness of God. Gilson argues that according to Bonaventure, the true metaphysician must rise to the likeness of all creation, who is its medium and through whom all things have been made. Christ is the center of all the sciences (*medium omnium scientiarum*).[42] All creatures proclaim the existence of God, because they reflect the one through whom all things were made. Gilson summarizes this point very well: "Thus, for him [Bonaventure], the philosophy of St. Albert and St. Thomas was of necessity in error because, while it situated Christ in the center of theology, it did not situate Him in the center of philosophy."[43]

It is the contention of this book that Bonaventure's thought presents us with genuine philosophy, whose content and spirit can be studied without entering formally into theology, in part, because he carefully distinguishes between arguments from reason and those from authority. This is not to say that Bonaventure would accept the rationalist thesis that the doctrines of the faith should be judged by reason. But according to Bonaventure, philosophy finds its completion in recognizing the likeness according to which creation has been made: the *Verbum* spoken from all eternity in the mind of God—Wisdom. According to Bonaventure, Wisdom is a person who calls us and beckons us to a journey of the mind to God.[44]

— II —

The Light of Philosophical Knowledge

Natural Philosophy

Physics

For those of us who live after the rise of modern science, it is difficult to understand that it is possible to become so focused on theological issues and the quest for the divine that the natural order falls out of intellectual investigation. Augustine's heartfelt prayer in his *Soliloquies* reflects this mind-set: "I desire to know God and the soul."[1] Augustine does not regard nature as unworthy in itself of being known, but diligent investigation of it seems somewhat idle, if not pernicious, compared with the exploration of the nature of an infinite and eternal God. Many ecclesiastical writers issued warnings against the dangers of idle curiosity, which they considered dangerous to the soul. Life is short; it is better to know a little about the most important and eternal things than a lot about the insignificant (at least by comparison) and ephemeral. This "forgetfulness of nature" seems to be exactly what happened until sometime in the twelfth century, when, in its course, certain questions came into focus and inspired an extraordinary degree of speculation about the changing world of the heavens and the earth, that is, "mobile being." In short, the twelfth century "discovered" nature. It is in the wake of this discovery that, in the 1250s, Bonaventure developed his view of the created world while commenting on the interpretation of the Genesis account of creation found in the church fathers, as these had been anthologized in Peter the Lombard's *Sentences*.[2]

The twelfth century's discovery was in no small part prompted by the one available text that seemed to shed some light on the most pressing questions of intellectuals about nature: Plato's sole work on natural philosophy, the *Timaeus*. This text possessed great appeal for Christian thinkers, especially because it presents the whole of reality as a cosmos, that is, a well-ordered coherent whole. But even more than this, Plato seems to have come to the view that this cosmos was formed by a divine craftsman who has made it in his likeness: "Then, God, having decided to form the world in the closest possible likeness of the most beautiful of intelligible being and to a Being perfect in all things, made it into a living being, one visible and having within itself all living being of like nature with itself."[3] It is not surprising then, that Plato's *Timaeus* helped spark a renewed curiosity about the cosmos and the natural world.[4]

While Plato's interest in the natural world was heavily confined to one text, his student, Aristotle, wrote a veritable library on the subject, during the course of his lifelong investigations. Aristotle had been absolutely fascinated with nature and had spent a great deal of his life observing it and trying to understand it. He was interested in it all: the basic elements, plant and animal life, the rational animal, the heavens, the overarching order of the whole, and its first movers. He wanted to understand everything that is, in other words, being itself, from its most general characteristics to its most fundamental cause.

In the light of the twelfth century's renewed interest in questions of natural philosophy, it is not surprising that the educated took up the study of Aristotle's texts on natural philosophy (especially his main one, *The Physics*) with vigor and alacrity. Few writers could seemingly have offered them more help than Aristotle; it is with good reason that some have called him "the father of Western science," for it is in his *Physics* that we find formulated for the first time the ideal of a scientific study of nature.[5]

It was not until 1234 that all of Aristotle's works were finally opened for study by the faculty at Paris. Nine years later (1243), the man who was to do so much to make Aristotle acceptable in Latin circles arrived in Paris—Albert the Great (ca. 1206–1280). Albert eventually wrote a commentary on the *Physics*, as did his most famous pupil, Thomas Aquinas, who followed Albert in his endeavor to understand and present Aristotle's teachings to the Latin-speaking world.

This medieval acceptance of Aristotle was to have far-reaching consequences. As one scholar has recently put it, "Medieval Latin scholars eagerly embraced Aristotle's methodology and his approach to the physical world, while adding important ideas about the cosmos from Christian faith and theology. The conscious and systematic application of logic and reason to the natural world was the first major phase in the process that would eventually embrace modern science."[6] The medieval Scholastics were to find in reason not only a handmaiden for theology, but also "the essential tool for explaining the operation of the entire physical cosmos."[7] Aristotle seemed the apotheosis of reason.

However, the arrival of Aristotle was not without difficulties and controversies. One scholar, David of Dinant (b. ca. 1200), for example, got himself into trouble because, in commenting on *Physics*, he identifies God with prime matter. This doctrine, along with some of those advanced by another thinker, Amaury of Bene (d. ca. 1204–1207), aroused suspicion and concern. Therefore, in August 1215, the papal legate, Robert of Courçon, prohibited the teaching of Aristotle's *Metaphysics*, *Physics*, and all books on natural science. In this prohibition, he included the teaching of the works of Amaury and David. This prohibition, issued under penalty of excommunication, was promulgated in the name of Pope Innocent III with the approval of the statutes of the University of Paris.[8] Sixteen years later, in a letter of April 13, 1231, Pope Gregory IV felt called upon to remind the faculty and students of Paris that the prior prohibition against Aristotle, and especially against the *Physics*, remained in force until the work could be submitted to editing and freed from error. On April 23 of that year, he appointed a commission to begin the task of preparing this edited Aristotle for teaching.[9]

Unlike his Dominican contemporaries, Albertus Magnus and Thomas Aquinas, Bonaventure never wrote a commentary on Aristotle's *Physics* (or, for that matter, on any of Aristotle's other texts). Nevertheless, we can find clear evidence that Bonaventure carefully studied the *Physics*, specifically in the section of his *Commentary on the Sentences of Peter Lombard* in which he comments on the six days of creation. This treatise, within Lombard's text, provided aspiring masters of theology with an occasion to give their views of creation and the natural world. Bonaventure comes to see the discipline of physics much as Aristotle did: a theoretical science concerned with the investigation of the principles or causes of the natural, changing world, that is, "mobile being." Its field of investigation is the whole material world; in modern parlance, it is a metaphysics of nature. But Aristotle separated physics from metaphysics, because the latter is more properly concerned with the supersensible.[10]

We find Bonaventure's view of the whole cosmos in his discussion of creation in the second book of his *Commentary on the Sentences*. In his discussion of the cosmos Bonaventure draws on a wide range of sources but with a singularity of purpose: trying to reconcile "the natural philosophers," above all Aristotle, with scripture and Augustine. His discussion constitutes a sort of a cosmic tour that would be familiar to his mid-thirteenth century contemporaries, who had been reading their Aristotle.[11] This cosmos consists of two main realms: the celestial or heavenly and the elemental, which is sublunar, since it is below the lowest planet, namely the moon. The earth is at the center of the cosmos. The celestial realm is made up of three heavens or spheres: the empyrean heaven, the crystalline heaven and the firmament of heaven. The empyrean heaven, Bonaventure thinks, is of one form, immobile, i.e., without motion, and made up of pure light.[12] The crystalline heaven is where we find the first motion.[13] The firmament is the orb of fixed stars.[14] Below the firmament are the planetary orbs or spheres (of which he thinks there are seven). Like other medievals, Bonaventure thinks that the stars of the firmament and the planets are incorruptible because they are made up a fifth element that is subject to the motion of change of place but not decay. Below the planets, in the sublunar world, we find the four elements: fire, air, water, and earth.[15] All the corporeal bodies of the sublunar world are made up of various combinations of these fundamental elements.

Bonaventure's account of the natural order unmistakably reflects the influence of Aristotle and the medieval commentators who came with him, but the principal guide for his views of these matters is Augustine. Bonaventure picks up and develops certain theories of the physical world that Augustine left inchoate. Indeed, he tells us that no one has ever described the nature of matter and time better than Augustine in his *Confessions*.[16] Bonaventure retains these theories from late antiquity—specifically, from Neoplatonic and Stoic sources—but develops them in conversation with the natural philosophy of Aristotle and his commentators.

Bonaventure became one of the most prominent critics of Aristotle in the 1260s. There are three opinions of Aristotle, all concerned with natural philosophy, that became the focus of Bonaventure's critique.

The first of these opinions and one of the most important and hotly debated issues that arose after the introduction of Aristotle's *Physics* was the eternity of the world. Aristotle clearly held that the universe had no beginning and no end—it always has been and always will be. Bonaventure argued adamantly that such an "eternal" universe is impossible. Although it is not clear that he regards his arguments as demonstrative in the strict sense of this term, he argues that the eternity of the world is impossible.[17] He states that creation is concomitant with time, and that God could not have created from eternity, for the two notions are mutually exclusive. Creation necessarily involves time. To prove that eternal motion or time without a beginning is impossible is to prove that the world is created.

Bonaventure has six main arguments against the eternity of the world.[18] Most concern the notion of infinity, and specifically the notion of infinite duration. The first is that it is impossible to add to the infinite. For example, if the world were eternal, there would already have been an infinite number of revolutions of the sun, and yet every day another is added. But it is not possible to add to the infinite; therefore, the world could not have existed from eternity.[19] Secondly, it is impossible to traverse an infinite series. If time were eternal, the world could never have arrived at the present day.[20] Thirdly, it is impossible to order infinite things. The very notion of an ordered series requires a first term or beginning. If the revolutions of the heavens were infinite, there would be no order, that is, there would be no one revolution before the others. But this is clearly false.[21] Fourthly, a finite power cannot comprehend infinite things. If the world did not have a beginning in time, a finite power must have comprehended infinite things. This view clearly relies on two underlying assumptions (both of which would obviously be very controversial): one, that only God has infinite power, and two, that the motion of the heavens has never been without a created spiritual substance that either caused the motion or knew it.[22] Another argument is that it is impossible for there to be in existence at the same time an infinity of concrete objects. If the world existed eternally, there would now be in existence an infinity of rational souls, but this is not possible.[23] The alternative in an eternal world to the infinity of souls would be that the soul is corruptible, that souls are transmitted from body to body, or that there is only one single intellect in all rational beings, all of which are unacceptable in Bonaventure's eyes.[24] Finally, the beginning of the world in time is clear from the very definition of creation: Creation is to have being after not being.[25] In short, the eternity of the world involves an inherent contradiction.

To Aristotle, one of the most striking characteristics of nature is that it constantly changes. His *Physics* is an investigation of "being" insofar as it changes. In other words, Aristotle sets himself the task of explaining how being (that which is) can change (become that which it was not). Aristotle inherited this problem from his pre-Socratic predecessors in the philosophical endeavor, Heraclitus (ca. 540–480 B.C.) and Parmenides (early to mid-fifth century B.C.).

Heraclitus teaches that all things are changing. He is famous for his claim that one can never step into the same river twice.[26] In such a view of reality, it is hard to claim that one possesses any knowledge, since any thing at any particular moment is becoming other than it was at any prior moment. When one goes to name a thing, whatever the "thing" is has already become something else, even if only in a particular way. At the other extreme, Parmenides seems to have denied the very existence or possibility of change. Being is; not being cannot be, for nothing comes from nothing. But the Parmenidean position seems utterly contrary to our experience of a world so thoroughly characterized by change.

Aristotle's solution to this problem was to hold that there are three principles involved in change: form (that which changes), matter (that which receives changes), and privation. When a substance undergoes a change, such that it ceases to be what it was, it is called a "substantial change." When a substance undergoes a change less drastic, for example, in quantity or in one of its qualities, it is called an "accidental change" (since what changes is not substance, but one of a substance's "accidents").

In other words, change does not involve being coming from sheer nonbeing, but being coming from being-in-potency. Thus, change is a movement from being-in-potency to being-in-act. There is no movement from nonbeing to being, for the fundamental reason that nothing comes from nothing.

In discussing Bonaventure's philosophy of nature, it is important to examine his own discussion of the problem of change; otherwise, we might fail to see the centrality of this problem in his own thought. It is precisely this problem that leads Bonaventure to develop his own idiosyncratic version of Aristotle's theory about change.

Bonaventure accepts in fundamental ways Aristotle's solution to the problem of change. Hence, Bonaventure holds the position that all things that change (mobile beings) are composed of two fundamental principles: first, one that makes each thing be what it is (a form); and second, that out of which it is made (matter). Hence, all finite things are composites of form and matter. This doctrine is referred to as "hylomorphism," from the Greek terms *hyle* (matter) and *morphe* (form). Bonaventure takes over many of the basic aspects of this doctrine from Aristotle, who is the originator of this thesis that form is immanent in things and enters into composition with matter. The conception of matter, however, involved in this version of hylomorphism, requires careful consideration, especially in bringing to light what aspects of Aristotle's theory have been modified.

First, matter is the principle of continuity in change; form is the principle that is transposed in any change, since change is precisely either the loss or acquisition of substantial form or the alteration of accidental form. All changing beings thus require matter as the underlying principle of continuity that undergoes change. Another way of stating this point is to say that matter is the intrinsic principle that permits a substance to be the subject of changes. All mutable substances are then necessarily ma-

NATURAL PHILOSOPHY: PHYSICS

terial. This is why Bonaventure does not limit matter to the corporeal. Matter, according to Bonaventure, is not coextensive with the corporeal. Even the spiritual beings, commonly referred to as "angels," are composites of form and matter. This variation on the Aristotelian doctrine is usually referred to as "universal hylomorphism."

In this conception, matter is considered the principle of receptivity, since form is act, and that which is other than pure form must include some such principle, which is at one and the same time a principle of alterity. Matter is that principle in things that makes possible the reception of form. Indeed, matter is the sheer capacity for the reception of form, much as a mirror has a capacity for receiving images, a favorite Bonaventurean analogy. This receptivity is really the distinguishing mark of matter. Act can only actuate that which can be actuated, but that which is actuated cannot be identical with that which actuates. Since form is act, matter must be the principle of potentiality that receives act.

Furthermore, matter is the principle of stability; it is that out of which things come to be in any way at all and without which they could not be in any way at all. For anything without matter is either pure act or absolute nonbeing. Hence, anything that is and that is other than God must be a composition of matter and form. Matter, in other words, is that which sustains form as act above sheer nonbeing. It is the principle that renders a substance capable of being a subject of existence.

Given this conception of matter, it should not be surprising that in his treatise on angels in his *Commentary on the Sentences*, Bonaventure treats the nature of matter at some length. Matter is knowable in two ways, either by privation or by analogy. In the first way, matter is considered stripped of every form to such a degree that its uncovered essence is seen and considered in itself. The way of privation consists in negating every form inhering in material things and yields, in the end, a view of matter as an "intelligible darkness" (*tenebra intelligibilis*).[27] When matter is considered by analogy, one considers the similarity of matter's disposition to form, as potency's disposition to act. Matter's relation to form is analogous to that of potency's relation to act.

Matter can also be considered either by metaphysics or by natural philosophy. Metaphysics considers matter insofar as it is a principle for being; natural philosophy considers matter insofar as it is a principle of motion, necessary for explaining change, whether it takes place among the corporeal substances here on earth or within the celestial bodies of the spheres or the angels in heaven. Hence, it is a principle of all created being, not just corporeal being. Although the spiritual creatures known as angels cannot undergo substantial change, they still undergo accidental changes and hence must possess matter. The metaphysical consideration of matter is important, because it yields an understanding of how a principle of stability is needed for any existing thing. Bonaventure says on a number of occasions that matter provides this stability, while form confers the actual act of being on a created substance.[28]

It is thus possible to speak about matter in two ways: (1) as it exists in nature, and (2) as it can be considered by the mind.[29] Matter, as it exists in nature, only exists in time and place, and is either at rest or in motion. Matter as existing is always united to form; it is always encountered in some *thing*. As matter is considered by the mind, however, it is unformed. When it is considered in this way, it is seen to be the sheer capacity for form. This unformed matter can never exist in this state in space or time; hence, it could not be created unformed.[30] It would not be any thing. Thus, care must be taken when interpreting Bonaventure on matter; one must know whether he is speaking about matter in its own nature (*secundum suam essentiam*) or as it is actually present in the things of nature (*secundum esse*). As Bonaventure puts it very succinctly: "Matter is able to be considered by the soul according to its own essence and as wholly unformed; but according to being it is not able to exist without any form nor was it created unformed."[31]

In its essence, matter is one and so serves as the undifferentiated *fundamentum* for existing things. In this view, it is the principle of existence and the foundation of being for every creature. All created things participate in matter since it is the essential possibility of existing for every form. The essence of matter is identical in all substances, and its being is conferred and differentiated by its form. Matter is one, even under the being of different forms, whether spiritual or corporeal. This gives them a common participation in existing. Things have the stability of existing from matter, since it confers a foundation for the substantial form, but it is the substantial form that confers being. For example, the spiritual matter in the human soul has being from its form, which gives an act of being to the soul, and this constitutes it as a being in the determinate existing of its matter.[32] "The being of a man comes from the form of his soul, which is united immediately to a spiritual matter. The existing of a man comes from the matter of his soul and of his body, which is united to the form of his soul by the mediation of corporeal dispositions."[33]

This distinction between formed and unformed matter is precisely one of the distinctive elements of Augustine's doctrine of matter. In Book XII of the *Confessions*, he says that unformed matter is "almost nothing."[34] This unformed matter never existed by itself in time, because at the moment that God created it, he also endowed it with forms. Augustine thought that matter in its essence is deprived of any distinct form. According to its proper nature, matter is the sheer possibility of form. In the order to time, however, it has never been totally without form, and, furthermore, its possibility for form must exist through some act in the order to time. As a result, matter is prior to form in the order of nature or of generation, but in the order of time, it is posterior, because the completion and perfection of matter depend on an ordination to form. As a result, form and matter are cocreated.[35]

One of the more difficult aspects of the problem of change is the nature of efficient causality, that is, how it works. Bonaventure considers some of the different theories that have attempted to account for the efficient cause of change. At one extreme, and the first he considers, is that of Anaxagoras (500–428 B.C.). This view regards efficient causality as almost nothing; the efficient cause merely discloses what is already there. Bonaventure understands Anaxagoras to have taught that the specific forms of new beings are already actually present in the matter involved in the change. The agent then produces them in the sense that the agent merely uncovers the form already present but hidden.

A second theory that Bonaventure considers, he attributes to Avicenna. In this theory, God is the only giver of forms (*Dator formarum*). Therefore, all forms are given directly and immediately by God; He is the sole efficient cause of substantial change. This truly robust view of efficient causality implies that the sole efficient cause is consistently effecting changes out of nothing. Concomitant with this, however, is a denial that any being other than God is in any real sense a cause. There are no secondary efficient causes; there is only the sole efficient cause. What we think of as events brought about by agents are merely occasions when God changes things. This view is often referred to as "occasionalism."

In his own account of efficient causality and change, Bonaventure gives considerable importance to a view advanced by Augustine—the doctrine of seminal reasons. According to this theory as Bonaventure interprets it, nearly all of the natural forms, such as the forms of elements and mixtures, are contained in the potency of matter and are reduced to act by a particular secondary agent. These inchoate forms, existing virtually in matter, are like seeds awaiting germination; they contain a plan for awaiting development; hence, they are referred to as *rationes seminales*. They are active potencies existing in matter. Matter is never inert and purely passive, but is always both passive and active. It is profoundly dynamic, because it is a seedbed (*seminarium*) in which corporeal forms exist in a virtual and germinal state. Bonaventure holds that the form, which exists in potency in the matter, is reduced to act by receiving a new mode of existence.[36] The secondary agent "creates," even in the case of animal reproduction, only in the sense of bringing out what already existed in potency. The secondary agent does not multiply forms, but on the other hand, form does not come out of nothing, even though a new essence is produced.

The problem with holding the theory that the secondary agent confers actual form, Bonaventure thinks, is that this view grants too much to the secondary agent, for such an agent, in conferring form, confers being. This understanding of change attributes to a secondary agent an activity too similar to the divine activity of creation.

All things then, except for the rational soul, arose from these germinal forms in prime matter. And the very first form to arise from a seminal reason is light. Robert Grosseteste maintained that light is the first form; specifically, it is the substantial form that all bodies possess.[37] The source of this theory seems to be Pseudo-Dionysius. Pseudo-Dionysius calls the Good "the spiritual Light," and maintains that this Light is the "fontal ray," because the visible universe is an unfolding from this Light in which it participates. Dionysius also sees light as the principle of activity in the universe: "Further also, it contributes to the generation of sensible bodies, and moves them to life, and nourishes, and increases, and perfects, and purifies and renews."[38] In Bonaventure's theory, light is the first form and disposes matter to the reception of any other form that is. In this view, the form of light (lux) is the first form that enters into union with matter, raises it above the level of sheer privation, and thus renders matter capable of entering into union with more complex forms. It is what renders matter ready for more forms. Only a minority of Scholastic thinkers holds this "metaphysics of light," as it is commonly called.

In this view, all of being is luminous, reflecting its source. Light is then an active principle in bodies shining forth in the activities of corporeal things, which flow from the basic operation of light, including sensible and intellectual cognition. This theme of light is found throughout Bonaventure's work. It is one of "the controlling ideas" of what the world is and of how knowledge is to be understood.[39]

Bonaventure held that the celestial bodies participate in the form of light, even though each one has its own form. Earthly bodies participate in an embodied light, which is not a substantial form, but is a virtual disposition to become colored under the influence of external light.[40]

One of the implications of the doctrine of seminal forms is that any given substance has a plurality of substantial forms, a suggestion that became one of the most highly debated issues of the late thirteenth century. Furthermore, there has been significant discussion of whether Bonaventure held that there is a plurality of substantial forms in a substance or simply one. Gilson thinks that he does hold to a plurality of substantial forms, but admits that Bonaventure does not explicitly argue for the position; he simply seems to presume it.[41] John Francis Quinn argues at great length that Bonaventure holds to a unicity of substantial form. The range of opinions has run the whole gamut of options.

On this issue, Bonaventure seems to have been influenced by his teacher, Alexander of Hales, and by the Arabic thinker, Avicebron (1021/2–1057/8), both of whom held a universal hylomorphist position.[42] Avicebron teaches in his famous work, Fons vitae, an extreme view on this question: A substance is composed of as many substantial forms as it can be divided into genera and species. The predication of any genus or species of a substance involves the identification of a substantial form. Accordingly, an individual human being would have one substantial form making him a substance, another making him a body, another making him alive, another making him rational, and so on.

Bonaventure clearly does not go to this extreme, especially with regard to positing plural souls, but he does consistently seem to take a plurality of substantial forms as a given (for example, see Collationes in hexaemeron, chapters 4, 10). Form is the principle that explains the perfections of being. In this view, each form prepares the matter for the reception of yet another form, until the appetite of any designated matter for form is exhausted. Hence, it is not any one particular form that confers a definitive unity on a substance. Rather, it is not until matter and form have exhausted all the possibilities for development that the opportunity for further composition with form is excluded. As already mentioned, this is way Bonaventure is quite comfortable saying that, although the soul is composed of matter and form, this does not preclude its entering into composition with a body and still forming a composite, unified human being.[43] What is important for composition is that matter and form be proportionate to each other.[44]

In the view of Aquinas, by contrast, there can only be one substantial form, which gives the thing its essence and makes it what it is. The substantial form delimits the being and thereby precludes any other substantial form. Any other perfections that a substance possesses must be accidental forms.

The question of whether or not there is a plurality of substantial forms in a substance has long struck readers as one of the more arcane debates among medieval thought. Part of this may be a function of the fact that the disputants themselves were not always fully aware of what was at stake, but were simply arguing party lines. There is no question, however, that this issue aroused considerable debate. In essence, the debate is an-other chapter in the Plato-Aristotle debate over universals. The pluralists, while adopting a hylomorphic theory that regards the individual as real, refuse to concede that form (the universal, or basis for the universal) is anything less than the really real. In other words, the pluralists are at-tempting to be Platonists and Aristotelians at the same time. For the defenders of unicity, hylomorphism requires a real composition of essence and existence, or, in other words, that the form-matter (essence) is in potency to the act of being. However, it was intolerable to the pluralists that form could in any way be a potential principle. Form is act, even when there is a plurality of them in one individual. What this makes the individual substance is a very interesting question.

There are different ways that being can be united. One is that beings may be juxtaposed with each other and thus closely related. Another way is for distinct beings to be mixed together to form a third being. A third way is for beings to be brought together so that their natures subsist without mixing or losing their identity. Thus, beings in this third way would be more than just juxtaposed, but not mixed; they would be neither separated nor confused, but would subsist.

In the theory of plural substantial forms, any particular substance con-sists of forms joined in the third way—without confusion and without separation. In this conception, a substance is a composite of forms and matter. The pluralists argued that these forms are joined in matter in a hierarchical order to form a specific individual. This hierarchy is made possible by the fact that each form itself reflects a hierarchy of being. In short, an individual substance is a hierarchy of substantial forms united in designate matter.

The pluralist doctrine is not a problem for the Platonist mind-set. However, the view of the rational soul as the form of the human body is a problem, for this view seems to cast considerable doubt on the possibility of the soul's immortality. Furthermore, the unicity doctrine implies that form is not being, since such a union could only take place if essence and existence are really distinct and enter into composition. Conversely, if form is being, and essence and existence are not really distinct, a plurality of substantial forms, when hypostasized or instantiated in an individual, remain distinct though hierarchically ordered. The unicity doctrine seems a first step on the slippery slope to nominalism.

Those who have defended the position that Bonaventure taught a un-icity of substantial form have argued that when a subsequent form brings about the generation of a new body, the antecedent form remains as merely a substantial disposition in the newly generated body.[45] Since the texts are not clear on the matter, caution is in order. At the very least, we should bear in mind that Bonaventure's disciples, who stand closest to him in time and doctrine—influential figures such as John Peckham and Matthew of Aquasparta—vigorously defended the pluralist position.

The elements also arose from seminal reasons, and each element has a substantial form that makes it a simple substance. The elements enter into composition with other elements to form bodies. Minerals, plants, animals, and human bodies are examples of bodies composed of the elements. The power of light harmonizes the contrariety of the elements in these composite bodies.[46] Such bodies are created by the form that arises from a seminal reason existing in the matter of the elements that go into shaping the mixture. The elementary bodies undergo a transformation such that a composite body is created with a substantial form. The elementary natures remain in the body as substantial dispositions contributing to the qualities of the compound. Animate forms inform complex bodies that have been rendered fit for union with a soul by the seminal reasons.

Furthermore, Bonaventure follows Augustine in maintaining that there are numbers in bodies, especially in sounds and voices. Indeed, since proportion, founded in numbers, is the primary requisite for beauty, and since number is a fundamental characteristic of all things, all things are beautiful and in some way delightful. "Number is the principal exemplar in the mind of the Creator."[47]

It is now necessary to turn to one of the more difficult aspects of any version of hylomorphism, namely, the human being as a composite of spirit and matter. The subtlety with which Bonaventure tries to explicate the relation between body and soul is easily overlooked.

Bonaventure agrees with Aristotle that the human being is a rational animal. This definition implies that the human being is a complex creature, a combination of rationality and animality, matter and form. It relies on the Greek view of the soul as the principle of life in living things: All living things are ensouled: plants, animals, and human beings.

Since Bonaventure thinks the distinctive characteristic of our animal species is rationality, and since he understands form to refer to the metaphysical principle that makes a thing be what it is, he holds that the substantial form of the human being is the rational soul. And it is this rational soul that makes rationality possible. Bonaventure speaks of the rational soul as "an existing, living, intelligent form having freedom of choice,"[48] or, as he puts it even more simply: The soul is a form endowed with being, life, intelligence, and freedom.[49] "Soul" is thus, most properly, a particular type of form, namely, a living one; and the rational soul is more specifically intelligent and free. Needless to say, the human soul is the noblest form of all natural forms found in the world.

First, Bonaventure believes that the soul is the perfection and motor of the human being—perfection with regard to substance, and motor with respect to the powers.[50] He defines the soul as the act and "entelechy" of the body. In discussing this definition, he explicitly quotes Aristotle's *On the Soul (De anima)*.[51] The term "entelechy" is taken from the Greek text and refers to an activating principle that transforms and shapes passive matter. It gives act and completion to the body.[52] If the relation between soul and body is that of act and potency, then it follows that the rational soul is "the perfection of a body intended by nature to be informed by rational life."

On these points so far, Bonaventure sounds like a faithful Aristotelian, but his position is not that straightforward. What adds significantly to the complexity of his view of the human being is his contention that the rational soul is itself a composite of form and matter. The matter of the soul, however, is a spiritual or noncorporeal matter. In this view, Bonaventure understands the spiritual matter that enters into union with the human form to be the sheer capacity or potency for form. The matter in the soul is the principle of its existing; the soul has its stability of being from matter as the receptacle or foundation for the substantial form. The implication of this view is that the rational soul is a substance in its own right, independent of its union with the body. In other words, the soul is a "this something" (*hoc aliquid*) in its own right.

This view is not as alien to the thought of Aristotle as some might think. After all, there are instances in *De anima* where Aristotle does tend to speak about the soul as a sort of substance. He writes:

> Therefore every natural body sharing in life will be a substance and this substance will be in some way composite. Since, however, it is a body of such and such a nature, i.e., having vitality the soul will not itself be the body. For the body is not one of the factors existing in the subject; rather, it is as a subject and the matter. It is necessary, then, that the soul be a substance in the sense of the specifying principle of a physical body potentially alive. Now substance is act; it will therefore be the act of a body of some sort.[53]

Aristotle, however, seems to mean that the soul is merely a substance in the sense of its being the form of the body potentially having life within it. Hence, he can dismiss the question of the soul's substantiality: "That is why we can wholly dismiss as unnecessary the question of whether the soul and the body are one: it is as meaningless as to ask whether the wax and the shape given to it by the stamp are one, or generally the matter of a thing and that of which it is the matter."[54] Passages such as this latter one made Bonaventure nervous, for Aristotle clearly seems to be eliminating the substantiality of the soul, thus its uniqueness and its separability. In the light of such a possibility, Bonaventure argues that the soul is a substance in the proper sense: a composite of form and matter that can exist on its own.

If one asks why such a composite soul requires a body at all, Bonaventure responds that the rational soul requires a sophisticated corporeal sensing system if it is to acquire knowledge. In other words, the human soul requires a body to exercise its power of sensing and knowing, for Bonaventure is unambiguous that knowledge begins in the senses, as Aristotle teaches.

As already mentioned, the rational soul is a composite of form and spiritual or incorporeal matter. In this way, the soul is a "this something." If the soul lacked matter, it would seem impossible for the soul to survive bodily death, since the soul would not itself be a substance, that is, a composite of matter and form, and hence capable of independent existence. In other words, the immortality of the human soul follows from its existence as a spiritual substance. Bonaventure's argument for immortality is thus not based on the simplicity of the soul, but on its substantiality. Nevertheless, Bonaventure concedes that, when the rational soul is separated by death from the body, it cannot properly be called "man."[55] The bodily death of the human being retains its unnatural character—an aspect of the natural order that cries out for healing. Bonaventure uses multiple arguments to establish the immortality of the human soul, drawn from the tradition he inherited, but the most important one for him is the argument from human teleology, specifically from the nature of human happiness and desire. This argument will be clearer after an examination of Bonaventure's eudaimonism in our consideration of his ethics.

Bonaventure does not think that the soul, as the substantial form of the body, is directly and immediately united to the body. O'Leary has argued that Bonaventure's doctrine necessarily entails, at the least, an intervening form of corporeity (*forma corporeitatis*), even though Bonaventure does not explicitly mention it.[56] At any rate, the matter must be disposed by a mediating principle, because matter is never a pure potency. Matter is disposed to form by seminal reasons, and the form must have an aptitude for the matter. The mediating principles of this union are unitability (*unibilitas*) and complexion.[57]

Unitability (*unibilitas*), or the capability of being united, refers to a property of the soul that disposes it for union with the matter (that is, the material elements) of the body without the mediation of anything else.[58] This property of the rational soul is like its other properties, such as rationality (*rationabilitas*), which renders it capable of rational thought, even though this "rational ability" may not always be in act. Unitability is a notion key to understanding the complexity of Bonaventure's view of what the human being is. This notion has received far less attention than it deserves. Bonaventure makes considerable use of this Scholastic notion, originally used to speak of how Christ can have one being with both a human and a divine nature.[59] Bonaventure uses this idea to explain how human bodies differ from other bodies in that they are unitable (*unibile*) to a human spirit.

Because the rational soul is unitable to the human body, it is able to perfect the human body and serve as the principle of its operations.

An implication of this position is that the human being is not simply a soul making use of a body; rather, the rational soul enters into composition with material elements, thereby perfecting these material elements into a living, sensing body and forming a composite, whole substance—a rational animal. It is important to note that the body is not a separate physical substance (as in a Cartesian view). Neither is the human being an angel, for an angel, as a rational spirit, could make use of a body, but could never be truly united to matter in such a way as to form a single, composite substance (a *hoc aliquid*, as is said in Latin).[60] Indeed, the angelic spirit lacks precisely what the human soul possesses—unitability (*unibilitas*). As one commentator succinctly summarizes this point, "Humans have their own bodies, but angels merely assume bodies."[61] As a result of this doctrine, Bonaventure can rightly speak of the soul, not merely as mover (*motor*) of the body, but also as the perfection (*perfectio*) of the body.[62]

The Powers of the Rational Soul

The rational soul, as united to the body, is its perfection and mover. In this latter role, the soul gives existence, life, sensation, and intelligence. The proper name for these abilities is "power," and Bonaventure thinks that the soul has a vegetative, sensitive, and intellective power. Through its vegetative power, the soul generates, nourishes, and increases the body; through its sensitive power, it apprehends sensible things, retains what it has apprehended, and combines and divides what is has retained. By the intellective power, it discerns truth, flees evil, and seeks good.

This first task of the intellective power—discerning truth—is cognitive, while its latter two are affective; hence, the rational soul, through its intellective power, is both cognitive and affective. Bonaventure further divides the cognitive into the intellect and reason. When carrying out its cognitive functions, the soul may be concerned either with knowing for its own sake or with knowing for the sake of doing something. Hence, the intellect may turn either to speculative matters or practical ones. This diversity of possible orientations in the intellect gives it a diversity of functions (though not a diversity of powers, as some in the thirteenth century argued).

Bonaventure further divides the affective power into the natural and selective will, though only the latter is properly called the will. And since the will, properly taken, is indifferent with regard to alternatives, it is referred to as the "free will." Free choice flows from cooperation of the powers of reason and will and their operations.[63] The free will is the greatest power in the universe next to God.[64]

Bonaventure labels the affective functioning of the soul as: (1) the irascible appetite through which it rejects evil, and (2) the concupiscible appetite through which it desires the good. The irascible appetite is a desire for the difficult good, but precisely as such an appetite, it also leads the human being to flee from evil that would render the good unattainable. The concupiscible appetite is the desire for the simple good.[65]

It is important to note here that Bonaventure identifies the appetites with the highest or intellective power of the soul, contrary to what one might expect. Contemporaries, following Aristotle's opinion, identify the appetites with the sensitive power of the soul. Not so, for Bonaventure. As explained below, this move would involve the claim that the higher, intellective power submits to the lower and sensitive power in many human decisions. Hence, this opinion fails to understand how freedom works, in that it misconstrues the sovereignty of the intellect within the human soul.

The soul can only exercise certain powers in union with the body, such as its power of sensing. According to Bonaventure, there are five external senses and a single internal sense. The five senses serve as "portals through which the knowledge of all things existing in the visible world enters the soul."[66] It is through the senses that we perceive not only particular sense objects—light, sound, smell, taste, and the four primary qualities of touch (cold, hot, wet, and dry)—but also the common sense objects (those perceived by more than one sense)—number, size, form, rest, and motion. By the internal sense, an animal determines at a basic level whether an object apprehended by the external senses is healthful or harmful.[67]

Bonaventure speaks of the sensitive power of the soul as "comprehending" sensible objects. He seems to mean by this that the sensitive power is capable of coming to a basic knowledge of sensible things without any special help. Furthermore, the sensitive power retains what is apprehended and can combine and sort what it has retained. It is the memory that retains, and the imagination that combines and sorts—it is the collating instrument of the soul.

Bonaventure informs us that the soul has three powers: memory, intellect, and will. Each of these powers can engage in three operations or activities. The memory can retain and represent present things, whether temporal or everlasting. It also retains simple things that are the principles of continuous and discrete quantities, such as, point, instant, unity. In this second activity of the memory, Bonaventure claims we can see that the memory is capable of being informed not only from outside by phantasms, but also from above, "by receiving and having in itself simple forms that cannot enter through the doors of the senses, nor through sensible phantasms."[68] Finally, the memory can retain the principles and axioms of the sciences, such as, "Every whole is greater than its part." Here too the memory receives its content from above, for the memory has present in itself a changeless light in which it recalls changeless truths. Adhering to Augustine's teaching in the *Confessions*, Bonaventure teaches that the memory retains the past by remembrance, the present by reception, and the future by foresight.[69]

In describing the process by which we come to know sensible things, Bonaventure draws freely from Aristotle. The senses receive a sensible likeness from things, which, in turn, stimulates the senses. Sense apprehension then prompts the intellect to go to work to grasp the object. The senses, however, are not purely passive, a point on which Bonaventure departs from Aristotle's account of sense cognition. Closely following upon apprehension of sensibles comes delight. Echoing Aristotle's first line of the *Metaphysics* ("All men by nature desire to know"), Bonaventure explains that proportional objects cause delight (*oblectatio*). Delight is the union of the suitable with the suitable.[70] After this apprehension and delight, a judgment (*diiudicatio*) is made, which determines certain basic characteristics of the thing (whether it is black or white), as well as why this object delights. "In this act there is an examining of the reason for the delight which is perceived from the object in the sense."[71] The reason for this delight is a proportion of equality, but the detection of this equality, which in itself is the same in objects regardless of their size and is neither extended nor mutable, already involves a spiritual sense. This judgment, therefore, is an action that purifies and abstracts the sensory likeness received in the senses and then causes this likeness to enter into the intellective power.[72]

Bonaventure thinks that we come to know things as they are, in other words, we can apprehend their natures, but the difficulty to be explained here is how the singular and concrete, which, in itself, is unknowable, can be rendered intelligible. To solve this difficulty, Bonaventure follows Aristotle in positing an agent intellect to help the passive intellect abstract out the intelligible aspect or nature of things. The agent intellect illumines the possible intellect so that it may abstract from the sense data it has received, the intelligible nature of the thing. The thing perceived by the senses is concrete and particular (e.g., this dog, Fido); but knowledge concerns the abstract and universal (e.g., dog or "dogness"). Fido is *this* furry dog, but we talk about "dogs" and can even write down everything we know about dogs in a book. Furthermore, even though we can't pet "dogness," this term applies to Fido, Rex, Lassie, and the like. In addition, while the concrete is mutable, the universal clearly is not: Fido is born, grows from puppyhood to mature canine, and will one day grow old and weak and then die. But while Fido is undergoing the ordinary vicissitudes of existence, dogness remains unchanged.

The agent intellect is a light that shines on the intelligible aspects of things and then abstracts this intelligibility from things and impresses it upon the possible intellect.[73] The agent intellect renders the potentially intelligible object actually so by abstracting the intelligible "species" or "likeness" from the object and impressing it on the possible intellect. "Likewise, the agent intellect is unable to bring to perfection its operation of understanding unless the summit of the possible intellect is informed by the very intelligible object."[74] They are not two substances, nor even two separate powers; they come together in one complete action of understanding. Bernard Gendreau discusses this point at some length:

> Thus in Saint Bonaventure we have a form of the theory of abstraction according to which similitudes or species are acquired from the senses and a form of self-sufficiency in knowledge according to which the mind by its own enlightening powers perceives and judges the value of its knowledge. Through sense perception, the similitudes acquired are purified and abstracted to be developed into intellectual species. This is done by an act of discernment or judgment which corresponds to a form of judicatory abstraction through the power of a natural judicatory light *"lumen naturale judicatorum"* and the act of discernment or of separation *"dijudicatio."*[75]

In an interesting variation from Aristotle's theory, Bonaventure denies that the passive intellect is purely passive or the active intellect purely active: "Nonetheless, it [the possible intellect] is not so active as the agent intellect, because it cannot through its own conversion either abstract a species or make a judgment about the species except through the aid of the agent intellect. Likewise the agent intellect is unable to bring to perfection its operation of understanding unless the summit of the possible intellect is informed by the very intelligible object."[76]

So, while it is by means of abstraction that we come to know natural kinds, or essences, such as "rock" or "horse," it also seems to be the means by which we come to such fundamental notions as "whole" and "part." (Bonaventure claims otherwise in his *Itinerarium*, but as Steven Marrone points out, "the reference is neither lengthy nor explicit enough to permit one to say how it ought to be related to the otherwise unambiguous rejection of such a view in the *Commentary on the Sentences*.")[77]

Abstraction, however, does not account for all our knowledge, for the soul knows itself and its qualities without reference to sensation or external species.[78] Furthermore, it is important to note that Bonaventure differs from Aquinas in maintaining that there is not an obligatory turning to the phantasm.

Bonaventure is aware of the Arabic positions on the question of the soul. He knows that Averroes ("the Commentator") argued that the soul or human intellect, both the active and possible intellect, was one in all men, since it is immaterial and incorruptible.[79] Indeed, Bonaventure discusses the Averroistic position at some length. He believes that it is wrong, not only for religious reasons, but also philosophical, among them being that different human beings have contrary thoughts and affections.[80]

The soul's desiring of goods may be carried out in two ways: one through instinct and another through deliberate choice. Hence, Bonaventure also speaks of an instinctive will and an elective will. It is only the latter that is "will" in its proper sense. Bonaventure seems to take it for granted that reason can apprehend alternatives and can deliberate about what choices to make. Augustine is now widely regarded as the first thinker to posit the will as a distinct power of human soul to choose freely, and, like his mentor, Bonaventure is deeply struck by the amazing nature of this power.

Certain actions seem clearly to be within our control. The human being then desires to act and to attain goods not merely through instinct as other animals, but also through deliberate choice. Indeed, truly *human* actions are those not fundamentally limited or determined, but rather those that flow from a fundamental ability to choose. Certain actions of the human being are "free" in this sense. The human being is a unique type of agent in the world: a free agent, we might say.

Medieval Scholastics debated whether free decision (*liberum arbitrium*) is an act, a power of reason and will, a power and faculty distinct from reason and will, or a habit of both reason and will.[81] Bonaventure speaks of it as a faculty or *dominium*. He argues that free decision is a habit of both the reason and the will, but which consists primarily in an act of the will. While free decision begins in reason, it is completed in the will.[82]

Freedom of choice is a power of both reason and will. Bonaventure quotes Augustine to defend the view that "When we speak of freedom of choice we refer not only to a part of the soul, but most assuredly to the whole."[83] It is only when reason and will work together that a human being acts with real freedom, and it is only the one who has acted with freedom who can merit and demerit.

Bonaventure describes the operations of the elective faculty or will as counsel, judgment, and desire. Counsel consists in determining what is better between two things. Judging involves conforming one's mental propositions to a law. The law that governs the judgment is a higher law that is stamped on the human mind. Desire (*desiderium*) is moved the most by love, and that which is loved the most is happiness.[84]

This ability to choose is precisely one of the two most ennobling features of the human being; the other is the ability to know. When it comes to determining which of these two abilities is greater, however, Bonaventure seems to regard the willing ability as the greater, for through the will we determine our destiny. The will is not compelled by the judgment of the mind; if it could be compelled, it would not ultimately be free. In this sense, the will has a certain priority or sovereignty within the soul.

Bonaventure clearly regards the human being as the greatest thing in the material universe. The human being is a unique combination of body and spirit, matter and form, encompassing the whole range of what is in the universe. And the noblest part of the human being is the human soul. "A great thing is the soul: in the soul the whole world can be delineated."[85] The human soul is a microcosm of reality, a microcosm of the macrocosm, an image of the world.[86]

Natural Philosophy

Metaphysics

Metaphysics, as a branch of natural philosophy, is concerned with the truth of "things," Bonaventure tells us. But unlike physics, which investigates things insofar as they change, or mathematics, which investigates things insofar as they are quantifiable, metaphysics goes beyond motion and quantity to investigate things simply insofar as they exist or are "beings." This investigation involves reducing things back to the most fundamental concept, namely, being. It has three main parts: (1) how things came to be from the First Principle, that is, why there is something rather than nothing; (2) how things reflect ideas or "exemplars" in the divine mind, in other words, how things are what they are and are intelligible; and finally, (3) how things "return" to their source, or, the ultimate meaning of things. These three aspects constitute the three parts of metaphysics: emanation, exemplarism, and consummation: "Such is the metaphysical Center that leads us back, and this is the sum total of our metaphysics: concerned with emanation, exemplarity, and consummation, that is, illumination through spiritual radiations and return to the Supreme Being. In this you will be a true metaphysician."[1] Each of these parts is integral to the whole: "For no one can have understanding unless he considers where things come from, how they are led back to their end, and how God shines forth in them."[2]

Emanation

Bonaventure's division of the subject of metaphysics reflects an understanding of the dynamic of being that became common doctrine among Scholastics: that of *exitus* and *reditus*, that is, a going out of all existing things from their cause and a returning back to their goal. It seems clear that the first Scholastic who set the precedent of structuring the science of being this way was Bonaventure's teacher, Alexander of Hales. He divided the four books of Peter the Lombard's *Sentences* into two groups of two each: The first two treat the going out of all things from God and the last two consider the return of all things to God.[3]

Bonaventure uses a method of "complete resolution" (*resolutio plena*) to arrive at the notion of being. In order to understand this method it is necessary to be aware of Bonaventure's distinction between the apprehending intellect (*intellectus apprehendens*) and the resolving intellect (*intellectus resolvens*). The former works to grasp the natures or essences of things; the latter resolves essences into more general concepts. This resolving intellect operates either in a full and complete way (*intellectus plene resolvens*) or in a partial way (*intellectus semiplene resolvens*). When the intellect performs a full resolution, it arrives at being.[4]

The starting point in this method is a thing's nature or essence. We can then reduce this general concept to an even more general one, until we have arrived at the most general concept: "being."[5] The concept of being is thus implicit in all others.

Bonaventure thinks, however, that the knowledge of the imperfect requires some grasp of the perfect; the finite requires some grasp of the infinite; and the changeable some grasp of the unchangeable. Indeed, the condition for the mind's attaining a notion of the limited and imperfect is that it has a knowledge of the infinite, perfect, most pure and absolute being.[6] "If, therefore, non-being cannot be grasped except through being, and if being in potency cannot be understood except through being in actuality, and if being designates the pure actuality of being, then being is that which first comes into the intellect, and this being is that which is pure act."[7]

Indeed, the intellect could not attain a single concept unless it knew what being is per se, and being per se cannot be known unless it is grasped together with its essential predicates—simplicity, necessity, absoluteness, and eternity. Ultimately, being could not be known unless the intellect were "aided by a knowledge of the most pure, most actual, most complete and absolute being, which is being unqualified and eternal."[8] In short, the being that comes first in the mind is pure act, that is, the Divine Being.[9]

This is not to say, of course, that the mind always adverts to this being. "But just as the eye, intent on the various differences of color, does not see the light through which it sees other things, or if it does see, does not notice it, so our mind's eye intent on particular and universal being, does not notice that Being which is beyond all categories, even though it comes first to the mind, and through it, all other things."[10] It is the light of being that makes possible all further knowing. Indeed, apart from the light of being, we could know nothing at all, much as apart from the light of the sun, we can see nothing at all.

Bonaventure is trying to maintain that the intellect knows being not only through species or likenesses abstracted from sensible things by the action of our active intellect, but also through an intuitive grasp of the Divine Being. Thomas Aquinas, by way of contrast, rejects the position that the mind first knows the Divine Being.[11] And although the process by which the first conceptions of the mind come to be is complex, being is nevertheless known strictly through likenesses abstracted from the sensible. The first principles are "the instruments" of the agent intellect, and it is by means of these that the intellect renders other things actually intelligible. Bonaventure thinks that the condition for the possibility of grasping finite being in the first place is that there is an intuitive grasp of infinite and absolute being. God is the light in which the intellect sees.

It is important to point out here, though, that the Divine Being is an objective condition for human knowing and operates within the human intellect, but is itself not identical to the mind. While Divine Being functions as an intrinsic, a priori condition of human knowing, it is not reducible to a subjective, a priori, and formal category of the mind as posited by Immanuel Kant (1724–1804). Efrem Bettoni explains the significant gap between what he calls Bonaventure's "innatism" and Kant's subjectivism:

> The discerning reader cannot avoid seeing a certain analogy between St. Bonaventure and Kant. For both rationality and its laws are within us: we apply them to experience, we do not derive them therefrom. The similarity, however, ends here. For Kant the "a priori" has its absolute foundation in the creativity of our spirit understood not as the empirical "I" but as the transcendental "I." For St. Bonaventure the "a priori" is merely a human participation in the divine thought which has created things according to the archetypes eternally generated with and in the word. Kant ends in absolute subjectivity while St. Bonaventure guarantees the objectivity of our thought by basing it on the absolute objectivity of divine knowledge.

And thus the abyss between the two thinkers remains intact: the abyss between immanence and transcendence.[12]

The human mind retains a receptivity and potentiality to what is, to finite being. But the condition for the possibility of such receptivity is a foundational apprehension of infinite Being, i.e., "that Being which is beyond all the categories [of thought]." This view of the soul's primordial awareness of God belongs in the tradition of Plato and Augustine. For Plato, knowledge involves *anamnesis* or reminiscence of the Forms. Augustine will modify this by holding that the soul's reminiscence or memory is not of the soul's preexistent vision of the Forms, but of the presence of God to the soul.[13] Bonaventure insists upon this presence as the condition for the possibility of knowing.

The Existence of God

Bonaventure regards it as self-evident that God exists—it is an indubitable truth. This view, however, requires some explanation. "But when I say that God exists, the existence predicated of God is totally identical with God, because God is His very existence. Therefore, nothing is more true or more evident than that proposition in which the existence of God is affirmed."[14] Bonaventure believes the human mind innately knows that God exists: "Indeed, it is certain as far as the knower is concerned, for the knowledge of this truth is innate to the rational mind in as far as it possesses the nature of an image."[15] He explains that since the mind is an image, it has an innate knowledge and memory of that of which it is an image, as well as an innate desire for union with this original. By this, Bonaventure does not mean that every human being has a clear knowledge of God. He is speaking objectively. Subjectively, however, the existence of God may be doubted. "A thing is said to be doubtful in two ways: either because of the process of reasoning or because of a defect in reason itself. The first way involves something on the part of the knower and on the part of the object known; the second way refers only to the knower."[16] In the first way, a truth can be doubtful if evidence is lacking either in itself, in its demonstration, or in the intellect that apprehends it. Hence, in this first way, there is no lack of certitude about the existence of God: "The existence of God is indubitably true, because—whether the intellect turns within itself or outside itself, or whether it looks above itself—if it proceeds rationally, it knows with certitude and without doubt that God exists."[17] However, in the second way, from the deficiency of reason, it can be conceded that it is possible for someone to doubt because of a threefold defect in the mind of the knower: in the act of apprehending, in the act of judging, or in the act of analyzing. In other words, doubt arises if someone does not understand the notion of God; or if in judging about evil or injustice, someone concludes that there is no justice. Doubt may arise from faulty analysis of reality, as when some people conclude that the sun is God, since it seems to be the highest corporeal substance.[18]

Bonaventure's most extended arguments for the existence of God may be found in his *Disputed Questions on the Mystery of the Trinity*, where he presents twenty-nine different arguments for the indubitable truth that God exists. He divides these into three general "ways": "proofs" based on the nature of mind, the notion of being, and the nature of truth (ideological),[19] which includes his treatment of the idea of God (ontological). Each of these categories of proofs leads to an indubitable truth: (1) Every truth that is impressed in all minds is an indubitable truth; (2) every truth proclaimed by all creatures is an indubitable truth; and (3) every truth, which in itself is most certain and most evident, is an indubitable truth.

In following the first of these "ways," Bonaventure believes the truth that God exists is impressed in every mind, though in different ways. First, for example, there is the inclination to the true and good, but such an inclination presupposes knowledge of these. "Therefore there is impressed in the minds of men a knowledge of the true and the good and a desire for that which is most desirable. But that good is God."[20] Therefore, God exists.

A variation on this sort of argument begins with a premise taken from Aristotle's *Metaphysics*: "By nature all men desire to know." The wisdom that is most desirable, however, is the eternal wisdom; thus, the human mind holds a desire for this supreme wisdom. But "love cannot exist unless there is some knowledge of the object loved. Therefore, it is necessary that some knowledge of that highest wisdom be impressed in the human mind."[21]

Bonaventure also presents other arguments from desire—for happiness, for peace, and even from hatred of falsehood (which, he argues, requires love of its opposite, namely truth).

Bonaventure classifies his second way of proving God's existence as defenses of the proposition that "every truth that is proclaimed by all creatures is an indubitable truth." In this way, of course, since "all creatures cry out (*clamare*) the existence of God,"[22] there are many different proofs. So, for example, "if there is possible being, there is a necessary being, since that which is possible implies indifference as to being or nonbeing." However, something that is indifferent to being or nonbeing cannot be, except through that which is necessary, that is, determined with respect to being. "Therefore if that necessary being in which there is no possibility of non-existence is none other than God, and if everything else has some degree of possibility, every category of being infers the existence of God."[23] Bonaventure presents the same type of argument with respect to posterior and prior being, with participated and unparticipated (essential) being, with being in potency and being in act, with composite and simple being, and with changeable and unchangeable being.

For his third type of argument, Bonaventure begins with the notion that "Every truth which is so certain that it cannot be thought not to be is indubitably true."[24] The existence of God is such a truth. Bonaventure says the first premise is self-evident; the second can be shown in many different ways.

In one of the ways he shows the second premise, Bonaventure presents a version of his "ideological" proof. He begins with the premise that whatever can be thought of is capable of being stated. However, it is impossible to say that God does not exist without also saying that God does exist. "This becomes clear in the following way. If there is no truth, then it is true to say: 'There is no truth.' But if this is true, then something is true. And if something is true, there is a first truth."[25] Thus, Bonaventure concludes, it is not possible to say, or even to think, that God does not exist. (Bonaventure appeals on various occasions to some version of the argument from truth. In his view, the affirmation of any truth affirms the cause of all truth.)[26]

It is among this third type that we also find Bonaventure's defense of Anselm's "ontological" proof: "God is that than which nothing greater can be conceived. But since it is true that that which cannot be thought not to be is more true than that which can be thought not to be, therefore, if God is that than which nothing greater can be conceived, God cannot be thought not to be."[27] In response to Gaunilo's objection about the best possible island, Bonaventure responds that there is no comparison, for while a being than which nothing greater can be thought is not a contradiction in terms, an island than which no better can be thought is. "For an island is a limited being, while the implication is proper to the most perfect being."[28] Limit necessarily involves imperfection and, therefore, something less than that which no better can be thought.

Knowledge of God

We have no external sense experience of God. He is not an object in the world that we can sense; in fact, God is beyond any genus we can even conceive of. "God and man do not share a common genus," Bonaventure says. Indeed, in certain respects, God and creatures may seem so unlike that one might conclude there is no way to bridge the gap between the infinite and finite. One might decide that all our talk about God involves such gross equivocation of terms that the person speaking about God is either talking nonsense or constructing an idol. Bonaventure does not take this view, but he is clear that our knowledge of God is limited.

Bonaventure argues that we can speak about God in two ways: (1) about what he is not, and (2) about what he is like. The negative way (*via negativa*) involves denying those characteristics that seem inappropriate to a perfect being. The positive way (*via positiva*) is more complex and difficult, since God and creatures do not belong to a common genus. Any positive, accurate judgments about God, of whom we do not have any sense experience and who is beyond all categories of thought, will be possible on the basis of those creatures we do know. Bonaventure clearly realizes this and so, at various points in his theological work, outlines a doctrine of analogy.[29]

Bonaventure understands analogy to be the middle position between two extremes: equivocity and univocity.[30] Univocity obtains when two things share a common nature, a common concept, and have the same name, as Aristotle makes clear in *Categories*.[31] Hence, we cannot make univocal statements about God. Equivocity obtains when two things share the same name but do not share a common concept or meaning. Analogy is operative in those situations where two things do not share a common nature, but rather a common concept. A stock example is "healthy," as in "healthy food" and "a healthy animal": Food is healthy insofar as it is a cause of health in an animal. In this example, "healthy" does not refer to a common nature shared by food and animal, but "healthy" is clearly related in the two usages.

Attempts to present Bonaventure's comprehensive doctrine of analogy have been complicated by the fact that he develops two different, though not unrelated, accounts of analogy: one for analogical names (a logical doctrine concerning the use of terms) and one for analogical resemblance (a metaphysical doctrine for how different things can be alike in reality without sharing a common nature).[32] Furthermore, there are two modes of resemblance: relational resemblance and simple resemblance. The former involves agreement between two and two; the latter, agreement between one and one, such that one thing simply is the likeness of the other.[33] The sensible likeness (*species*) of an object, for example, simply resembles that of which it is a likeness. Terms predicated analogously must have a foundation in the real, even if the foundation is merely a sameness or equivalence of relationships.

The Nature of God

These theories of analogical names and analogical resemblance make possible Bonaventure's discussion, in his *Disputed Questions on the Mystery of the Trinity*, of the perfections (or attributes) of God. In this text, Bonaventure argues that the Divine Being is simple, infinite, eternal, and immutable.

The Divine Being is supremely simple because he lacks not only actual composition, but potential composition as well. He explains that a being can fail to realize the highest unity for only three possible reasons: (1) because it is composed of different elements, (2) because it is a component part of another being, or (3) because it has a capacity for entering into composition. But certainly it cannot be the case that God is composed of part of another: then he would not be first. Nor can God be a component part of another being, for then he would not be perfect, and what is perfect cannot enter into the constitution of another being. Nor can the Divine Being have the capacity to enter into composition, for then he would be ordered to another being and would not be the Ultimate Being.

Because God is supremely simple, the Divine Being and power are infinite insofar as the infinite denies any limit with respect to quantity of power. When infinite is used negatively, it negates all limit and finitude, but this can be understood in two ways: in accord with the two meanings of end. An end can refer both to end-as-limit and end-as-completion. "Infinite" thus can be predicated in two ways, either by negating end as limit or end as completion. Limit can be understood with regard to material quantity or to spiritual quantity. The first refers to a quantity of weight, the second to a quantity of power. When infinite is predicated as the negation of a limit in the quantity of weight, "infinite" refers to some degree of incompleteness. When infinite is predicated as the negation of a limit in the quantity of power, it refers to a perfection, not contrary to simplicity.[34]

Because the Divine Being is simple and infinite, it must be eternal. Because it is infinite, it lacks either a beginning or an end. Because it is simple, it lacks both prior or posterior, both of which would include diversity and composition. "Therefore, supreme simplicity involves total simultaneity; supreme immensity involves total interminability; and when both of these attributes are joined together, they constitute eternity. For eternity is nothing other than the 'simultaneous and total possession of interminable life.' "[35]

Bonaventure argues that twelve "predications" can be made of the "highest excellences" of the Divine Being. By our intelligence, we can judge that certain perfections, because they are superior to their contraries, must belong to a supreme and perfect being. For example, since we understand that living beings are superior to lifeless ones, we must say of the Divine Being that it is supremely alive; and because sensing is better than lack of sensation, God must perceive all things. In this way, Bonaventure derives a list of twelve excellences that can be predicated of God: supremely alive, perceiving all things, understanding all things, immortal, incorporeal, i.e., a spirit, omnipotent, utterly just, supremely beautiful, incorruptible, immutable, perfectly good, and completely happy. These excellences can be reduced to three—eternity, wisdom, and happiness—and these can be further reduced to one: wisdom, by which is meant, the begetting mind (mens generans), its begotten word (verbum proles), and the love that binds them (nectens utrumque).[36]

God is almighty in that he is the all-powerful principle and ruler of the universe. But this omnipotence does not mean that God can carry out acts that contradict the very notion of divinity. Bonaventure does not think that God can execute certain types of acts. For example, God cannot commit any "acts of culpability" (or wrongful acts); he cannot lie or intend evil, that is, what is contrary to the natural order and the divine plan. Nor can God undergo any "acts of penalty," that is, defective acts made possible by the sinful Fall, such as feeling sorrow or fear. God cannot make something greater than himself or create some being that would be infinite in act, or make a square circle. Bonaventure is particularly insistent upon the last type of acts. He quotes Anselm to support his exclusion of contradictory acts: "Whatever is contradictory, be it the smallest thing, is not found in God."[37] This point is especially clear when we consider that God's power must be orderly. A well-ordered power does not do the impossible, and whatever contradicts "the primordial and eternal principles and causes" is impossible. Bonaventure thus concludes that it is impossible "to produce some being infinite in act," or "to make something to be and not be at the same time," or "to make a past event as never having happened."[38]

God is all knowing. God's wisdom extends to all things: actual or possible; good or evil; past, present, or future. "On account of this utter perfection, He knows all things most distinctly in all their actual and possible states."[39] This wisdom, insofar as it is aware of all possibilities, is referred to as knowledge or cognition. Insofar as this wisdom is aware of all that occurs in the universe, it is referred to as vision. Insofar as it is aware of all that is done well, it is called approval. Foresight refers to the divine wisdom's awareness of all that is to come about. Providence is divine wisdom's awareness of what God himself will do. Preelection is this wisdom's awareness of who is to be rewarded, and reprobation refers to its awareness of who is to be condemned.

In his discussion of divine wisdom, Bonaventure argues that God knows each and every thing in the most distinct fashion, conceiving them all most clearly and perfectly. God thus knows the multiplicity of things, because he possesses the determining principles and ideas of all individual beings; but he possesses this knowledge of the many in such a way that it does not threaten his unity because "all the likenesses of these beings are one in this divine wisdom."[40]

⌈ It is important to touch upon what God wills. The fact that God does not will to exist everything he knows is implicit in the distinction Bonaventure makes within God's knowledge between the actual and possible divine ideas. God knows more than he says, for the exercise of the divine will is precisely what makes the difference between merely possible beings and actual beings. God has chosen what comes to be from the infinite range of possible things. Bonaventure unambiguously rejects any sort of necessitarian view of creation in which everything God knows would necessarily have to be. Hence, when Bonaventure speaks of his metaphysics being concerned with emanation, he does not mean a necessary emanation as we find in certain Neoplatonist metaphysics. Creation reflects the choice of the divine will and is thus an act of love. ⌋

Since the first principle is the highest Being, he must possess a will and in the most noble manner. The will of God must be completely righteous and effective. It must be perfectly righteous, because in him will and truth are one; it must be perfectly effective, because in him will and power are identical.[41] In other words, in God there can be not even the slightest deviation from truth, nor any defect in power. Hence, it is the very norm of righteousness and the origin of all efficiency. As a result, "nothing can be accomplished without it, nothing can prevail against it, and there is nothing it cannot do."[42]

Concurrence

Bonaventure never ceased to be amazed by the very fact of the existence of any created thing. That there is something rather than nothing is a theme to which Bonaventure returns with frequency. For him, creation from nothing means "to be" after not being. A creature is a being from nothing. And every creature bears the mark of its origin—its nothing-ness—in at least three important ways. Together these marks establish the radical contingency of things, that they are not the cause of themselves.

First, there is, what he calls on numerous occasions throughout his writings, a fundamental "vertibility" in things. That is, all created things retain a disposition to revert to the nothingness from which they came and from which they are preserved at every moment by the will of God.[43] In other words, existence is always, at every moment, a gift, and not something accruing to a thing as an aspect of its being. God alone is invertible, for he alone is being. That which has come from nonbeing is thus not invertible in its nature. Another way of putting this point might be to say that existence includes no "right" to existence. It is only by the first principle's concurrence that things are sustained in being. Indeed, the continued existence of finite and changing being is the primordial evidence of the first principle's goodness.

Two other metaphysical qualities that all creatures have are also "possibility" (possibilitas) and "vanity" (vanitas). Both of these qualities are found in creatures because they are from nothing. Bonaventure argues that, since every creature receives being (esse) from another, it is not its own being. Implicit in this argument is the premise that that which receives being must not already possess it. But a being that receives being is not pure act and so is radically contingent, that is, able to exist but not existing of itself, i.e, possible.

Every creature also possesses "vanity" (vanitas) because it was produced from nothing. The vain thing is not able to sustain itself. But no thing is able to sustain itself in being that has received being from nothing. Bonaventure describes a being that is from nonbeing as "vain." "Vanity" is his term for a finite being's inherent vertibility. He contends that all things are vain; every thing is sustained by the presence of truth. That a thing exists is as if someone were suspending a heavy body in the air.[44]

The power of bringing something to be from nothing could only be unlimited and hence belong to God alone. In addition, if he creates the world, he must bring it out of nothing for he cannot possibly make it of his own substance.

All things abide by the first principle. Furthermore, the distinguishing characteristic of the creature is its utter dependence, for it could not be apart from God. "Of itself, therefore, the creature is nothing. Whatever it has it is indebted for. Thus it is that the creature, because of its deficiency, always remains dependent upon its Principle."[45] God's constant presence, clemency, and influence maintain the creature in existence. "Such concurrence, although it applies to all creatures, is called a grace, for it derives, not from any obligation, but from the liberality of divine bounty."[46] In short, it lacks stability, "and therefore is not able to be except by the presence of the one who gave being to it."[47] "An example of this is clear in the impression of the form of a seal in water, which is not preserved for a moment unless the seal is present."[48]

Indeed, the divine will is so utterly efficacious that "no one can effect anything unless that will operates and cooperates with him."[49] The divine will is beneficent, a will of good pleasure as Bonaventure calls it. Indeed, he has a strong notion of the divine will's constant and ever-present work in creation. "Everything that occurs in the universe comes about by this will of good pleasure."[50] He quotes approvingly Augustine's claim in *De Trinitate* that nothing occurs apart from the divine will: "Nothing visible and sensible ever occurs in the immeasurably vast and comprehensive empire of the created world that does not proceed by either command or permission from the inner, invisible, and rational authority of the supreme Emperor."[51]

Exemplarism

In *Eighty-three Different Questions* (*De diversis quaestionibus LXXXIII*), Augustine posited the Platonic forms as ideas in the divine mind. The Neoplatonist, Philo of Alexandria (ca. 15 B.C.–50 A.D.), had made the same move in his work, *De opificio mundi*. It is through the Augustinian text, however, that Philo's thesis came to influence Christian philosophers in the West. This is no small move. This move also means that created natures reflect the divine mind. Creation expresses the divine truth, the divine exemplar; it "speaks" of that of which it is the likeness.[52] Reality has meaning—not only in the sense that there is a ground for the universal that the mind forms from the concrete singular, but also in the sense that the concrete thing is a likeness of the divine mind.

As already seen, Bonaventure's threefold division of metaphysics highlights an important intermediate step in the larger dynamic of exitus and reditus—his theory of exemplarism. Bonaventure's exemplarism is not an aspect of his thought, but its heart and center. His theory will therefore

be given considerable attention. Bonaventure argues that the metaphysician proceeds from the consideration of finite, particular substances
to the infinite, universal substance. Insofar as he considers all things in
reference to the first principle of the universe, he is like the natural philosopher; insofar as he considers all things in reference to the final cause,
he is like the moral philosopher; but insofar as he considers the exemplary
cause of all things, he shares this subject matter with no one else. Indeed,
so central is exemplarism to metaphysics that the only real metaphysician
is the one who considers being in the light of that principle which is the
exemplar of all things.

Having come to a basic notion of God, and having established that
God is all knowing, we can now take up the nature of the divine mind.
In a famous sermon, Bonaventure praises Plato for preserving the way of
wisdom, while Aristotle, the way of science. Bonaventure wants to bring
these two together. Aristotle was correct to criticize Plato for limiting
knowledge to an ideal world, but he was wrong to neglect the eternal
ideas. Indeed, Aristotle is not a true metaphysician, because he rejected
transcendent form and so failed to perceive the transcendent cause of the
world. He compounded the error by holding that the world is eternal.
Plato was right to turn to the eternal, and thus preserve the way of
wisdom.

> Because Plato related all certain knowledge to the intelligible or ideal
> world, he was justly criticized by Aristotle, not because he was wrong in
> affirming the Ideas and the eternal reasons, since Augustine praises him for
> this; but because—despising the sensible world—he wished to reduce all
> certain knowledge to the Ideas. In doing this, he would seem to provide a
> firm basis for the way of wisdom which proceeds according to the eternal
> reasons; but he destroyed the way of science which proceeds according to
> created reasons. On the other hand, Aristotle provided a firm foundation
> for the way of science while neglecting the way of wisdom. It seems,
> therefore, that among the philosophers, the word of wisdom is to be granted
> to Plato and the word of science to Aristotle.[53]

Bonaventure contends that it was one of Augustine's great insights that
he understood this. Augustine preserves both the way of science and the
way of wisdom. Bonaventurian realism insists that Plato, Aristotle, and
Augustine sit at the feet of the same master and speak of the one truth,
but it is Augustine who is preeminent. While taking account of many
Aristotelian doctrines, Bonaventure painstakingly attempts to reconcile
Plato and Aristotle on the issue that most radically divides them, namely,
the transcendence of form. Bonaventure thinks that Plato, with his doctrine of forms as the ultimate basis of thought and reality, understood

rightly that forms must transcend the singular and sensible, but that Aristotle correctly understood that forms must be immanent in finite singular things. It is Augustine, Bonaventure thinks, who saw that both Plato and Aristotle must be right in different ways—that form must be transcendent and immanent, both present in the concrete singular and yet beyond any passing things. Augustine is the one who corrects Plato by positing the forms as ideas in the mind of God. As divine ideas, the forms find their "home" and can thus serve as exemplars for the things that come to be. One implication of the positing of the forms as divine ideas is that there is an infinitude of possible beings, for the mind of God is infinite. The only restriction on these ideas is the law of contradiction. A square circle or a goat-stag cannot exist in reality, because neither can be thought by that mind that makes it possible for anything to be at all; and these contradictions cannot be thought, because they are not really thoughts at all—they are contradictory, which is to say, incoherent and meaningless.

⌈The view that the divine mind is the ultimate locus of forms of being is referred to as "exemplarism." Bonaventure regards exemplarism as the heart and center of metaphysics. The central concern of metaphysics, then, is the ultimate ground of being under a particular aspect: namely, as the source for reality's having meaning or making sense at all, as the source of things being what they are and not other things, and as the source for being graspable by mind at all. To deny form is to deny that the real is attainable by mind, but Bonaventure thinks that to deny the forms as divine ideas is to fall short of seeing the necessary ground or condition for the possibility of truth. The metaphysician, however, does not stop at the fact that God is the exemplar cause of all things; he must also consider the nature of such a making cause.⌉

In a late work, the *Disputed Questions on the Knowledge of Christ*, Bonaventure takes up the question "whether God knows things by means of their likenesses or by means of their proper essence."[54] The underlying premises of Bonaventure's response are that God must know his own creation and must know in a way appropriate to him.

God cannot know things by means of their proper essences, for then there would be plurality in God. It is the representative likenesses that are the principles of knowledge, "since knowledge, precisely as knowledge, involves expression and assimilation between the subject and object."[55] Bonaventure explains that the eternal ideas cannot be distinct from the Creator, and so, they must be the representative likenesses (and exemplary forms) of created things.[56]

Bonaventure is then careful to distinguish two different types of likeness: a likeness of imitation (*similitudo imitativa*) and an exemplary likeness

(*similitudo exemplativa*). For the former, Bonaventure gives the example of
the creature who is a likeness of the Creator. For the latter, he gives the
example of the exemplary idea in the Creator, which is also a likeness of
the creature. In both of these, the likeness is expressing and expressive.[57]

Bonaventure then goes on to explain that there are two ways of knowing: one that causes things to be and one that is caused by things. The
latter requires a likeness of imitation;[58] the knowledge that causes things
to be, however, requires an exemplary likeness.[59] "Such a likeness does
not come from outside; hence, it implies neither composition nor any
imperfection."[60] Bonaventure takes as given that the divine intellect is
"the supreme light, the full truth, and pure act," then he argues that just
as the divine power that can produce things is sufficient in itself, "so the
divine light and truth is sufficient in itself to express all things. And since
this expression is an intrinsic act, it is eternal. Because an expression is
a form of assimilation, the divine intellect—expressing all things eternally
in its supreme truth—possesses from eternity the exemplary Ideas of all
creatures."[61] God creates on his own; God knows on his own; and because
of what it means for God to know, it must be from all eternity.

It is the likeness of exemplarity that grounds knowledge, and this type
of likeness is found in the Creator by which he creates.[62] Bonaventure
explains that if our intellect were fully in act, it would need no likeness
from outside, but it too would still use a likeness for knowing beings.[63]

Bonaventure argues that truth is "a principle of knowledge" (*ratio cog-
noscendi*), and this can be understood in two ways. First, it is identical
with the "entity of a being" ("*rei entitas*"). "To this, Augustine writes in
his *Soliloquies*, that 'truth is whatever exists.' " Second, "truth is the expressive light in intellectual knowledge." Bonaventure quotes Anselm for
support: "Truth is a rightness perceptible only to the mind." He then
explains that in the first way, truth is the remote principle of knowledge;
but in the second way, it is the proximate and immediate principle.[64]
Truth is found in the supreme degree in the likeness that is the exemplar
of creation. "Such a likeness expresses the creature more perfectly than
the created being itself can."[65] Indeed, no truth can be seen apart from
this first truth.[66]

Bonaventure thinks this exemplar is accessible to human reason.[67] Being (*Ipsum Esse*) has expressed himself perfectly in an intrinsic word that
is the *similitudo expressa*. It is this likeness that is the exemplar for all
things. This medium is the key to the whole: "If you understand the Word,
you understand all knowable things."[68] Bonaventure thus makes the uncreated Word the center of reality and therefore of metaphysical investigation.[69]

To explain, Bonaventure thinks that mind, engaged in thinking, necessarily generates an interior "word." In a question on whether the divine Word is spoken of essentially or notionally, Bonaventure discusses speaking to oneself:

> To speak to oneself is nothing other than to conceive something by the mind. The mind, however, conceives by understanding, and by understanding another conceives a likeness to the other, by understanding itself conceives a likeness to itself, because the understanding is assimilated to the thing understood. The mind therefore, by speaking to itself within itself conceives a likeness to itself, and this is the conceived word.[70]

Speaking to oneself is a conceiving in the mind, and this requires a likeness. This conceiving is a speaking because one cannot conceive without speaking an interior word. "In another way to speak to another is to express the 'concept' of the mind and to this [speaking] corresponds the word brought forth."[71] There is an intrinsic fecundity to thought such that it naturally produces its term—the Word.

This is not to say, however, that the metaphysician attains a notion of the Trinity. Indeed, he does not come to see the medium of being as the "Christ" or Messiah, nor as the revealed Son of God:

> Although the metaphysician is able to rise from the consideration of created and particular substance to that of the universal and uncreated and the very notion of being, so that he reaches the ideas of beginning, center and final end, yet he does not attain the notions of Father, Son, and Holy Spirit. For the metaphysician rises to the notion of this being by seeing it in the light of the original principle of all things, and in this he meets physical science that studies the origin of things. He also rises to the notion of this being in the light of the final end, and in this he meets moral philosophy or ethics, which leads all things back to the one Supreme Good as to the final end by considering either practical or speculative happiness. But when he considers this being in the light of that principle which is the exemplar of all things, he meets no other science, but is a true metaphysician.[72]

Augustine made the fundamental move of positing the ideas in the divine mind. These ideas of all things are expressions from the Word. The ideas of all creatures are in the Word; they are one with the divine essence. However, since there can be no real distinction in God except between the subsistent relations that are the three Persons, there is no distinction in what these ideas are; there is only a distinction in what they connote. They only are because he thinks them—they are expressions of his mind, but his mind would still be what it is even without these ideas. These ideas include everything actual or possible, all universals and all individuals. There is thus an infinite number of them, indeed, "an infinity of infinities."

It should be clear from even this brief overview that Bonaventure was deeply aware of Aristotle's errors and their interrelatedness. His suspicion of Aristotle increased, presumably as a result of the development of the extreme Aristotelianism of the Averroists. The only proper reading of Aristotle is a critical one; an uncritical reading leads to a whole mesh of errors. If one affirms the eternity of the world, then one denies creation, for creation is necessarily in time. If one denies exemplarism, then God does not know his creation. It follows that God knows only himself, as Aristotle implies in his *Metaphysics*. If God does not know his creation, then he can exercise no government or providence over it. All events would then transpire as a result of chance or necessity. Of course, if there is no providence, there is no ultimate justice in the world. There is no ultimate reward and punishment. All of these views flow from the denial of exemplarism.[73] It is difficult to overstate the centrality of this doctrine in Bonaventure's whole synthesis.

An implication of Bonaventure's expressionism is that the universe is like a book reflecting, representing, and describing its Maker. Indeed, there is a hierarchy of expressions, for all things reflect God as a trace, rational spirits as images, and the God-conformed as likenesses. The universe reflects the wisdom of which it is an expression.

Another implication of this expressionism is that all sensible things are a lie in comparison with the Word.[74] Everything exists more nobly, even if not more truly, in the eternal art. Bonaventure could be easily misinterpreted here. When this statement is placed in the context of his larger philosophy, it seems clear that he does not mean that God lies in creation, but that the dissimilarity is great enough between exemplar and exemplified, i.e., between sign and signified, that the hearer can be easily misled into thinking that the sensible stands alone and has no significance.

According to Bonaventure's exemplarism, reality reflects the divine ideas that are exemplars in the divine mind. As noted below, Bonaventure thinks that knowing truth involves attaining or "glimpsing" these eternal reasons, though in an opaque manner. Therefore, while Bonaventure maintains with Aristotle that cognition is a mode of being and thus a way of union, the union is never just between the object and the knower, for the object is also a sign that points to a transcendent order, which is found in the mind that knows all forms. Reality is the expression of the Mind that knows it; hence, our knowing is always a journey of the mind to God.[75] Bonaventure develops what may be called a semiotic metaphysics. All things or substances are signs, intentionally expressed by a sign-giver. Indeed, so thoroughly is the divine mind and its own interior word expressed in the universe that the world is truly a book—an intelligible, coherent, structured monograph expressing the Great Mind of all the ages.

Consummation

The study of Aristotle in the thirteenth century led scholars to a larger view of the human capacity to know.[76] Although Aristotle's theory of cognition is ambiguous on a number of points, it could easily be interpreted to imply that cognition is a strictly natural process without need of divine or heavenly assistance. This naturalistic interpretation seemed, in the view of many thirteenth-century thinkers, to run counter to the long-established view of Augustine that the human mind is not sufficient in itself to carry out its basic operation of knowing truth, but is in need of divine assistance, usually described in terms of light imagery or "divine illumination." In the thirteenth century, a number of writers attempted to defend this illuminationism, which they saw as the immemorial Christian view. They appealed to Augustine, who, in fact, did not develop a systematic theory of illumination, but rather alluded to it in some rather loosely scattered and often ambiguous references in his corpus. William of Auvergne and Robert Grosseteste were among the earliest of these "Augustinians"; others followed in their path: Alexander of Hales, Jean de la Rochelle, and Richard Rufus of Cornwall, to name a few. As the influence of Aristotle increased, there was increasing pressure to be logical, systematic, and scientific, according to the canons established by Aristotle.[77] In the late thirteenth century, John Peckham (in his *Commentary on the Sentences*, 1266–1268), Matthew of Aquasparta (in his questions *De fide*, 1277–1278 and in *De cognitione*, 1278–1279), Roger Marston (in his questions *De anima*, 1281–1282) all defended theories of illumination,[78] but the most prominent, and perhaps most extreme, theory of illumination was advanced by Henry of Ghent (ca. 1217–1293). Out of the work of such men from the 1250s forward developed for the first time a complete doctrine of divine illumination.[79]

In the 1290s, Duns Scotus reacted against Henry's interpretation with such a thorough critique that his attack seemingly brought an end to theories of illumination for generations. "Bonaventure's Questions ceased to be copied, and his Sermon survived to our day in only one manuscript."[80] It was not until the Renaissance revival of Scholasticism, and specifically, until the work of certain Capuchin Franciscans, that an illumination theory returned. The Capuchins made an effort to return to the teachings of Bonaventure, but their sources were very limited.[81]

"Illumination" is an analogous term, borrowed from the corporeal world to describe an immaterial activity. It is also important to keep in mind that, for Bonaventure, there are three lights at work in human understanding: (1) the natural light of the intellect itself; (2) the light of cognitive objects in the sensible world; and (3) the most problematic, the eternal light of God.[82] When we talk about illumination theory, we are usually speaking of the role of the last light, the divine light, in human knowing.

Like "recollection" in Plato's own writings, its main point is to insist that the mind attains reality, indeed, that the highest goal of human cognition is the contemplation of "the permanent things," or the eternal truth (in Bonaventure's theory). Precisely because this knowing is the attainment of the permanent things, of eternal truth, an activity that allows the mind to transcend the temporal illumination must be invoked. Recollection and illumination fulfill similar roles in this regard. Unlike "recollection," however, "illumination" stresses the human mind as passive, rather than active.

There are occasional hints of Bonaventure's theory of illumination in his early *Commentary on the Sentences*; it is only in other texts that he commits himself to such a theory. His *Disputed Questions on the Knowledge of Christ* (*Quaestiones disputatae de scientia Christi*) and his sermon, *Unus est magister vester, Christus* are two key texts, *loci classici*, for his illumination theory. A close examination of these works, however, rules out certain interpretations and shows that Bonaventure's doctrine of illumination is concerned with the judgment and its mode of certitude.[83] In fact, it becomes evident in the course of analyzing the various texts below that Bonaventure's so-called "illumination theory" is fundamentally "a metaphysical analysis of certitude."[84]

There have been four major interpretations of Bonaventure's illumination theory: (1) ontologistic, which tends to see illumination as giving the human mind immediate access to the divine mind; (2) ideogenic, which sees illumination taking place in the formation of our basic ideas or concepts;[85] (3) formal, which sees illumination taking place in the judgment;[86] and (4) synthesizing, which combines theories two and three.

In 1874, the fourth question *On the Knowledge of Christ* was published. Ontologists seized upon the question as evidence that they belonged in a long and distinguished line of thinkers that went back through Nicholas

Malebranche (1638–1715) and Bonaventure to Augustine, the Alexan-drines, and finally Plato.[87] One of the leading ontologists of the nine-teenth century, Vicenzo Gioberti, cites the *Itinerarium* in his introduction to philosophy.[88] Indeed, in 1859, G. C. Ubaghs of Louvain set out to show that Bonaventure was the source of ontologism.[89]

The Franciscan, G. Ortoleva, was perhaps the first to "rescue" Bona-venture from the Ontologists by situating his doctrine in the context of all his writings, that is, the *Sentences*, the newly found *Questions on the Knowledge of Christ*, the *Itinerarium*, and the *Collations on the Six Days* (*Collationes in hexaemeron*).[90] The debate, however, between the ontolo-gistic and the non-ontologistic reading of Bonaventure's theory raged into the 1890s, with the coup de grâce delivered by one of the editors of Bonaventure's *Opera omnia*, Ignatius Jeiler, who vigorously refutes the on-tologistic reading in the scholion to the *Itinerarium*, published in the crit-ical edition of 1890.[91]

The synthesizing interpretation of illumination has been advanced by Bernard Gendreau, who argues that even "on the level of apprehension and definition there is a role played by the eternal ideas to assure the value of the knowledge."[92] In other words, divine illumination is required for certitude about the content of the knowledge acquired naturally, even beginning in sense perception: "The genesis and acquisition of knowledge itself would thus be achieved by human reason alone, while the certainty and the infallibility of the acquired or arrived at knowledge would be based upon the eternal reason and would require divine illumination to be realized."[93]

Bonaventure's illumination theory has to be interpreted, however, in the light of two key doctrines that help clarify the theory and how it works: first, a sophisticated exemplarism that is the ultimate context in which illumination operates; and second, an Aristotelian abstraction the-ory, which includes a doctrine of the agent intellect. Bonaventure com-bines both illumination theory, which he borrows from Augustine, and an abstraction theory, which he borrows, with change, from Aristotle. Placed in the context of exemplarism and abstraction theory, we can see that Bonaventure holds illumination to fulfill an epistemic and normative role rather a noetic and ideogenic one.[94] In other words, illumination functions within the judging acts of the human mind to clarify, stabilize, and confer certitude on particular types of judgments.

First of all, it should be pointed out that the ontologistic and ideogenic interpretations of Bonaventure's illumination theory would render an agent intellect and the activity of abstraction as utterly superfluous. In attempting to account for knowledge, the whole role of such theories is to explain how that which is not intelligible is made so by an activity of the intellect. Bonaventure, however, clearly defends such an intellectual activity on the part of the individual human being in the texts from his *Commentary on the Sentences.*

Bonaventure is keenly aware of the mutability of things. Therefore, it seems that there are two fundamental problems in knowing the particular: first, there is a gap between the particular and the universal in what we think and talk about; second, the sensible is mutable, the universal is not. Hence, the aspect of knowing that is difficult to explain, as Bonaventure conceives it, seems not to be in sense perception, nor in the uncovering of the intelligible in the sensible. The agent intellect, working in close conjunction with the passive intellect, is capable of the requisite abstractive activity. The aspect of knowing that is really difficult to explain seems to be how a mutable mind, which at one time did not exist, could make necessary and immutable judgments about mutable concrete things, or about immutable universals, which still at some time did not exist, for the necessity and immutability of these judgments seem to be of such a nature that they could not not be true at any time. In other words, the judgments made by the mind possess an absolute necessity and certitude so great that they are truly outside of time—they are eternal. For example, there is no time at which it is not true that every dog is a mammal.

The key point to understand, then, is that illumination in Bonaventure's theory is necessary to explain this final "gap" encountered in knowledge: the gap between the intelligible and the absolute necessity of certain judgments—a necessity that renders these judgments such that they could not exist otherwise under any conditions, and such that there is no time at which they are not true. The judgment, "Every dog is a mammal," is true, even if no dog ever exists. This truth is eternal. But neither the mind nor the thing could provide this eternal character, because neither the mind nor the thing is eternal. It must be that mind, in coming to this judgment and seeing its necessity, has been aided by a standard, a cause that is eternal. Illumination, then, is necessary to explain the modality of true judgments.

The adoption of an abstraction theory implies that the mind is the agent in rendering the concrete and particular as universal, or, in other words, the sensible as intelligible. An alternative to this explanation for speaking accurately about cats and dogs and other universal terms is to adopt an intuition theory, which holds that the mind directly intuits the universal in the particular, or the intelligibility of the sensible in the concrete, sensible thing. Bonaventure, however, clearly does not adopt an intuition theory. Furthermore, if illumination functioned at the level of sense perception, there would also be no need for an abstraction theory, because the heavenly light would presumably have already rendered the particular universal and the sensible intelligible. It would then merely be necessary for the judgment to start connecting the dots: Fido is a dog, and dogs are animals.

The human mind, Bonaventure says, can be in one of four states about any given proposition: ignorance, doubt, opinion, or certitude. The last state occurs when there is such firm adherence to a proposition that the mind recognizes it cannot be otherwise than it is, either because it would violate the principle of noncontradiction, or nature would have to be other than it is under ordinary circumstances. However, in order for the mind to adhere so firmly to a proposition, it must recognize some quality that warrants such firm devotion. Thus, we may speak of both objective and subjective certainty. That is to say, we may speak of a mind "being certain" or of a proposition "being certain," meaning a given proposition warrants the former state of mind. Bonaventure holds that in order for the human mind to recognize this quality of a proposition, it must receive assistance from the objective standard of all truth. This standard must illumine the intellect such that it can recognize the objective quality of the proposition and so warrant the intellect's firm adherence. This is not to deny that one can have subjective certitude about a false proposition, but this misjudgment is not the failure of illumination, but of the judge.

The judgment, Bonaventure says, has to be made by reason that abstracts from place, time, and change. Everything that we judge with certitude, we judge by a standard (*regula*) that is immutable and beyond limits in time or space. "But nothing is absolutely immutable and unlimited in time and space unless it is eternal, and everything that is eternal is either God or in God." Consequently, Bonaventure concludes that we judge by a higher light than just our intellect. The intellect is not sufficient in itself to explain knowledge, since knowledge seems to involve characteristics that cannot be derived either from things themselves or from the mind. Seemingly, we have guidance from divine reason, an infallible rule, and the light of truth itself. These immutable and eternal standards serve as laws by which we judge all sense objects. Bonaventure quotes the second book of Augustine's *De libero arbitrio*, "No one judges them, but by them."[95] These laws exist eternally in the eternal art, "by which, through which, and according to which all beautiful things are formed." "This is the Being that contains the form in all creatures, and is the rule that directs all things. Through it our mind judges all things that enter it through the senses."[96]

De scientia Christi requires careful consideration, because it is crucial to establishing that illumination applies to the judgment. In question 4, Bonaventure asks "whether that which is known by us with certitude is known in the eternal reasons themselves."

In the response to the fourth question, Bonaventure argues that the human intellect attains to the eternal reasons "as that reason which regulates and moves,"[97] if it attains certain knowledge. It is important to notice here that Bonaventure is not saying that the eternal reasons are the only principles of knowledge by any means, nor that they are attained with clarity—they are realized only obscurely and as in a mirror; nevertheless, they are necessary principles for certain knowledge.

Bonaventure outlines three ways it could be said that everything that is known is known in the light of the eternal reasons. The first way would involve knowing with certitude only the intelligible and archetypal world, but then, we would not know the sensible world. The second way would involve postulating that the eternal reasons are an influence of the uncreated light, but this is to make the light a creature and thus to demand of it more than it can give. This interpretation of illumination defeats the whole purpose of the theory; for the theory attempts to explain how the human mind can attain to the immutable and unchangeable, precisely what creatures are not, even created influences divinely given. Bonaventure points to the problem with this interpretation: "The nobility of knowledge and the dignity of the knower necessarily require that, in the case of certain knowledge, our mind must in some way attain to those rules and unchangeable reasons."[98]

The third way, Bonaventure claims, is the middle way. It holds that "for certain knowledge, the eternal reason is necessarily involved as the regulative and motivating principle."[99] It obviously is not the sole principle, nor is the eternal reason seen with full clarity. "But along with the created reason, it is "contuited" (or glimpsed) by us in part as is fitting in this life."[100] Bonaventure is thus affirming that the eternal reasons are necessary to attain certain knowledge. They are the regulating and moving principles of that knowledge, but they are not attained in clarity and fullness—they are contuited.

Bonaventure then gives the argument that the nobility of knowledge requires this divine illumination. First, "there can be no certain knowledge except where there is immutability on the part of the object known and the infallibility on the part of the knower."[101] Bonaventure summarizes these points succinctly:

But if full knowledge requires recourse to a truth that is fully immutable and stable and to a light that is completely infallible, it is necessary for this sort of knowledge to have recourse to the heavenly art as to light and truth, a light, I say, which gives infallibility to the knower, and a truth which gives immutability to the object of knowledge.[102]

A cause must be adequate to its effect. And the natural light of the intellect is not a cause adequate to certain truth, for truth is immutable and infallible. Truth does not just involve an intrinsic necessity.

Bonaventure then proceeds to argue that it is the higher part of the rational spirit that adheres (*inhaerescit*) to the eternal rules, "and by them it judges and defines with certitude whatever it defines."[103] In this text, Bonaventure is explicitly tying the role of illumination to judging and defining. Given what he said immediately before about immutability and infallibility, it seems clear that Bonaventure is arguing that judgments require divine illumination to meet these conditions for truth. Thus, the eternal reasons make possible certain judgments, even though essences come to be in the mind through abstraction. Here, we find what has been called an association of illumination and Aristotelian science.[104] The mind must have a measure for all its judgments, and nothing less than the supreme measure will do.[105]

Bonaventure reaffirms this understanding of illumination as applying to the judgment: "Therefore, natural things are known in the eternal reasons by the power of judgment that is natural to reason."[106] This is a key quote. Bonaventure is not claiming that God somehow causes knowledge at the level of ideogenesis. The eternal reasons are not the formal cause of knowledge, for obviously, then, our knowledge would not be of worldly things.

In this regard, Bonaventure found precedent in Augustine. Augustine has a passage in his *De Trinitate* where he clearly speaks of divine illumination with reference to practical judgments about right and wrong (Bonaventure quotes part of it in question 4 of *De scientia Christi*):

Yet it [the mind] is reminded to turn to the Lord as though to a light by which it went on being touched in some fashion even when it turned away from him. It is in virtue of this light that even the godless can think about eternity and rightly praise and blame many elements in the behavior of men. And by what standards, I ask you do they judge, if not by ones in which they see how a man ought to live, even though they do not live like that themselves? Where do they see these standards? Not in their own nature, since there is no doubt they see them with the mind, and we all agree that their minds are changeable, while anyone who can see this sort of thing can see that these standards are unchangeable. Nor do they see them in the attitude of their own minds, since these are standards of justice, while it is agreed that their minds are unjust. Then where are these standards written down, where can even the unjust man recognize what being just is, where can he see that he ought to have what he does not have himself? Where indeed are they written but in the book of that light which is called truth, from which every just law is copied and transferred into the heart of the man who does justice, not by locomotion but by a kind of impression, rather like the seal which both passes into the wax and does not leave the signet ring?[107]

In another of the replies, Bonaventure makes an important distinction, which he had made in passing in the conclusion. Truth is immutable in two ways: absolutely and conditionally. If truth is something above the mind and is God, then it is immutable absolutely. But if truth refers to something created, then it is not immutable in an absolute sense, but only in a conditional sense, "because every creature comes from non-being and can return to non-being"[108] (a creature's "vertability"). There are levels of signification: Truth can be signified either as it is in matter, in the soul, or in the divine art, or in all three places simultaneously. Truth in the external sign is a sign of the truth in the soul. Since the soul occupies the middle place between God and created things, it is related in its superior part to the higher things; in its inferior part, it is related to lower things. "Therefore it receives a relative certitude from below, so it receives an absolute certitude from above."[109] The sort of truth that is above the soul is absolutely immutable, but the sort of truth that is immutable in a relative sense is "multiplied" in diverse being, and it is this sort of truth that is the concern of demonstration. "But that truth which is absolutely immutable can be seen only by those who are able to enter that innermost silence of the soul, and to this no sinner is able to come, but only one who is supremely in love with eternity."[110] This reply and its distinction between absolutely and relatively immutable truth are crucial to eliminating an ontologistic reading of Bonaventure. He is not saying that the knower reads the divine mind or a transcendent real.

In a text from early in his career, *On the Free Choice of the Will*, Augustine writes: "Whatever I may experience with my bodily senses . . . I cannot know how long it will endure. But seven plus three are ten not only now but forever. There has never been a time when seven and three were not ten, nor will there ever be a time when they are not ten."[111] According to Augustine, truth is necessary and immutable, and what is immutable can never cease to be—truth is eternal. Neither the finite mind nor the thing known is sufficient cause for the eternal character of truth. Truth cannot be accounted for by the created order. Truth is neither inferior to our minds nor its equal—it can only be superior and more excellent. In order to attain the height that is truth, the ever-changing human mind must receive illumination from an eternal and immutable source.[112] In other words, only illumination from an eternal being can account for the human mind's attaining truth. Augustine bequeathed this understanding of truth to the Latin Middle Ages, during which time, illumination was a dominant epistemological theory.[113]

Bonaventure was to return to the topic of illumination on at least three other occasions. One of these is his sermon, "Christ the One Teacher of All." "Certitude can be had neither from a principle that can be deceived nor from a light that can be obscured. The necessary light is not that of created intelligence but that of uncreated Wisdom which is Christ."[114]

In *Collationes in hexaemeron*, he clearly ties the operation of the divine truth on the human intellect to the judgment. He says, "Truth is the light of the soul."[115] In this same place, Bonaventure speaks of a *triplex veritas*: a truth of things, a truth of signs or words, and a truth of behavior. This is an intricate teaching, but for our purposes, it is worth noting that Bonaventure speaks of truth from the viewpoint of the receiving subject as "the reason of understanding." The truth of words comes from the reason of understanding. On the part of the receiving subject, truth is operative, making possible the apprehension of the truth of things, of words, and of things to be done. The supreme truth makes possible the apprehension of the *triplex veritas*.

The eternal art is that by which we judge, even though it is not the object of cognition. It illumines our judgments, even if it does not provide the objects of those judgments. But the necessity and timelessness of right judgments cannot be derived from the things themselves. The standard by which things are judged seems to be unchanging and not subject to time, but the only thing not subject to change or time is God. Bonaventure thus holds that the divine light illumines our judgments in that it provides the standard by which the judgment is made. This light from above provides our judgments with a certitude that they would otherwise lack.

Bonaventure's theory is admittedly not completely clear. It is difficult to determine with precision exactly what "regulating and moving cause" means. Gilson correctly states the nuances of Bonaventure's theory: "It [divine illumination] does not simply sustain it [knowledge] as a cause, and it does not transfigure it from within as does a grace, but it moves it [knowledge] from within as a hidden object."[116] In short, divine illumination applies primarily to the judgment in the order of certitude.

The light that Bonaventure posits is neither just a general influence of God nor a special light of grace.[117] On this problem, it is probably best to take Bonaventure at his word and reject attempts to read divine illumination as either grace or as a created influence. At the very least, there may be all sorts of reasons to reject divine illumination, but one of them cannot be that it is impossible for God to illumine the intellect. It is evident that God is not the sole means of our knowing: If he were, wisdom would be identical with knowledge of temporal things, that is, natural science. Nor is God's mind the direct object of our cognition: If it were, then the beatific vision would be superfluous. Nor can God be the exclusive means: If he were, we would not need sense experience.[118]

With this said, divine illumination's operation on the judgment would seem to apply in two areas: with regard to achieving certitude both in speculative and in practical judgments. For example, knowing the principle of noncontradiction is of such a character that involves divine illumination. To say that this is an eternal and immutable truth is to say that it transcends all time; there are no real or possible conditions under which it is not true.

However, one might immediately object that the human intellect, where this truth resides, is not eternal and is not immutable. On the contrary, there was a time when this intellect was not, and this mind changes, but Bonaventure's theory insists that there is a truth in things themselves insofar as they reflect and express the divine exemplar. This is where Bonaventure's adherence to the Anselmian notion of a twofold truth becomes important. Things themselves "speak" this truth, and this truth is also in the divine and supreme light. There are no conditions under which it is not true, even if no intellect ever knows it. The principle of noncontradiction was true even before any human intellect existed, and since this truth is also in the divine light, it is beyond time and beyond the finite minds that may know it. Hence, when a mind does come to know it, it has moved beyond the passing hour and day and touched the eternal.

Thirteenth-century Scholastics, such as Thomas Aquinas and Duns Scotus, took a dramatically different turn on the question of human knowledge. Thomas argues that the human intellect possesses an imprint of the First Truth and so needs no other light in order to know. Certitude is ultimately derived from the first principles; the certitude of any proposition depends on its reducibility to the first principles of knowledge. Question 20 of Aquinas's *Disputed Questions on Truth* seems clearly to respond to the seventh question of Bonaventure's *On the Knowledge of*

Christ. Ultimately, Aquinas and Scotus executed a dramatic shift in the medieval understanding of knowledge. There are two theses that constitute the heart of this change: (1) the human mind guarantees the certitude of its own judgments, and (2) truth is necessary, but not eternal. These theses are a significant departure from the older, Augustinian conception of truth that dominated in the West. After Scotus, truth involves necessity but not eternity; after William of Ockham (c. 1285–1347), the necessity involved in true propositions is logical and no longer metaphysical.

For Bonaventure, as for Augustine and all the Scholastics, the cognition of truth involves immateriality and necessity: We know material things in an immaterial way and what we know has an intrinsic necessity or it would not be knowledge. The Augustinian school, however, insists that knowing involves eternity, which can come from neither the world nor the human mind. Knowing truth involves glimpsing eternity.

Journey of the Mind to God

One of the classic texts on the theme of consummation is Bonaventure's *Itinerarium mentis in Deum.* In this work, Bonaventure sees the world as a ladder of ascent to God. The journey of the mind in each step is made possible by divine illumination. He follows the Augustinian method of ascent to God found in the *Confessions,* in which Augustine speaks of returning to himself and then entering into his inward self in order to behold the inner light. From within, he looks above.[119]

The journey begins by looking for the vestiges of God in the external, sensible world (chapter 2). The next step is the consideration of God through the image ensigned in our natural powers (chapter 3). The journey proceeds from without to within, to above, that is, to the consideration of God in his image, found in the soul, reformed through the gifts of grace. The last steps of the journey of the mind to God are found in the consideration of the one God as *Ipsum Esse* and of the triune God as Goodness (chapters 5 and 6, respectively). The final step involves a sabbath rest for the mind as the affect totally goes out to God (chapter 7). Philosophy thus finds its fulfillment in a mystical union with God, but it is important to be aware of the deeply rational character of this mysticism. Affect and reason are not opposed to each other in this journey. There is a constant complementarity between them, not unlike the relation between *eros* and dialectics in Plato's philosophy.

In this text, the metaphysical reflection on the transcendentals comes to fruition in the mind of the faithful pilgrim, for the metaphysics of the transcendentals enriches the believer's contemplation of God. Indeed, the faithful pilgrim receives a foretaste of the delights of the beatific vision. The transcendentals emerge as the primary theme of the branch of metaphysics that Bonaventure's refers to as "consummation." The transcendentals are the path to the First Principle.

We can see the centrality that these transcendental conditions of being occupy in the thought of Bonaventure in his consistent reference to what he regards as the universal characteristics of being: "Every creature is one, true, and good; has mode, species, and order; and has measure, number, and weight—for weight is defined as an orderly tendency. All this applies to every creature in general, whether material, spiritual, or composite, as is human nature."[120] It is worth considering exactly what Bonaventure means when he says that every creature is one, true, and good.

Bonaventure tells us that we may examine the unity of every being from two aspects: from its relation to matter or from its relation to form. By reason of its relation to matter, a being is in itself undivided, even though it is potentially divisible. By reason of its relation to form, a being is distinct and limited. In other words, every being is itself and not another being (i.e., it is "this thing"—hoc aliquid) and it is what it is.[121] Bonaventure refers to this condition of all beings in the term "number." Every thing has number, for every thing is itself and not another thing.

Since the First Principle is supreme and perfect, there must be found in it the highest and most universal properties of being: oneness, truth, and goodness. "One" describes being insofar as it is whole, by reason of inner indivision. "True" describes being in that it is intelligible by reason of its indivision between itself and its proper likeness, i.e., the Word. "Good" describes being in that it is communicable by reason of its indivision between itself and its proper operation.[122]

An early thirteenth-century thinker, Philip the Chancellor (ca. 1160–1236), seems to be the first to propose the definition of the oneness of being as indivision; Alexander of Hales then picked it up and bequeathed it to Bonaventure.[123] "One" signifies the indivision of a thing; in other words, its intrinsic unity.

At the basis of Bonaventure's thought is an understanding of God as the self-diffusive Good who is the origin of all. "Now just as being itself is the principal root of the vision of the essential attributes of God as well as the name through which the others become known, so the good

itself is the principal foundation of the contemplation of the emanations."[124] He describes the "first principle" (*"primum principium"*), that is,
God the Father, as *"fontalis plenitudo."* He applies to the fontal plenitude
a principle taken from the *Book of Causes* (*Liber de causis*) that the more
primary a thing is, the more fecund it is.[125] "The opinion of the Philosopher also obtains, who says that principles, the more primary they are,
the more powerful they are—and the first cause exercise more of an influence—and that which is simply first has the highest influence in every
way."[126] Indeed, it is accurate to say that the principle underlying the
entire Bonaventurian synthesis is that the good is self-diffusive and that
the highest good is the most self-diffusive.

It should not be surprising then, that all the branches of knowledge
lead to theology and the contemplation of God. *De reductione artium ad
theologiam* is a presentation of the theme of consummation, but in the
context of education. Bonaventure gives systematic expression to Hugh
of St. Victor's reform of education, which he set forth in the *Didascalicon*.
All knowledge, as found in the arts and sciences, is a return to God
through Christ. The *reductio* is first a leading back of all the disciplines
to theology, the center of Christian culture. All knowledge leads up to
the study of sacred scripture, the study of God's own revelation, which
by definition must be the height of wisdom. Philosophy, as the height of
natural wisdom, is the culmination of the liberal arts, and the others find
their summit in it. But philosophy itself, of course, is no longer centered
on the investigation of *physis*, as the materialists would have it, but on
God and the soul, as Augustine would have it. Philosophy's culmination
is found in the ascent from being and its principles to God.

Bonaventure's *De reductione* is a reassertion of the Augustinian view of
Christian *paideia* (education). It offers a comprehensive and synthetic
view of education in which all human knowledge and art is grounded in
the exemplar ideas of the Word of God. In this regard, Bonaventure's
work is a medieval renewal of the Augustinianism found in *De doctrina
christiana*, as filtered through Hugh of St. Victor. Bonaventure again follows, in this text, the Augustinian method of ascent to God found in the
Confessions, wherein Augustine speaks first of returning to himself and
then entering into his inward self in order to behold the inner light from
above. Bonaventure considers four lights that are ultimately the one light:
the exterior light, the inferior light (the senses), the interior light, and
the superior light. This fourfold light is the illumination of all human
knowledge.

It is important to note the parallels between this work and the *Itiner-*

arium De reductione seeks not only to reassert the Augustinian educational program, but also to show how all knowledge and art reflect the font of intelligibility. The leading back of which Bonaventure speaks is ultimately an ascent of the mind to God—now, however, in and through the arts and sciences.

Moral Philosophy

A Moral Philosophy

An account of Bonaventure's moral philosophy should begin with a brief defense of ascribing to him any interest at all in philosophical ethics. Some might think that Bonaventure would have believed a moral philosophy to be impossible, for, as Augustine seems to teach, the virtues of the pagans are really well-disguised vices and, hence, the only account of right human action is found in moral theology. While it is true that Bonaventure thinks the ancient pagan philosophers were ignorant of a doctrine absolutely essential to understanding human behavior—namely, original sin—he nevertheless unambiguously presents moral philosophy as a distinct branch of study in *On the Reduction of the Arts to Theology*. Bonaventure divides moral philosophy into three branches: personal (*monastica*), domestic (*oeconomica*), and political (*politica*). According to Bonaventure, moral philosophy investigates the truth of morals and the right order of living (*rectitudo vivendi*), specifically, the right order in man's actions as an individual (ethics), as a member of a household (economics), and as a member of the city (politics). Human beings are able to know the right order of living through the natural law, which consists of both the dictates of right reason and God's eternal law impressed on the human soul. Furthermore, while it is also true that Bonaventure spent far more time developing moral theology than a philosophical ethics, as we can see in his *Commentary on the Sentences*, it is nevertheless clear that he does sketch the main elements of reason's role in pursuing the good human life.

It is important to understand Bonaventure's moral philosophy in the context of his metaphysics of emanation and return: All things have come forth from God; all things are to return back to him. It is the rational creature, endowed with a will and capable of choice, that is the agent for reality's return to its source. Man as a rational animal is the bridge between lower, material creation and a higher, spiritual creation. The human being unites all the elements, and so, as the lynchpin in creation, man "speaks" for creation. God, who is the cause of being and the principle of knowledge (as Bonaventure repeats with some frequency) is also the order of living.

Happiness

Bonaventure holds the view that happiness is the ultimate end sought by man, because it is desired just for its own sake and not for some other end. Indeed, all men desire happiness by nature.[1] Hence, we can say that Bonaventure was a eudaimonist, that is, someone who views happiness or well-being as the goal of human life. As we shall see, Bonaventure's eudaimonism more resembles Augustine's than Aristotle's. They differ, above all, on what ultimately constitutes human happiness.

Aristotle defines happiness as "an activity of soul in accordance with perfect virtue," and therefore proceeds to argue that, since happiness is found in living the virtuous life, it must culminate in our highest activity, which turns out to be the intellect's contemplating—the contemplation of truth, especially about the highest being.[2] Aristotle, however, presents us with an activity that only attains a fleeting glimpse of the highest being. There is certainly no union or possession, nor is there permanency for this height of human happiness, since Aristotle is vague as to the immortality of the soul.

There are three foundational difficulties that Bonaventure has with Aristotle's eudaimonism: (1) this contemplation lacks the permanency of immortal life; (2) abstract truth is inadequate to making the human being happy; and (3) the human being cannot attain this end through any natural means.

With regard to the first issue, Bonaventure accepts the Augustinian critique of ancient eudaimonism found in *The City of God*. How, Augustine asks, can the human being be truly happy if he is conscious that he must die, and that death is either the end of his existence or involves a life separated from the supreme good? A being that longs for immortality and perfect happiness cannot be happy while conscious of its mortality and its coming to an end apart from the highest good, no matter how beautifully he perfects his natural capacities and governs his soul by the light of reason. As Augustine argues in *De Trinitate* and *The City of God*, a rational soul, conscious that at some time it would not be, could not attain happiness, for such a soul would also be conscious that its most fundamental good would be lost. In other words, if the soul is not immortal, there is no happiness, for the human soul is conscious of itself, which is to say, it is present to itself and aware of its being, its living. It has a natural desire for always possessing life. Indeed, the condition for the possibility of supreme happiness is the immortality of the rational soul. Hence, the rational soul must be immortal or our natural desire for beatitude would be in vain. Aristotle, however, taught that nature does nothing in vain.

The soul's awareness of being present to itself also means that it has some understanding of what being absent is, of not being. Indeed, it loves its life so dearly, that if the possibility of losing this life were present, this evil's presence, even if only a distant thing, would make miserable such a creature's every moment. Nothing is capable of beatitude except what is immortal, and to be immortal, something would have to also be indissoluble.[3] Bonaventure thus accepts much of Augustine's critique of ancient eudaimonism. Out of his sheer goodness, God has communicated his beatitude to lower creatures, such as the angels, but he also has granted the possibility of beatitude to a corporeal spirit, that is, the human being. Beatitude, however, is not truly beatitude unless it can never be lost, so nothing but what is indissoluble and immortal is capable of beatitude.[4]

Abstract truth, even about the highest being, which Aristotle does call "god" in the *Metaphysics*, is not adequate to the task of making the human being happy, given the nature and capacity of human longings. Bonaventure thinks that human beings ultimately want union with the supreme good and infinite truth. Hence, it is not surprising that Bonaventure believes every human being has a natural desire to know and love God.[5] This knowledge and love of the perfect being will alone prove adequate to fulfilling human desires. The rational soul has a capacity for God (*capax Dei*), and thus, nothing less than God will do. *Beatitudo* is Bonaventure's term for this true happiness that can only be found in God.

There is still a further problem with Aristotle's eudaimonism: Given that every human being has a natural desire for beatitude, which is only found in union with God, the human being cannot attain the supreme transcendent good with his own powers. In other words, nature cannot achieve the proper end with its natural powers. There are natural appetites that simply cannot be fulfilled, that is, they are in vain, barring some divine intervention. However, since nature does nothing in vain, God will have to make up for the weakness of natural virtue. Bonaventure, like Augustine before him, was deeply conscious that the acquired virtues are ultimately vain in that they cannot bring man what he most longs for. Only grace can do so, and without grace—specifically, without the grace of charity—the natural virtues do not merit the human being his beatitude. Behind the Bonaventurian position is the view that the good human being is the one who is meritorious before God. This is to say that perfect happiness is a gift, not something we achieve on our own, though God does not give this gift without our cooperation. The human being's true goodness can only be measured by his progress in salvation—all other attempts to reckon goodness are vain and devoid of lasting significance.

Beatitude consists more in an activity of the will than of the intellect. In other words, the primary intentionality of the human being is through the will's act of loving, and not through the intellect's act of knowing. On this issue, Bonaventure is reflecting a common Franciscan view that the human being is primarily perfected and thus made happy by rightly loving rather than by knowing. Hence, although love and knowledge are inseparable since we cannot love what we do not know, it is, nevertheless, in the intentionality of loving that the human being most unambiguously achieves his fulfillment.

That the human being will engage in loving is beyond question. What needs to be answered is how we love: whether we love the supreme good enough, that is, above all else, or whether we love more the lesser finite goods, which are also mutable. And of course, in agreement with Augustine, Bonaventure says that the love of lesser goods over the supreme good is not really love at all, but only the simulacrum of true love, which he calls "covetousness." The bride who loves the ring that is given to her by the bridegroom more than the bridegroom himself does not possess true love, but is, in fact, lost in greed. This is not to say that the human being ought not to love creatures at all. On the contrary, man's familial, matrimonial, and civic loves have their proper place in his life and indeed will largely determine its course. Love is our weight (*pondus*), our destiny.[6] The virtuous and the vicious are alike in loving, but unlike in how they love. The question is whether these loves will be ordered by reason (and by grace). Nevertheless, the central dynamic of every human life is the movement of the will's acts of love. Thus, the central story of every human life is the tale of the turnings of the heart: whether it turns upward to love God or downward to love itself or creatures more than God.

Given this understanding of the supreme good and our relation to it, it should not be surprising that the dominant notion in Bonaventure's moral theory is rectitude (*rectitudo*). Indeed, Bonaventure regards rectitude as the principal concern of moral philosophy. This rectitude consists in the rightly ordered will; to be more precise, it is a will conformed to a rule or objective standard, and this standard is that of divine law.[7] He argues that rectitude involves the *concuspiscible* or desiring power of human nature clinging to the good.[8] Bonaventure clearly recognizes that human action flows from the dynamic relation of the various elements of the human soul. Nevertheless, there is a certain primacy given to the will in his account of human action. While the intellect disposes the will to move, it is the will that moves and commands the intellect and the powers of the soul.[9] Free choice, or decision, consists principally in the will. The central moral task for the human being is to achieve this rectitude of the will, and when it is achieved, the human being is transformed by being made "deiform," Godlike in his being.[10]

Even though Bonaventure thinks the perfect happiness that fulfills the human being is only attainable by grace, and then only in the eternal life of union with God, this is not to say that the acquired moral virtues are of no value: They are perfections that enable the human being to do morally good acts.[11] The virtues, however, will be understood primarily as rightly ordered loves, that is, as dispositions in the rational part of the soul to choose rightly. Aristotle understood the virtues as states of character involving the control of the passions, neither suppressing them nor allowing them to overwhelm the agent. Courage, for example, involves fearing rightly, not so much as to play the coward, nor too little as to be a fool. For Bonaventure, as for Augustine before him, virtue is not so much a question of the control of the passions as of rightly loving, of loving creatures in due measure. The acquired virtues are loving rightly, and when we love the good, we do the right.[12]

Like Augustine, Bonaventure tends to think that a fundamental human problem is that we do not desire the supreme Good sufficiently: We settle for too little, we are easily content with the basic necessities of life, and we often work to attain physical or external goods (e.g., honor, friends) without realizing that we desire much more. However, to realize the deeper desires of human nature, the individual must make an effort at self-knowledge, for it is only in this way that one can come to know human nature's desire and capacity for truth, beauty, and goodness. Ultimately, the desires of the rational agent are such that they can only be satisfied by perfect truth, perfect beauty, and perfect goodness. Anything less leaves the human heart wanting more and thus not truly at rest, and not happy in the profoundest way that a rational agent is capable of being.

It is not enough for the rational agent to know the nature of his desire; he must also love truth, beauty, and goodness. The human being who lives without this love of higher things easily wallows in superficial pleasures and impermanent goods. In a sense, then, sloth is the ever-looming tendency for the human animal, who may easily live and die forgetful of his high calling. Sloth, the failure to love the supreme good sufficiently (with all one's heart), is what leads the human being to settle for the lesser goods. This primordial, ever-looming sloth, however, goes hand in hand with pride; indeed, they are two sides of the same dynamic. For sloth is the lethargy of not loving the good sufficiently, while pride is excessive love of self, to the exclusion of external good, and so too involves an inadequate love of the supreme good.

The antidote to sloth and pride is humility. Bonaventure thinks that humility is essential to living the moral life (as well, the Christian life) and to being wise. Humility is, at root, living in accord with a metaphysical truth. Hence, the first step to attaining humility is recognizing the fundamental metaphysical truth that one is nothing in oneself, indeed, that all things are nothing in themselves: "Therefore, since all things which have been made abide by the one principle and were produced from nothing, that man is truly wise who really recognizes the nothingness of himself and of others, and the sublimity of the First Principle."[13]

The Virtues

Bonaventure tells us in his *Commentary* that "virtue" (*virtus*) can be understood in three ways: commonly, properly, and more properly. In a commonly understood sense (*communiter*), it has to be defined either in relation to act or in relation to act and the last end. Aristotle's *On Heaven and Earth* supplies Bonaventure with the first definition of virtue as the definitive potency of a thing.[14] In this sense, virtue is a perfection. Aristotle's *Physics* supplies Bonaventure with the second definition as the disposition of the complete to the best.[15] These definitions, taken from Aristotle's natural philosophy, understand virtue in its widest sense to include the full realization in act of any potency. Hence, Bonaventure can speak of "natural virtues," that is, perfections of the natural order; both the natural and moral virtues fall under this sense.

In its proper sense (*propie*), however, virtue refers to the moral virtues alone, whether political or gratuitous. In this sense, virtue has to be considered either in relation to act itself or in relation to its directive principle. Under the first consideration, Bonaventure points to Aristotle's definition of virtue in the *Nicomachean Ethics*: "Virtue is a *habitus*, which perfects its possessor and renders his work good."[16] Aristotle again provides Bonaventure with the definition of virtue in the second of considering it: "Virtue is a voluntary *habitus* (habit) consisting of a mean, determined by right reason, as a wise person would determine it."[17] This quotation is, of course, Aristotle's classic definition of virtue, which Bonaventure repeats with slight variation in his *Collations on the Six Days*.[18] Bonaventure regards these Aristotelian definitions as reconcilable both with Cicero's definition ("Virtue is a habit of the mind that concurs with the way of nature of reason") taken from his *De rhetorica*, and two taken from Augustine ("Virtue is a habit of the well ordered mind," and "Virtue is the equality of life concurring with reason in every way").[19]

When discussing virtue in this proper sense, Bonaventure is careful to explain that virtue involves the good use of a rational power, namely, the will.[20] In addition, this *habitus* involves an inclination to action, so that Bonaventure also speaks of virtue as a weight (*pondus*) or disposition inclining and moving the agent to the mean.[21] The literal translation of *habitus* is "habit," but Bonaventure does not mean that this is something a person falls into without thinking or even choosing. *Habitus* is a fixed disposition of soul that prompts its possessor to act in certain ways, whether the act is of the mind or an external action. As a fixed disposition of soul, a *habitus* falls in the category of quality.

In its more proper sense, however, "virtue" refers to the habits given by God as a grace and infused into the soul (*virtutes gratuitae*). Both the theological and moral virtues are types of gratuitous virtue. Indeed, the theological virtues can only be had by grace, but the moral virtues can be acquired by grace as well as by habit. These infused virtues not only habituate us to morally good works, but also elevate morally good acts to being meritorious works.[22] All of the gratuitous virtues are supernatural (*supra naturam*) because they elevate a power above itself and the acts of that power above what they lack in themselves, namely, meritoriousness. The gratuitous virtues have as their end the union of the soul with God.

Bonaventure examines the meaning of virtue in relation to its end, its subject, its act, and its source, that is, its four causes. In relation to its end or final cause, Bonaventure borrows the definition from Augustine's *Soliloquies*: "Virtue is right reason attaining its end."[23] Examined with regard to the agent in whom it inheres, that is, its subject, "virtue is a good will," as Augustine says in *The City of God*.[24] In relation to its formal cause, virtue is "the order of love or ordered love," again as Augustine says in *De moribus ecclesiae*.[25] Finally, in relation to its efficient cause, Bonaventure turns to Augustine's *On the Teacher* (*De magistro*) for the understanding of virtue: "virtue is a good quality of the mind . . . by which we live rightly . . . of which no one can use them wrongly . . . [and] which God works in us without us."[26] In this sense, Bonaventure includes the theological virtues, as well as the cardinal virtues informed by grace and charity and infused into the soul. These infused virtues have three tasks: (1) to lead the soul to its final end, that is, union with God; (2) to rectify the passions of the soul—sorrow, joy, fear, and hope—and make them holy; and (3) to heal the diseases of the soul—weakness, ignorance, malice, and concupiscence. Bonaventure does not think that a human being can accomplish these tasks, apart from grace.[27]

In an article addressing the question whether it is appropriate to posit cardinal virtues in addition to the theological ones, Bonaventure is surprisingly insistent that it is appropriate, since the human being is ordered, not only to God, but also to neighbor and self. Hence, although the theological virtues are meant to invigorate and rectify the powers of the soul with respect to God, the cardinal virtues principally rule and rectify the powers of the soul with respect to neighbor and self.[28] Bonaventure responds to the objection that since grace and the theological virtues reform the powers of the soul, no other virtues are necessary by saying that the theological virtues are principally for reforming the soul with respect to the uncreated good and bringing man to his final end, but other virtues, namely the cardinal ones, are necessary for reforming man with respect to the created good and to those things ordered to the final end.[29] Hence, he speaks of the cardinal virtues as political because "they render man well ordered to living among men."[30] This discussion is particularly important for understanding Bonaventure's moral philosophy.

The theological virtue of charity is the form of all the virtues, because it makes the natural virtues efficacious, that is, conducive to meriting union with God. In this way, charity vivifies all the virtues and the whole moral life. Apart from charity, the virtuous life is not exactly a simulacrum of the real thing—a charlatan—but it is incipient and deeply imperfect, for it cannot lead to beatitude or true happiness. Natural virtues are vir-

tues in potency that remain inchoate and undeveloped, precisely because
they lack the form that actualizes them—charity.

Virtues of the Will

One of the points of considerable discussion about the virtues among
Scholastic authors was their locus within the soul. Some, like Aquinas,
held that certain virtues, such as prudence and justice, reside in the rational part of the soul, but other virtues, such as temperance and courage,
reside within the concupiscible and irascible appetites, respectively. These
appetites are animal powers of the soul, and can only be called "rational"
insofar as they are obedient to reason. In this conception, temperance is
a disposition to restraint within the desiring or concupiscible appetite
itself (as the Scholastics called it); likewise, courage is a disposition to
moderation in the irascible appetite itself. Hence, the temperate human
being does not desire physical goods excessively, nor does the courageous
person fear excessively.

Bonaventure explicitly discusses this opinion in his *Commentary on the
Sentences*, and rejects it. He admits that this view might seem probable
to moral philosophers, but it does not seem reasonable to the theologian,
because all the cardinal virtues are equal with respect to their dignity in
meriting eternal life. All the virtues are sources of merit. Furthermore,
since merit is found in free choice, it follows that the virtues, whether
cardinal or theological, are found only in those powers containing free
choice. And since free choice is a habit of the rational part of the soul
(will and intellect working together), the virtues must reside there.[31] Indeed, one can understand how the naturally acquired virtues must especially reside in the rational part of the soul, because it commands the act
of virtue and directs the sensible power.[32] Virtuous acts come from the
rational power of the soul, even if they govern a lower power that serves
as the subject matter for command. Finally, "the dignity" of the virtues
requires that they reside in the rational part of the soul, since they may
have an origin in grace and are thus nobler than knowledge (*scientia*),
which is certainly in the rational part of the soul.[33]

The first virtue that should be discussed is justice, since Bonaventure
speaks of it, generally, as a synonym for the virtuous life itself. Justice, in
this sense, is simply rectitude of the will: "Since the intention of moral
philosophy is concerned principally with rectitude, it treats general justice, which, as Anselm says, is a rectitude of the will."[34] Bonaventure also

speaks of general justice as rectitude of the soul and involves the avoiding of evil and doing of good.[35] This general justice involves the unity of all the virtues in an ordering of the human being to the good. It is the virtue of justice that embraces all the human being's relations: to God, himself, and his neighbor. All the commands of the Decalogue may be reduced to one command of "Do justice": The first table (first three commandments) is concerned with our relations with God, the second table (the remaining seven commandments) with our relations to fellow human beings.[36] Hence, moral philosophy is a science meant to lead the human being to justice, which involves, first and foremost, rectitude of the will.

In his *Collations on the Six Days*, Bonaventure tells us that temperance is the virtue concerned with the mean with regard to pleasure and pain. He takes over Cicero's definition from *De rhetorica*: "Temperance is the firm and measured dominion of reason over passion and over other movements of the soul that are not righteous."[37] Hence, its parts are sobriety with regard to taste, chastity with regard to touch, and modesty with regard to the other senses.

This virtue is necessary from childhood to old age and especially needed to control our desire for food and money. The insatiable desire to possess and retain is "the death of men." Bonaventure says that temperance is the virtue that restrains this desire without falling into the two extremes: considering possessions as our greatest good or considering them as the greatest evil.[38] We see in this understanding of temperance that it involves both an accurate judgment about the value of external goods and rightly desiring them on the basis of this evaluation. For this reason, temperance with regard to possessions is not a question of things, but of "the soul's desire." "For if you desire these things in order to be sustained by them, be they your own or those of others, you keep the middle way. If you overestimate them as if happiness were to be found in them, you are at one extreme; if you spurn them as being wicked, you are at the other."[39] Bonaventure points to the Manichees as an extreme of the latter sort, because they believed that sexual intercourse was wicked, even with one's spouse, and that all possessions were wrong. "The middle way, then, consists in being sustained either by your own goods or by those of another."[40]

According to Bonaventure, since the virtue in the sphere of possessions involves the proper valuation and concomitant right desire for these goods, even the very poor (no doubt, he has the religious mendicants in mind) keep the mean. To those who would say that one must have a modicum of possessions to keep to the mean, Bonaventure makes the analogy that this view is like someone saying that the extremes with regard to sexual intercourse are knowing no woman or knowing all women and the mean being only knowing half of all women.[41]

Fortitude is concerned with fear and acts of valor; it is a virtue necessary to avoid either cowardice or rashness. Hence, it involves confronting and attacking dangers and then enduring them. Its parts are confidence, patience, and perseverance. Bonaventure thinks that fortitude is in the soul, not in the flesh, and that it confers a "nobility" to the soul, for it is the virtue that restrains anger and irascibility—"not that man should never be angry at all, but that he should be so only in the right circumstance of place and time."[42]

In addition to the general justice already discussed, Bonaventure speaks of justice as the virtue concerned with our relations with others. "Justice is a disposition which attributes to each one his deserts, once the common good has been served,"[43] or, as he puts it even more succinctly, "Justice consists in attributing to each man what is his."[44]

Prudence is a virtue perfective of the rational power of the human being. It is concerned with truth, not speculatively, but as a rule of action; hence, if there is a virtue that directs the intellect in judging about true and false, so there is a virtue that directs the intellect in choosing what is to be done and what is to be avoided. Prudence not only directs what is to be done, but also how it is to be done. Knowing, willing, and doing are involved in any action, and prudence is the virtue perfective of the knowing power's contribution to action. It plays a crucial function in the whole moral life, for it is the virtue concerned with finding the golden mean involved in various virtues. At times, Bonaventure sees Aristotle's notion of the mean and his notion of virtue as a "proper measure" as one and the same. Hence, he will say, "Prudence finds this proper measure, so that you do not go too far in anything, but remain close to the center."[45] This is why Bonaventure calls prudence the moderator (*moderatrix*) of the whole virtuous life.[46] It is the indispensable virtue for all the spheres of human life: "Great prudence is required for the governance of oneself, still greater for the governance of a family, and the greatest for the governance of the city."[47]

We find Bonaventure's most extensive treatment of the intellectual virtues in his *Collations on the Six Days*. Following Aristotle's enumeration of these virtues in Book VI of his *Nicomachean Ethics*, Bonaventure discusses five intellectual virtues: science, art, prudence, understanding, and wisdom.[48] As virtues, they are perfections of the intellect eliciting acts ordered to truth.[49]

It is important to recall that, prior to Bonaventure, Christians had long regarded the virtues to be supernaturally infused dispositions of the soul that enable us to do meritorious acts. One of the challenges that Aristotle poses to Christian thought is that he presents a complete theory about naturally acquired virtues. This Greek view understands the virtues to be naturally acquired dispositions that make us good human beings. In Aristotle's account of "virtue ethics," the virtues are not gifts from God, that is, graces that transform us within, making us worthy of eternal beatitude. On the contrary, we slowly build up dispositions to act in particular ways as a result of our own efforts at governing our soul and controlling our passions. This theory prompted some Scholastics to posit that there must be two types of virtues: the supernaturally infused and the naturally acquired. Much discussion then transpired in Scholastic circles about how these virtues are related to each other and to supernatural beatitude. Closely related to this is the issue of what happens to the acquired virtues when gratuitous virtues are conferred.

Bonaventure's two major treatments of the virtues—his early *Commentary on the Sentences* and, later, in his *Collations on the Six Days*—makes clear that he read and studied with care Aristotle's newly translated *Nicomachean Ethics*. (Robert Grosseteste made the first complete translation of the *Ethics* in 1246–1247, prior to which only the first three books of the *Ethics* had been available.) But Bonaventure's assessment of Aristotle's virtue theory is not exactly clear, especially in light of his later *Collationes* and so there has been considerable scholarly controversy. Did he regard Aristotle's account of the virtues as fundamentally reconcilable with Christianity or did he consider it as a rival account that one chose only to the exclusion of Christian ethics? In other words, did he regard the *Nicomachean Ethics* as a "bad book" that leads one away from being a true Christian (as René Gauthier has implied), or as a valuable, albeit limited book that takes the reader some distance in ethics, but which lacks those Christian doctrines that truly illumine human conduct, such as original sin and humility?[50] The problem in determining Bonaventure's interpretation of the *Nicomachean Ethics* is that there are two redactions of *Collationes in hexaemeron*. We find one version of this text in the Quaracchi edition of his works, and another, somewhat different version in a single manuscript edited by Ferdinand DeLorme, OFM (Order of Friars Minor), in 1947. These two redactions contain different interpretations of Aristotle's virtue ethics. The Quaracchi edition presents a far more negative assessment of Aristotle: One must choose between Aristotle or Christ, for Christian virtues, such as humility and charity, preclude one from achieving Aristotle's ideal of a magnanimous or great-souled man. The Delorme edition consistently attempts to reconcile Aristotle's account of the virtues with Christianity.[51] It is also important to keep in mind that while both versions are *reportationes*, the scribe of the Delorme edition informs us that Bonaventure saw and approved his transcription.[52]

Another virtue that Aristotle regards of great importance but which seemingly conflicts with Christian notions is that of magnanimity or greatness of soul. Bonaventure treats this important Aristotelian virtue in the fifth conference of his *Collations on the Six Days*; he describes it as the virtue "through which great things are appreciated and vile things despised." He equates magnanimity with humility, which is not fooled by appearance but sees through the appearance of the small to appreciate greatness in reality. With regard to Aristotle's contention that the magnanimous human being desires honor, Bonaventure replies that this is not the case unless we amend this honor in eternal things.

If Aristotle is right in his discussion of incontinence or weakness of will in Book VII of the *Ethics*, the truly virtuous and temperate person no longer struggles against disordered desires: Someone who is authentically virtuous not only knows the right, but also takes delight in it, and can do so because he has thoroughly submitted desire to the rule of reason. Aristotle contrasts the truly virtuous with its simulacrum—continence. But continence is the not-authentic virtue because the continent human being knows the right, but finds doing it unpleasant and difficult. At first glance, the Aristotelian notion of temperance would seem to be in conflict with Augustine, according to whom disordered desire, and the accompanying internal conflict, are part of the human condition. This is so because Augustine posits (1) that the cause of weakness is found in the will (and hence not in reasoning or the practical syllogism), and (2) that the will is not in its primordial state. Augustine thus sets down a distinct path for solving a problem that bedeviled ancient ethics, namely, the failure of human beings to pursue the good, even when they know better. The ancient Manichees explained this *akrasia* (weakness) by insisting that there are two souls, one good and one bad. Platonists attributed weakness to the effect of the body on the soul—it is as a prison on the prisoner. Augustine rejects this solution in his book, *On Free Choice of the Will*. It is not ignorance, or the body, or an evil soul that accounts for human weakness[53]—it is our will. Bonaventure follows down the path Augustine marks.

Bonaventure lists kindness among the virtues as the one concerned with seeking someone else's good. On this point, he corrects Aristotle, who had said that it is fitting to do good to friends and evil to enemies.[54] Bonaventure appeals to Christ, who recommends, instead, that every person be loved and all be given things useful to them. "If I love you and grant you some favor or freedom which you will misuse as soon as you receive it, I am not being kind, but rather malicious; and so, in order to be kind, I will not give it to you."[55] Accordingly, a father does not flatter his son, lest the son become proud; nor does a friend give his friend a position of power that will corrupt him.

Bonaventure calls vice the sequel to sin, because he understands vice to be a quality of the soul that is built up as a result of repeated sin. This *habitus* of the soul disposes the agent to commit more easily certain types of wrongdoing.[56] In this regard, it is a real quality of soul and not a negation, but it is a negation in that vice disorders the powers of the soul and disposes them to acting in ways destructive of the true good of the agent. It can corrupt our acts, then, either by providing the main impetus for a particular act or by accompanying certain otherwise good actions, such as when a person gives alms but is quite vain about the fact of having done so.

The Natural Law

The eternal law is the ultimate rule or measure of all human activity. Augustine identifies the eternal law with God's wisdom. He writes: "That law which is named supreme wisdom cannot be otherwise understood than as unchangeable and eternal."[57] This identification of the eternal law with divine wisdom and thus with the divine mind has profound implications for Bonaventure. The moral order of things is not rooted in the arbitrary rules of a mercurial dictator; rather, the moral order reflects God's rational plan for the entire cosmos. The moral law flows from the divine intellect and thus God's plan for the whole universe.

Bonaventure seems to recognize that "natural law" can be used in different senses. Some use it to refer to that law that nature has taught to all animals and dictates how each operates and conducts its activity. In another sense, "natural law is that which is common to all nations and this law is what right reason dictates."[58] The natural law is a reflection of the eternal law; it is a collection of precepts. These precepts are known innately, much as the first principles of the speculative intellect, that is, the principle of noncontradiction, the principle of identity. Among these first-known precepts are such things as the golden rule—do not do to another what you would not have done to yourself—or that God is to be obeyed. If the will is naturally bound to this law, it seems that this law must be naturally known by the soul.[59] In fact, at one point in his writings, Bonaventure defines the natural law as an impression (*impressio*) made in our soul by the eternal law.[60] So deep is this impression that God will punish wrongdoers, even those without the written law (i.e., the written Mosaic law).[61]

Bonaventure posits that there is a threefold way in which the natural law obligates. These differing modes of obligation correspond to the threefold status of human nature: before the Fall (*status naturae institutae*), after the Fall (*status naturae lapsae*), and after the written law or the law of Moses (*status legis scriptae*). The written law makes the natural law obligation explicit. Under the status of fallen nature, this obligation is implicit in the two precepts of the natural law: Do unto others as you would have them do unto you; do not do unto others as you would not have them do unto you. The obligation of the natural law under the status of created nature was both implicit and explicit: The precepts ordered to God obliged man explicitly; the precepts ordered to the neighbor obliged man implicitly. The precepts only unfolded after the multiple disorders that followed the first transgression.

The entire unfolding (*explicatio*) of the commandments of the Decalogue only came about after the first sin, on account of which the light of reason was obscured and the will disordered. Because of the multiple disorders of the fallen will, it was necessary to bind it through multiple commands. So, for example, it was only after the Fall that the wrong actions governed by the second table of the law became explicit. This is not to say that the natural law changed, but that it became explicit on these points.

The problem lurking for the Christian exegete, who would want to defend some version of a natural and universal law, is how to explain the fact that the written law seems to contain some explicit violations of the natural law (or perhaps dispensations from this law): for example, the command of Abraham to sacrifice Isaac; the permissibility of divorce.

Since sin brought with it disorder in the three powers of the human psyche, the commands of the law must reorder each power—the rational, the concupiscible, and the irascible. To the irascible power correspond the commands that order the human being: (1) to his superior through reverence and honor, namely, "Honor your father and mother"; and (2) to peace and tranquility with his neighbor, "Thou shalt not kill." The command against bearing false witness is particularly aimed at the rational power and the fulfillment of its intrinsic purpose, knowing and communicating the truth. Do not steal and do not covet your neighbor's wife or property are aimed at the concupiscible power.

The natural law, as a body of precepts, can be the object of either the conscience or *synderesis* (the will's inclination to the good). Bonaventure takes into consideration the different ways in which people use the term "conscience." Conscience can refer to what directs human judgments about whether or not particular actions ought to be taken; in this way, it refers to the law for our mind. "Conscience" can also refer to a conscious potency. Finally, the term is also used to refer to a *habitus* of the practical intellect, specifically, the *habitus* by which we know the law; it is through the conscience that we know the natural law.[62] (Human beings were originally created with rectitude of conscience.) Bonaventure thinks that the last use is the most precise in getting at what the conscience actually is. It is a *habitus* of the mind perfecting the practical intellect through its precepts. Bonaventure, however, distinguishes conscience as an innate *habitus* from the conscience as an acquired *habitus* that originates in the free choices of human beings.

Synderesis is nothing other than the will's inclination to the good.[63] It is the will's natural inclination to move toward the good as dictated by conscience and known by natural law.[64] Bonaventure draws a parallel between reason and will in their natural orientation: When the natural light of reason is directed to right action, it is called "conscience"; the natural inclination of the will to right action is called "synderesis." *Synderesis* consists of a threefold action in the will: it stimulates to the good, it fights against temptation, and it protests against evil committed.[65]

Bonaventure explains that it is reality under the aspect of goodness that arouses our appetite, that is, the first appetible, but that the good is twofold: the eternal and the temporal. This twofold good generates in us a twofold love: charity and lust. Charity is love leading to eternal things (*rediens ad aeterna*); lust is love leading to earthly things (*ad terrena*). Love has led to the formation of two cities: the things of the world attract under the aspect of good; they are to be scorned under the aspect of vanity.

The world is like a ring from the spouse to his beloved: It is to be loved insofar as it is a sign, but it is not to be loved insofar as it is a thing in itself; in this regard, it is to be scorned. The human love of this given sign can be either chaste or adulterous. Love is chaste when it is seen for what it is—a sign. "Out of love for the spouse, chaste love loves the ring in memory of the spouse; adulterous love loves the ring more than the spouse."[66]

There is a twofold contempt for the world. One of these gives glory to the spouse, the other does not. The improper contempt of the ring, insofar as it is a small and vile gift, redounds to the bridegroom; the "contempt" of the ring as nothing in comparison to the love of the bridegroom, is for the glory of the bridegroom.[67]

Vanity and the Correct Valuation of the World

In speaking of the material cause of the book, Bonaventure says that the vain or fleeting is referred to in two ways. In one way, it is spoken of simply insofar as it is a lack of the true and the good; this vanity is not in the universe. However, there is another way of speaking about the vain: by a comparison to the initial end in that all things are from nothing.[68] The vain bespeaks the mixture within every creature between being and nonbeing:

> In another way the true is said according to which it joins being unmixed to non-being, the former in no way has a potency to the latter; and so it is said to have true being that has immutable being; and in this way the fleeting (*vanum*) is truly opposed to that which is mutable and transmutable. And so every creature is fleeting, because subjected to fleetingness, that is, changeableness.[69]

Here, Bonaventure understands vanity as a metaphysical quality of created being. It is this metaphysical vanity that accounts for the instability of things. Every creature bears the mark of its original movement from nonbeing to being.[70]

Bonaventure then explains that the vain, spoken of in the book of Ecclesiastes, refers to the vanity of mutability: "From the third way, namely from the changeableness of the creature, knowledge is *per se*, as is clear from the motion of the sun and the spheres and the other things. In this book [Ecclesiastes] the fleetingness of changeability or nature is treated, because it is beautiful and fitting, and about the vanity of sin; it does not treat another vanity, namely, of privation of all kinds because about that there is no science nor doctrine."[71] In other words, there cannot be *per se* knowledge of the vanity that is privation; there can only be knowledge *per accidens* by its relation to being, as medicine is a science of health and sickness, of health *per se*, and of sickness, *per accidens*.

Bonaventure sets out to prove the mutability in the existence of creatures. He begins this proof by explaining that creatures have a threefold being (*esse*):

> And because creatures have a threefold being, namely in the Word, by reason of exemplarity; in the universe, through the mode of materiality; in the human soul through the mode of abstraction; the first being is unfailing and immutable; whence it has no fleetingness; but in the others, there is vanity; and therefore this part has two: because in the first the vanity of

changeableness is indicated in the things according to the being that they have in the universe; in the second, insofar as to the being that they have in the human soul.[72]

In the universe, all things have this vanity of mutability: rational creatures, heavenly creatures, and the elemental. There is a vanity of mutability (*vanitas mutabilitatis*) to things according to the *esse* that they have in being. Bonaventure presents a key text in explaining the first of these mutabilities: "And the word by which we recognize all things is twofold: namely, the divine word and the human word. Every creature is a divine word which God speaks; this word the eye perceives."[73]

It is because of this vanity intrinsic to things, that curiosity is reprehended. There is the curiosity of the works of prudence (or of philosophy) and a curiosity of the mechanical arts. The first has two parts: to the consideration of natural things and to the consideration of moral things.

Occupatio is a distraction of the mind that diverts, pulls apart, and entangles the soul. Curiosity is like a prostitution of the human intellect indiscriminately embracing any truth and committing adultery with it, because the first truth is the only bridegroom.

Politics

"Man is an animal of social nature."[74] This social nature of man is rooted in two fundamental characteristics: affection and dependency. We see this fundamental fact in that man possesses a social affection (*affectus socialis*) by which he desires the companionship of fellow human beings.[75] Man is a rational animal, but one that is dependent; he needs the help of other human beings. Bonaventure sees this affection and dependency functioning in three social orders—the conjugal, the domestic, and the civil. Each is a true society possessing its own proper authority: matrimonial (of husband over wife), parental (of parents over children), and civil (of superior over subordinates).

The dependency of the human being is found at the most basic level in the fact that the continuation of the species requires the cooperation of a man and woman in a union of common purpose and mutual aid. The marital state is necessary for the procreation and education of offspring. Husband and wife need each other to provide mutual help for this task. In attempting to fulfill this task, they develop a common will or unity of purpose—"a conformity of will" (*conformitas voluntatis*). Furthermore, such a union, in order to fulfill its task, must be permanent and exclusive. Hence, we find Bonaventure's teaching on man's social nature presented in his discussion of marriage as the foundational relationship of human society.

What is true of marriage and the family is also true of society. Society too requires mutual help and a common will.[76] Goods received should be shared, whatever these may be.[77] A society has a unity of nature, purpose, and activity. This threefold unity of society is built on that of the marital union and family. There is thus an organic unity to society from the most basic of its units to its wholeness. Indeed, a society is like a living organism in which the members depend on each other for mutual aid and common purpose.

In the body politic, there is a diversity of members. There are three main groups amidst this diversity in any society: those who work, those who fight, and those who pray.[78] Bonaventure's tripartite division of society was commonplace in medieval thought;[79] it was believed that each had its own unique role in the larger society. And society, as an organic body, must have an order in which each part is delineated, and ordered within the whole. Without order, there could be no common life.

Furthermore, this order necessarily requires a hierarchy of members. Indeed, the hierarchy of human society simply reflects, and is part of, the other hierarchies of the universe. Bonaventure thinks that there are three main hierarchies in reality: (1) the divine hierarchy (the Trinity), (2) the angelic, and (3) "the ecclesiastical" or human. This universal "ecclesiastical" hierarchy is, in turn, made up of three orders: (1) the monastic, that is, those who live the purely contemplative life; (2) the clerical, or those living both the active and contemplative life; and (3) the lay, or those living the active life. The lay order of the hierarchy includes three other hierarchies: rulers (*principes*), ministers (*consules*), and the people (*plebs*). The hierarchies of this lay order concern themselves with temporal affairs, that is, with the goods of nature, the fortunes of private individuals, and the commonwealth, respectively.

Political virtues are necessary because man is a "social animal," as explained by Bonaventure in the following passage:

> The good men in the government take counsel from them, and guard the cities; by these they venerate their parents, love their children, and are kind to their neighbors; by these, they take care of the welfare of the citizens; by these they protect their companions through careful foresight, attract by a just generosity, and through these they make others remember them for their merit.[80]

Bonaventure distinguishes three states of human nature—created, fallen, and glorified[81]—and then employs this distinction when discussing the power of ruling. He subsequently tries to show that there are three different types of dominion corresponding to the different states of human nature: (1) a dominion over things or possessions (whether movable or immovable goods), (2) a dominion over others who are capable of reason and precept, and (3) a coercive dominion of superiors over subordinates. The first type of dominion is found in every state of nature, the second only in created and fallen nature, and the third is found only in fallen nature. It is important to note in this discussion that the coercive power or ruler is remedial and not natural; thus, the dominion of the political order is tainted by being associated with fallen human nature.

The Light of Theological Knowledge

———————————————————————— 6 ————

The Triune God

Theology is a science concerned with the First Principle or God, but also with all other things insofar as they are related to God. Bonaventure calls theology the perfect science, because it alone traverses the whole, going from the First Principle to the final end; it alone begins with the highest, God, and descends to the lowest, hell. Theology begins where philosophy ends—with God.

Bonaventure frequently identifies theology with sacred scripture; indeed, he uses the term "scripture" as a synonym for theology to the extent that he refers to the whole of what God has revealed for the salvation of the human race. Hence, he speaks of "holy Scripture, which is called theology."[1] But as Henri de Lubac points out in his important study of medieval exegesis, this understanding of sacred scripture was traditional and common. St. Thomas Aquinas, for example, also speaks of "Theology, which is called Sacred Scipture."[2]

This is not to say, however, that theology or scripture are identical with revelation. Revelation is an "unveiling of the hidden" (as Bonaventure speaks of it in his later *Collations on the Six Days*), and so includes more than what is merely written down as a result of the act of disclosing.[3] It is abundantly clear in Bonaventure's view that God is certainly more than anything that could possibly be said about him, whether in speech or in writing. But in the *Hexaemeron*, "revelation" also refers to the unveiling of the future and the mystical knowledge given to certain individual believers. Hence, there is no exact equivalent in Bonaventure's writings to the notion of "revelation" as the entire content of what God has disclosed. Indeed, it is more proper to speak of individual revelations that have occurred throughout the course of salvation history.[4] Near equivalents to the notion of the whole content of what God has unveiled and asks us to believe would be "doctrine" (*doctrina*), "the faith" (*fides*), or probably closest of all, "scripture."[5]

Perhaps the best place to begin to understand Bonaventure's view of sacred scripture is with the conviction that he held with other medieval believers, that God has written three books—one within, one without, and one for sinners to return home. The first book is the First Principle's perfect expression of himself in an interior Word that was generated from all eternity. The second book is creation, but we human beings fail to read this book rightly because of sin. As a result of the original sin, our intellect became clouded by ignorance and our will disordered with concupiscence. So God wrote another book to help us read aright the second book—this third book is sacred scripture.

We must take caution in understanding this. In Bonaventure's eyes, scripture is not merely the literal meaning of the text. When Bonaventure speaks of Scripture, he means Scripture as revealed in the fullness of its meanings, above all, in its allegorical interpretation. We can find the full deposit of faith in Scripture as long as we understand the spiritual meaning of Scripture. Bonaventure clearly does not regard the Scripture in its mere literal meaning to be the whole of theology. The Bible as a written document does not constitute the whole of revelation, especially not as literally interpreted. Bonaventure is in no way advancing an early version of *sola scriptura*.

Furthermore, he does not leave the interpretation of the spiritual meaning of scripture to the decision of the individual. The spiritual meaning of scripture is found, in part, in the teachings of the church fathers and in the faith of the church. Scripture in its full meanings is referred to as "theology," but this notion of theology includes both the Bible and the understanding of the Bible in the faith of the church.[6] There is an organic unity to divine revelation, and so the problem of how scripture and tradition are related does not come to the fore. Indeed, scarcely any Christian thinker has had a keener sense of the fundamental unity of divine revelation; for it is a unity that is located not only in its source (God), but also in its end (salvation) and in its material.

Bonaventure repeatedly attempts to bring to light the unity of its material content through the application of his theory of the "senses" or meanings of scripture. He is constantly looking for parallels between the two major divisions of the text. For example, he divides the books of the

Old Testament into four categories: legal, historical, sapiential, and prophetic, and then attempts to see how the New Testament mirrors the categories of the Old Testament: The gospels, Bonaventure says, correspond to the legal books, the Acts of the Apostles to the historical, the epistles to the sapiential, and the Apocalypse to the prophetical. "For the Old Testament is contained in the New, and vice versa."[7] The legal books are symbolized by the face of a lion because of their authority, the historical by the face of an ox because of their examples of moral strength, the sapiential by the face of man because of their keen wisdom, and the prophetical by the face of an eagle because of their penetrating vision.

With these cautions in mind, we can go on to examine Bonaventure's understanding of scripture.

Scripture is the key to understanding reality. It describes the breadth, length, height, and depth of the entire universe "in so far as this knowledge serves the purpose of salvation." Indeed, the subject matter of scripture is nothing less than the meaning of the whole, for it presents all things in the light of eternity. The whole universe can be understood fully only in the light of its relation to God. Scripture sums up the content of the entire universe (the breadth of the whole), describes the whole course of history (the length), displays the glory of the saved (the height), and reveals the triumph over evil (the depth).[8]

Scripture describes the whole course of history. There are three main phases in history: the period under the law of nature, the period under the written law, and the period under the law of grace. Within these three phases can be distinguished seven ages: from Adam to Noah, from Noah to Abraham, from Abraham to David, from David to the Babylonian exile, from the exile to Christ, from Christ to the end of the world, and the last which runs concurrently with the sixth, from the placing of Christ in the tomb until the universal resurrection. These seven ages parallel the seven days of creation described in Genesis and both parallel the life of every man, for the microcosm contains the macrocosm. So tight is the order of the universe that it is like a "beautifully composed poem," which every mind may discover. And just as one must comprehend the entire poem to appreciate the beauty of it as a whole, one must have an integral view of the whole universe. "And since no man lives long enough to observe the whole with his bodily eyes, nor can anyone by his own ability foresee the future, the Holy Spirit has given us the book of the Scriptures, whose length corresponds to the whole duration of God's governing action in the universe."[9]

Bonaventure compares sacred scripture to a vast and complex forest. Scripture is wide-ranging, complex, and filled with many dark and foreboding obscurities that seem impenetrable to the mind; the theologian's task is to find a way through this forest, but this requires perceiving the organization and ultimate unity in God's revelation in scripture. Theology is meant to be a kind of travel guide through the intricate pathways of the forest that is divine revelation. The theologian's task is to serve as a good guide through this forest and not to let his ward become lost, a task that is thus eminently practical.

In addition, because human beings are not disembodied minds devoid of will and emotions, God, as the author of scripture, has written it in a way that stirs the love and hearts of his readers and entices their minds to contemplate its intricate mysteries. To achieve its purpose, scripture must lead the soul to the love of God and the virtuous life. God has carefully fit or proportioned scripture to man's capacity. For example, fear plays an important role in scripture's task.[10] Bonaventure views the reports of punishments, as well as the threat of punishments in the eschatological passages, as playing a crucial role, since fear prompts us to choose the good and do the right.

In the *Breviloquium*, Bonaventure presents succinctly what came to be the four standard "senses" or meanings of scripture as distinguished by medieval authors. First, of course, there is the literal sense of the text; in addition, there are the allegorical, the moral, and the anagogical. Allegory signifies something other than the literal that is in the realm of faith. The moral sense involves learning what we must do through the example of another. The anagogical concerns the eternal happiness of the elect. Scripture has this depth (as Bonaventure explicitly calls it) because of the extent of its content, as well as the diversity of its hearers. With regard to its content, scripture has to treat of God, Christ, the works of salvation, and the things of faith. Scripture is addressed to every kind of hearer and therefore must have a manifold sense in order to appeal to so many different minds. It must reprove the proud, drive away the insincere, and awaken the slothful to search for mysteries.

We find an example of these four senses applied to one verse in Bonaventure's exegesis of Ecclesiasticus 24:12: "He who has created me has rested in my tent (*tabernaculum*)." Bonaventure writes:

> According to the literal understanding, it applies to the Virgin Mary, in whose tabernacle the Lord rested bodily. According to the allegorical, it applies to the Church Militant, in whose tabernacle the Lord rests sacramentally. According to the moral, it applies to the faithful soul, in whose tabernacle the Lord rests spiritually. According to the anagogic understanding, it applies to the heavenly court, in whose tabernacle he rests eternally.[11]

The four senses of scripture are also necessary for achieving the sacred text's very purpose. We need to be led to eternal life, which is our goal, but this cannot happen unless "our intellect knows what truths to accept, our will chooses the good that is to be done, and our heart yearns to see God, and to love Him, and to enjoy Him." Another way of putting this is that the scriptures are God's third book, which is intended to teach us how to read rightly his second book, creation. The third book uses a threefold method to achieve its end: (1) by tropology it teaches us how to act; (2) by allegory, it shows us what to believe; and (3) by anagogy, it reveals what to desire.[12] Bonaventure clearly thinks that scripture is designed to move our hearts as well as our minds, our intellect, and will. In order to prompt us in the journey to heaven, it therefore, like a good teacher, varies from telling stories to presenting poems to issuing commands and prohibitions. In this way, it attempts to serve as a guidebook to the journey home. Bonaventure implies that it would have been a mistake if the Bible were strictly scientific in its method, that is, if it were to proceed "by way of definition, analysis, and synthesis in order to prove the properties of some subject matter, as do the other sciences."[13] If a person is not moved by command, he might be led by example; if not by the latter, then perhaps by "terrifying threats" or "trustworthy promises."

The Triune God

Scripture tells us about God, and the central truth about God that it speaks is that there is only one God, who is three in "person"—Father, Son, and Spirit. The doctrine of the Trinity is not a professorial obscurity or an addendum to revelation or Christianity. On the contrary, when we read Bonaventure, as with other patristic or Scholastic theologians, we quickly discover that he regarded Christianity to be fundamentally about the Trinity. In his *Disputed Questions on the Mystery of the Trinity*, he says that the article of the faith that God is triune, is "the foundation of the entire Christian faith."[14] That is to say, the teaching on the Trinity is so central that it is accurate to say that the Christian faith is, in essence, the belief that God is triune; to be a Christian is to believe that God is triune. This doctrine about God has priority over doctrines concerning either what God is, in his various perfections—for example, omniscient, provident—or what God has done for us, such as creating the world or redeeming the human race.

According to its long line of critics beginning in the Renaissance and continuing through the Enlightenment and modernity, Scholastic Trinitarian theology represents the worst tendency of Christians to engage in arcane and abstruse speculations about God. The critics have charged Scholastics with violating the canons of reason itself in their endless attempts to reconcile the unity of the Godhead with Nicea's Trinitarianism (i.e., Father, Son, and Spirit are three hypostases; the Son is the same substance [homoousios] as the Father). Medieval Scholastics attempted a defense of Trinitarianism by trying to explain how there can be a real distinction without separation in one being.

One of the chief accusations made by other Christians against Scholastic Trinitarian theology is that it separated out the doctrine about the Trinity (de deo trino) from that concerning the nature of God (de deo uno), thereby subordinating the Trinity to the unity of God. However, the reader will search in vain for such a separation in Bonaventure. Whatever path one takes to God, whether scriptural or philosophical, one will find the Trinity of persons. Everything that exists proclaims the triune God.

Bonaventure belongs in the long tradition of Christian thought that has attempted to take seriously what scripture says about God, while also respecting the principles of logic and rules of inference. He inherited a doctrine about God that came with its own specialized vocabulary and taught that God is one ousia (one being or substance) and three hypostases (three subsistencies or persons). This seemingly obscure vocabulary had been enshrined in the creedal formulas of two fourth-century general church councils—Nicea (325) and Constantinople (381)—from which no Christian who wished to remain within the church could depart.

Bonaventure had at his disposal two different models of Trinitarian theology: the psychological or intellectual model of Augustine, and the social model of Richard of St. Victor (d. 1173). Richard's approach is neatly summarized in the following quote: "In order for the charity to be true, it demands a plurality of persons; in order for charity to be perfected, it requires a Trinity of persons."[15] Even Richard's social model has precedent in Augustine; in book 8 of De Trinitate, Augustine presents a model of Trinitarian love—the Father is the lover, the Son the beloved, and the Holy Spirit the mutual love that passes between them.[16] In book 15, Augustine returns to this analogy of love. Richard's innovation therefore seems to be his insistence that perfect love requires the presence of a third who shares in the mutual love and rejoices in it.

Drawing on Augustine, Bonaventure argues to the Trinity from the notion of God as mind; drawing on Richard, he argues to the Trinity from the notion of God as love. It seems that Bonaventure attempted to use them both in order to create a synthesis rooted in a metaphysics of being, goodness, and love. One finds this synthesis presented in the *Itinerarium*: "The first approach fixes the soul's gaze primarily and principally on Being Itself, declaring that the first name of God is *He Who is*. The second approach fixes the soul's gaze on the Good Itself, saying that this is the first name of God."[17] It is the contemplation of God as Good that leads Bonaventure to a consideration of the emanations of the Trinity:

> Having considered the essential attributes of God, we must raise the eyes of our intelligence to the contuition of the most Blessed Trinity, so as to place the second cherub facing the first. Now just as Being itself is the principal source of the vision of the essential attributes of God, as well as the name through which the others become known, so the Good itself is the principal foundation of the contemplation of the personal emanations.[18]

Bonaventure then proceeds to argue that since the good is self-diffusive, the highest good must therefore be the most self-diffusive. This principle is central to Bonaventure's Trinitarian theology. Furthermore, the greatest self-diffusion cannot exist unless it is actual and intrinsic, substantial and hypostatic, natural and voluntary, free and necessary, lacking nothing and perfect. More specifically, Bonaventure's attempt to synthesize Augustine's intellectual model with Richard's social model creates a balance between God as self-subsisting mind and God as self-giving love. Mind achieves perfection in self-presence; love achieves perfection in communion. God is the Supreme Spirit who has no need of the world; the world is radically contingent, and thus any danger of pantheism is eliminated. On the other hand, the world is not unrelated to God; it is really related to God both for its being and form. As Supreme Spirit, God freely expresses himself in creation; and as love, he freely pours forth a share in his being in creatures. The world is God's book, his love letter, and thus any danger of nihilism is eliminated. The world is enchanted, since it speaks of the God who is spirit and love. Trinitarianism becomes a necessary condition for understanding God, man, and the universe.

Bonaventure does not think that there can be demonstrative proof for the triune nature of God, but he does think there are arguments showing why belief in the Trinity does not contradict reason and is, in fact, congruous with rationality and the mind. He presents arguments of congruence or fittingness for the triune nature of God[19] that are "testimony" of the Trinity. We know the Trinity because God has gradually revealed himself to us in different ways, or books. The triune God has written three books: the Book of Creation, the Book of Scripture, and the Book of Life.

In the Book of Creation, every creature, and especially the rational creature, bears witness to the triune nature of God. Every creature is a vestige of God; every rational creature is also an image of God: The vestige bears witness indistinctly, the image more clearly. Every creature has measure, species, and order; unity, truth, and goodness; or measure, number, and weight, which by appropriation correspond to the Trinity of persons and thus give witness to the fact that God is the Trinity. An intellectual creature is an image that testifies to the threefold character of God from near at hand, because an image is what Bonaventure calls "an express similitude." "The intellectual creature has memory, intellect, and will; or mind, knowledge, and love. Mind is like a parent, knowledge like the offspring, and love like a bond proceeding from both and joining them together. For the mind cannot fail to love the word which it generates."[20]

In the Book of Scripture, we have the clearest testimony for the Trinity from two sources: the Old and New Testaments. The testimony of the Old Testament is implicit, while that of the New is explicit and unambiguous. It is in the latter that we find the command of Jesus Christ that the truth of God's triune nature should be preached clearly and openly throughout the world. Before the coming of Christ, human beings were obliged to believe in the Trinity only implicitly, but after the coming of Christ, they are obliged to believe explicitly (Matthew 28:19). "It must be believed by reason of the promulgation of the truth of the gospel."

In the Book of Life, we have explicit and express testimony to the eternal Trinity. God has provided this witness of his triune nature, Bonaventure tells us, because not all listen to the gospel and because this is a truth beyond reason: The Divine Wisdom provided an eternal testimony for these reasons in the Book of Life, which provides a testimony for the souls on earth through the influence of light. This illumination can be received in two ways, either through an innate light or from an infused one. That God is triune is dictated not by the innate light itself, but by the infused light from which, together with the natural light, it can be concluded that God should be thought of as one who generates and spirates one coequal to, and consubstantial with, himself.

The central question became how to understand God as one in substance and nature and yet three in person. In his book, *On the Trinity*, Augustine set down the theology of the Trinity that became normative in the Western church. There are at least three distinctive points found in Augustine's Trinitarian theology.

First, he views the divine nature as prior to the persons. Augustine clearly believes the starting place of Trinitarian theology to be the divine nature or essence, not the Father or the manifestations of the three persons. Hence, in the West, the question will always be: After Augustine, how can the one God be three in person? This understanding of the central question of Trinitarian theology is different from the approach taken in the church in the East, for which the question is: How can the three persons be one God? The Greek theologians tend to see the persons as logically prior to the nature, while for the West, following Augustine, it is the divine nature that is seen as logically prior.

Second, Augustine insists that every operation of God is due to the entire Trinity. Third, in order to explain how the one God can be three, he develops an analogy between human thought and will and the divine processions (of the Son and Spirit). This mental analogy for the divine processions is usually referred to as a psychological view or model of the Trinity. The warrant for this analogy comes from the biblical teaching, found clearly in Genesis, that man is the image of God. Augustine thus looks for God's image in the human soul, which he comes to see as the mirror of the divine. This approach had a lasting influence in the West. An implication of this psychological model is that the Trinity of persons must in fact be subsistent relations within the Godhead, since the persons cannot be distinguished by any unique essential attribute. Since there is no opposition between spiration and either paternity or filiation, there is no reason for a fourth person. The West, following Augustine's lead, came to see Father, Son, and Spirit as three subsisting relations within the one God.

However, Augustine did not have the last word in the West. Beginning with a landmark study in the late nineteenth century by Théodore de Régnon, it has become clear that there were different traditions even within Western Trinitarian theology.[21] De Régnon, in particular, pointed out some of the important differences between Aquinas and Bonaventure. Since De Régnon's study, there has been considerable discussion about how Bonaventure fits within the different approaches to Trinitarian theology. De Régnon saw Bonaventure as belonging to a tradition that went back through Alexander of Hales and Richard of St. Victor to Pseudo-Dionysius. He placed Aquinas in a distinct tradition that went back and through Anselm and the Lombard to Augustine. Other scholars followed this main line of argument set down by De Régnon,[22] but in 1966, Olegario Gonzalez set forth a somewhat different account of the history of Trinitarian theology. While De Régnon had presented Richard as one more deeply influenced by Greek Trinitarian theology and thus the medieval founder of a tradition that competed with Augustine, Gonzalez argued that Richard of St. Victor was heavily influenced by Augustine on a number of points.[23] In addition, more recent studies have indicated that

Richard belongs solidly in the Latin tradition. There are two distinct ideas present in his Trinitarian theology: first, his notion of the good seems to depend heavily on Anselm's "that than which no greater can be thought"; second, the dominant idea in Richard's thought is dependent upon a psychological analysis of love. Given the dearth of influence from Pseudo-Dionysius, it is now clear that Richard is not the founder of the Greek tradition. Richard held what has come to be called a social model of the Trinity.[24] In this view, perfect love requires a beloved. Self-giving love requires one to receive the love; hence, there must be at least two persons in the Trinity. But Richard also argued that love between two is less perfect than that among three, because a third is necessary for the love of the two to be recognized and intensified; only a circle of love is truly complete and perfect. Richard also proposed as the definition of person, "an incommunicable existence of the divine nature."

Bonaventure, however, unambiguously belongs in a tradition influenced by Pseudo-Dionysius. It seems clear that Bonaventure learned of both Richard and Pseudo-Dionysius through Alexander of Hales. Alexander and the work for which he is largely responsible, namely the *Summa fratris Alexandri*, are deeply influenced by a Dionysian concept of the good. Indeed, Bonaventure develops a metaphysics of the good, which serves as the foundation for his Trinitarian theology. Into this metaphysics, he incorporates his principal argument for a plurality of persons, an argument from an analysis of love. Gonzalez concludes that there is a distinct tradition of Trinitarian theology in the thirteenth century, but that the founder of this tradition is not Richard of St. Victor, but in fact, Bonaventure.[25] The sources of Bonaventure's distinctive Trinitarian theology are, proximately, Alexander of Hales, but more remotely, Pseudo-Dionysius and Aristotle. Bonaventure incorporates elements from Augustine and Richard into this foundational metaphysics of the good. De Régnon was correct in saying that there are two distinct traditions of Trinitarian theology, but the originator and source of these two traditions have been radically revised.

Anselm was a thoroughgoing Augustinian on theological matters in general and on Trinitarian theology in particular. But Anselm, while drawing on Augustine's psychological model, is considerably more confident of what reason can attain, and therefore he presents necessary reasons for the Trinity. In his *Monologion*, Anselm argues that God, while remaining one in essence, must have three relations within himself. God as the Supreme Spirit must thus be knowing or rational in order to know what he has created. Since created beings clearly indicate rationality and design, there must be a designer who knows created beings, just as a craftsman who is to make something must know what he is going to make. This knowing must involve reasoning about what will be made. "For a maker makes something rationally, if and only if, there is already something there in his reasoning—as a sort of exemplar."[26] But knowing involves an interior speaking to oneself. "Before a craftsman makes something by means of his craft he first expresses it within himself by means of a mental conception." Indeed, the Supreme Spirit, in knowing himself, gives perfect expression to all that he knows in a single, but definitive, word. In other words, God is mind. The word is the eternal interior expression of God's knowing himself. And what is known is also loved, and the love binding together mind with its expression is the Holy Spirit.

Bonaventure approaches the doctrine of the Trinity by asking the classic question of how the unity of substance and nature can be reconciled with certain "pluralities" that are associated with God: the plurality (1) of persons, (2) of manifestations, and (3) of appropriations. We are led to the conclusion that God is three in one for two general types of reasons, depending on whether we are considering God as the good or as mind.

When we consider God as the good, we are at the heart of Bonaventure's whole metaphysics and theology. The supreme instance of the good's self-diffusion is "that in which the diffusing good communicates to another his whole substance and nature."[27] This point is key to understanding Bonaventure. It is the good's first self-diffusion that is the medium of creation. This self-communication of God is a word begotten from all eternity, but it is not subordinate in being to the First Principle; it is coequal and through which all things have been created and through him all things are governed.

"For the diffusion that occurred in time in the creation of the world is no more than a pivot or point in comparison with the immense sweep of the eternal goodness."[28] This self-diffusion of the Good is the supreme self-communication of God: "He supremely communicates Himself by eternally possessing One who is beloved and One who is mutual love."[29]

We can also consider God as mind, and Bonaventure thinks we are again led to a Trinitarian view by this consideration. Implicit in the excellences predicated of God is the view that God is the supreme mind. In other words, once it is granted that God must be rational and thus understanding, then God must possesses mind. Or, to be more precise, since there is nothing that God can possess as an attribute, God must be mind. And there are necessary reasons why mind begets an interior word that is a likeness of itself, and this likeness is loved; a fortiori, God must beget a word that is the perfect expression of the Godhead, and God must love this word, and the word must love what it expresses. There are thus necessary reasons why the Godhead must be one in three, triune.

Bonaventure therefore develops three basic arguments for the plurality of persons: an argument from the nature of the good, an argument from the nature of mind, and an argument from love. The essential premises of these arguments are that the good is by nature self-diffusive, the mind is by nature self-knowing, and love is by nature self-communicative. Bonaventure employs different arguments in the course of his career to defend the Trinity of persons. He argues that the concepts of goodness, privacy, love, perfection, and simplicity all reveal why there must be no fewer than three persons. But it is the concept of primacy that lies at the heart of Bonaventure's doctrine of God. The argument is that a being is the cause of others because it is first. The divine nature is absolutely first with respect to all other essences, and thus is the only being in the fullest sense of the word. Bonaventure defends the Scholastic view that within the Godhead are two modes of emanation, three hypostases, four relations, and five concepts.

Before discussing the two modes of emanation, it is perhaps important to say a word or two about the very notion of person. Boethius had defined a person as "an individual substance of a rational nature," but this definition, taken by itself, could lead one to become a tritheist. In attempting to apply this notion to Trinitarian theology, those theologians relying on Augustine came to understand the divine "persons" as constituted by relation; those theologians relying on Richard tended to see the divine persons as constituted by difference of origin. Bonaventure seems clearly to side with Richard. This is not to say, however, that Bonaventure completely abandons any notion of the persons as subsistent relations, but only that it never takes on the centrality that it has for Aquinas. If a relation arises from procession, it would seem that the first procession logically presupposes a person who actively generates; but if this were so, the first person would have to be prior to the relation by which he said to be constituted. Hence, Bonaventure will maintain that primacy has a logical priority over paternity.

From the First Principle, there are two perfect emanations: one through nature and one through will. The first emanation from the very nature of the First Principle is referred to as generation; the second emanation from will of the First Principle is spiration. Both of these emanations are perfect in the sense that both involve a complete pouring forth of the Godhead: one emanation that involves a begetting of the perfect image that reflects God fully, and a second emanation that involves a procession of the perfect love of God.

Each emanation further involves a twofold relation, since a real emanation involves a principle, a term, and their relation. The emanation must be real, and not merely logical or mental. Because there are two emanations, there must be four relations: two of origination (paternity and spiration) and two of procession (filiation and procession). In other words, there are four relations in God: the relationship of the Father to the Son (the active generation), the Son to the Father (the passive generation), the Father and the Son to the Holy Spirit (the active spiration), and the Holy Spirit to the Father and the Son (the passive spiration). Furthermore, these relations must be subsistent, and not accidental, for whatever is in God must be his essence, or one in being with him. These relations must also constitute the distinction between the persons, since the persons cannot be distinguished by any absolute attribute, for every absolute attribute must belong to the divine nature as such and so be common to all persons. Hence, the distinction between the persons is found in the relations alone. It is true to say, then, that the Father is the Divine Paternity, the Son the Divine Filiation, and the Spirit the Divine Procession.

Bonaventure discusses each person of the Trinity in terms of the three names. He treats the first person of the Trinity as the Unbegotten One, as the Principle who proceeds from no other, and as the Father. "The Unbegotten One" designates him by negation; "Principle who proceeds from no other" designates him by an affirmation and a negation; "Father" designates him positively, properly, and completely.[30] The Father is the "ancient of days" "whose antiquity is eternity."[31] In his *Sentences* commentary, Bonaventure compares the emanation of the persons (*personarum emanatio*) to a river because when one stands at some point beside a river, it seems to have no beginning and no end.

The second person of the Trinity is the Image, the Word, or the Son. Image designates him as the expressed likeness of the Father. Word designates him as the expressing likeness, and Son as the personal likeness. The Word proceeds from the First Principle as the term of an intellectual procession in a way analogous to the generation of a concept in the human mind. As an act of intellectual conception, the Word must be a likeness of the object known—in this case, the First Principle.

The third person of the Trinity is the Gift, the mutual Love, and the Holy Spirit. Gift designates him as being given through the will; Love as the one given through the will as the Gift par excellence, and Holy Spirit as the one given through the will who is a person. As the Son is the term of the act of the divine intellect, so the Spirit is the term of the act of the divine will. As in human love, the act of love arouses an impression of the object loved, so does God's act of love for himself proceed forth into the Spirit.

Bonaventure discusses Aristotle's ten categories of being—substance, quantity, relation, quality, action, passion, space, time, position, and possession—in terms of their applicability to God. The last five of these do not properly apply to God because they pertain only to beings both bodily and mutable, and they may be used of God only in an analogical or figurative way. The first five are applicable to God insofar as they betoken completeness without contradicting the divine simplicity. In other words, as Bonaventure explains, whatever is predicated must be identical with God such that any predicate is understood as substantive. "The only exception is relation, which has a twofold reference: the subject in which it exits and the object to which it points."[32] The relation that refers to the subject in whom it exists is substantive; the relation that refers to the object is not substantive, but exists only because there must be distinction.

Bonaventure then sets down a rule to govern the distinct modes of predication: "Terms predicated as substances of all three Persons are predicated severally and jointly, and in the singular; while terms predicated as relations cannot be predicated of all three Persons; and if they apply to more than one Person, they are predicated in the plural, designating them as related distinct, similar or equal by reason of their intrinsic relationship." What this amounts to is that some terms may be predicated of only one of the persons, and only in the singular: Father, Son, Spirit, begotten. Other terms may be predicated of two of the persons, in the singular or in the plural depending on whether they apply to one or both: The Son proceeds from the Father, the Son and the Holy Spirit proceed from the Father. Still other terms may be predicated of all three persons, either in the singular or the plural: All three persons mutually dwell within each other.

After Trinitarian theology has addressed the question of how to reconcile the unity of nature with the plurality of persons, it must take up the question of reconciling the divine unity with a plurality of manifestations. These manifestations, to which Bonaventure refers, are the appearances or theophanies of God at various moments in salvation history, such as when he appeared to the patriarchs and prophets.

In discussing these manifestations, Bonaventure begins with the foundational view that the Principle has revealed himself through the effects that emanate from him, that is to say, in all creatures. But within this general revelation found in all creatures, there are special manifestations that make God known through particular effects. First, there are indwellings that are spiritual effects that make God possess us and be possessed by us. Bonaventure had in mind here sanctifying grace, which makes us sharers in the very life of God. Second, there are manifestations properly so-called that are effects perceivable by the senses, such as when the Holy Spirit appeared as a dove.

The final plurality that Trinitarian theology must treat is the plurality of appropriations. Hugh of St. Victor had developed the notion that it is right to think of each of the persons as particularly involved in certain works. None of this is to deny the fundamental principle, established by the church fathers, that what one person does, all do. But particular persons of the Trinity may be said to be especially at work in certain actions.

Following in the Victorine's path, Bonaventure unambiguously holds that all essential attributes apply to all three persons, but certain attributes are "appropriated" to just one of the persons because they apply to that one in an especially appropriate way. For example, oneness is appropriated to the Father, truth to the Son, and goodness to the Holy Spirit. These terms are not properly predicated of the person since they are always common, but they are useful in understanding the distinct persons within the Trinity.[33] As already seen, oneness, truth, and goodness apply to God as the supreme and perfect being insofar as it is a whole, intelligible, and communicable. But each of these terms is appropriated to a particular person in the Trinity, such that oneness refers uniquely to the Father, truth to the Son, and goodness to the Spirit. There is a certain logic to this: "The Supremely One is supremely first because He is absolutely without beginning; the Supremely True is supremely conforming [to the One] and beautiful; the Supremely Good is supremely satisfying and beneficent."[34]

There is a second series of appropriations: eternity, splendor, and fruition. Eternity is in the Father, since he has no beginning and is first in every respect; splendor is in the likeness, since he is supremely beautiful; fruition is in the Holy Spirit, since he is supremely beneficent and generous. Bonaventure quotes Augustine for support on this second mode of appropriation.[35]

The third mode of appropriation flows from the second in that supreme oneness implies principle and origin; supreme beauty and resplendence, expression and exemplarity; supreme beneficence and goodness, the end. As a result, in this third mode, efficiency is appropriated to the Father, exemplarity to the Son, and finality to the Holy Spirit.

Finally, since all power derives from the one supremely first, all wisdom flows from the supreme exemplar, and all will tends toward the supreme end, omnipotence, omniscience, and benevolence may be appropriated to the Father, Son, and Spirit, respectively.

The Creation of the World

Why does Bonaventure explicitly include creation as a distinct subject area in his division of theology? What does theology add to
our understanding of creation that has not already come to light in examining nature?

First and foremost, according to Bonaventure, theology reinforces our
awareness of the nothingness of creation. It is this fundamental nothin-
giness that we must recall if we are to understand Bonaventure's doctrine
of creation. In recalling this doctrine, however, it is also important to
keep in mind that Bonaventure believes creation *ex nihilo* (from nothing)
can be known by reason alone. Theology reiterates and reinforces with a
higher authority what the reflective mind already knows. Bonaventure's
constant reiteration of the nothingness of creation has a twofold aspect:
(1) creatures are made by God from nothing; and (2) even in their being,
creatures are almost nothing in that they participate in a finite way in
being, and they are radically contingent, for they come to be and cease
to be.

Like other Christians, Bonaventure affirms the goodness of creation,
but for him, it is part of a larger mysticism that he inherits from Franciscanism. Francis of Assisi popularized a view of nature that looked upon
the created world as a reflection of the Creator.[1] One of Francis's biog-
raphers, Thomas of Celano, tells us:

> [W]hatever he discovers in creatures he guides to the Creator. "He rejoices
> in all the works of the Lord's hand" (Psalm 92:5), and through their de-

lightful display he gazes on their life-giving reason and cause. In beautiful things he discerns Beauty Itself; all good things cry out to him: "The One who made us is the Best." Following the footprints imprinted on all creatures, he follows his Beloved everywhere; out of them all he makes for himself a ladder by which he might reach the Throne.[2]

Francis was deeply struck both by creation and by our kinship with it, a view that he expresses in his famous hymn that calls upon "Brother Sun" and "Sister Moon" to join him in praising God. In Bonaventure's hands, this nature mysticism receives a new philosophical depth thanks to his semiotic metaphysics rooted in divine exemplarism.

In addition, theology adds to the doctrine of creation a clear knowledge of the divine Word's central role in creation. Bonaventure's view of creation is thoroughly Logos (Word) centric. Christ is the Word of God through whom all things have been made.

A Trinitarian View of Creation

Bonaventure's view of creation, in addition to being Logos centric, is also Trinitarian. Bonaventure develops a Trinitarian view of creation by building on the foundation laid by Augustine in *De Trinitate*. The whole world reflects the triune God in different ways and to different degrees.[3] Bonaventure is quite fond of seeking out trinities in creation and relating them to the triune God. This endeavor involves two steps: first, seeking an analogy between and unity in its conjoined trinity and then, "appropriating" the trinity of characteristics to the divine persons. This two-step process is followed again and again. Obviously, this endeavor relies on analogous reasoning, with the analogies found in creatures, in the human soul, and in the soul's operations. The soul, with its unity of essence and three powers, is an image of the Trinity. But the free will in itself is a sign of the Trinity because insofar as it is a power, it bears the mark of the Father; insofar as it is rational, it bears the mark of the Son; and insofar as it is free, it bears the mark of the Holy Spirit.[4]

Every creature has measure, species, and order; unity, truth, and goodness; or measure, number, and weight, which by appropriation correspond to the Trinity of persons, Father, Son and Spirit, respectively, and thus, to Bonaventure's mind, give witness to the fact that God is the Trinity. The intellectual creature is an image and testifies to the threefold character of God from near at hand, because an image is an expressed similitude. The intellectual creature has memory, intellect, and will; or mind, knowledge, and love. Mind is like a parent, knowledge like an offspring, and love like a bond proceeding from both and joining them together. "For the mind cannot fail to love the word which it generates."[5]

Bonaventure reiterates on many occasions that the First Principle has disposed all things by measure, number, and weight. In this way, he indicates that every thing is an effect of the creating Trinity. Every thing that exists is brought about by the Trinity, which is the efficient, exemplar, and final cause. The Trinity's efficient causality, in bringing any thing to be, is manifested in its measure, that is, it is one and is dependent upon the efficient cause. The Trinity's exemplar causality is reflected in the thing's number, in other words, it is true (conforms to its exemplar cause) and has a distinct existence; the Trinity's final causality is reflected in the thing's weight, that is, it is good and ordered to its final cause.[6] Bonaventure is saying that every being is one, true, and good; has mode (a dependency upon the efficient cause), species (a conformity to its exemplar cause), and order (an ordination to its final cause).[7]

Bonaventure appeals to the reader to support his view that the created image provides testimony of the Trinity. " 'In the state of innocent nature' the Book of Creation had not been obscured nor had the eye of man darkened. It was sent the weekend human vision and the mirror of creation was made dark and obscure. And the ear of our inner understanding was hardened against hearing that testimony."

The Hierarchy of Creation

In the actual production of physical nature, the divine operation was threefold: creation, division, and provision. God created out of nothing and this was before any day. Then there was an act of division that took place over three days. Bonaventure describes the works of these days according to their relation to light. On the first day, God distinguished between the luminous, the translucent, and the opaque natures, that is, light (fire), air and water, and earth, respectively. On the second day, God brought about distinctions between the translucent natures. On the third day, there was a distinction made between the translucent and opaque natures.

Finally, over the course of the next six days of creation, God made provision for the various natures. On the fourth day, God provided for the luminous nature by the forming of the stars. On the fifth day, there was a provisioning for the translucent natures when fish and birds were made to fill the water and the air. On the sixth day, there was a provisioning of opaque nature when animals were made, and then, finally, man.

"God could have brought all this about in a single instant. He chose instead to act through time, and step by step."[8]

Angels

Bonaventure holds that angels are incorporeal spirits. At the very moment of their creation, God gave the angels special perfections: simplicity of essence, individuality of person, rationality, and freedom of choice. It was the exercise of the last perfection that made all the difference in the history of the universe. For in that first instant, the angels had the choice to either cling to or turn away from the good, to their own finite good. A certain, particularly eminent angel, the glorious "Bearer of Light" ("Lucifer"), did turn away. Indeed, this angel loved his own glory and his own gifts more than God and wanted yet more of them. "The sight of his own beauty and eminence having made him fall in love with himself and his private good, he presumed upon the lofty state already his, to aspire to a further height that he did not possess."[9] Thus, in that first instant of creation, one of the spiritual creatures, employing the very gift that was the condition for the possibility of its being a spiritual creature, turned away from the good and thus brought about disorder into God's creation. The will of the intelligent being is made to choose the good, but in order for it to be able to fulfill its very purpose, it must be able to choose something else. So did the will of one such spiritual being, and the disorder of sin entered into the world. Bonaventure is keenly aware of the problem of evil, and because he thinks the origin of evil is an action of the will, he is also deeply aware of its explosive power. The fate of the universe rides on the movements of this power.

Because of the nature of angels as purely spiritual beings, they were capable of a single definitive choice in a way that corporeal beings are not. Precisely because their first choice was definitive, Lucifer and the angels who followed his lead became immediately obstinate in their evil choice, and blind to truth, lawless in their action, and deficient in their powers. In other words, the rebellious angels sunk even further, and by a similar dynamic, the faithful angels, who turned to the good, were confirmed in the very good they chose. The bad angels were fixed in their impenitence, and the good angels were confirmed through grace and glory. The good angels thus possess a "God-formed" intellect and a will irrevocably fixed on the supreme good as a result of their first and definitive choice. Because the angels behold God face to face, they move in God wherever they may be sent.

Bonaventure discusses in detail the heavenly hierarchy, in which there are three orders of spirits: the first consists of Thrones, Cherubim, and Seraphim; the second of Dominions, Virtues, and Powers; the third of Principalities, Archangels, and Angels. It is of interest here that Bonaventure follows the enumeration of the angelic hierarchy provided by Pseudo-Dionysius in his *On the Heavenly Hierarchy* (*De caelestia hierarchia*).[10] Gregory the Great (ca. 540–604) had provided a slightly different listing of the hierarchy.[11]

God has given the administration of the universe to the angels in that they are to move the heavenly bodies. They receive from the first cause an influx of power to preserve the natural stability of things. The faith teaches that the angels also have special roles in the works of reparation.[12]

The Human Being

The origin of the rational soul has long proven a difficult issue for Christians. The two main opinions on this matter are the traducianist and the creationist. The defenders of traducianism held that the soul is generated with the body, "led out" of the matter, so to speak (hence, the name from *traducere*, "to lead out"). The creationists argue that God directly creates the human and immortal soul and infuses it, at some moment (another point of dispute) into the body. The problem for the traducianist is immortality: If the soul is generated with the body, why does it not die when the body dies? The problem of the creationist is original sin: If God directly creates the human soul, how does it incur original sin and its effects?[13] Augustine himself had been unclear on this issue and bequeathed the problem to his commentators in the Middle Ages.

Bonaventure discusses different theories about the origin of the soul at some length.[14] He holds the view that God directly creates the rational soul with the body, or perhaps following the body.[15] God reserves the creation of the soul to himself alone because the form that is the soul cannot be brought into existence by generation since all that is generated is naturally corruptible, but the soul is not;[16] it is the substantial form of the human being. Bonaventure quotes Aristotle to support his contention that the intellect has to come from an extrinsic, nonmaterial source.[17]

Human reason can be analyzed in three different ways: innocent, fallen, and glorified.[18] The human being was happy in paradise as God originally intended. Paradise, as the condition of creation as God originally intended it, plays a paradigmatic role in Bonaventure's thought. The source of this prelapsarian happiness was man's ability to read the two "books" God wrote. One is the external book or the book without, that is, the perceptible world. For "the first Principle created this perceptible world as a means of self-revelation so that, like a mirror of God or a divine footprint, it might lead man to love and praise his Creator." The second book is the book within, for it is inscribed in nothing less than God's eternal art, that is, his mind and that mind's definitive expression of itself, the eternal Word. "Accordingly there are two books, one written within, and that is God's eternal art and Wisdom; the other written without, and that is the perceptible world."[19]

The Corruption of Sin

Good and Evil

Bonaventure rejects any sort of fundamental dualism between good and evil. "A first and absolute evil does not and could not exist," Bonaventure argues, because the very notion of First Principle implies supreme plenitude.[1] There cannot be two supreme beings. The First Principle must necessarily exist for his own sake and not for another. The one Supreme Being is utterly without defect; it cannot be lacking in existence and cannot fail in operation, nor can the First Principle be the cause of evil in any manner. Indeed, the First Principle is the cause of everything that comes about in the universe except sin. The question then becomes, whence comes evil?

Bonaventure follows Augustine in distinguishing between natural and moral evil, or, to use the terminology from Augustine's *On Free Choice* (*De libero arbitrio*), the evil of penalty (*malum poenae*) and the evil of guilt (*malum culpae*). The former is an evil we suffer, while the latter is a privation of righteousness that we cause. The evil of penalty is just and comes from divine providence. Although the stain of original sin is blotted out in the soul by baptism, the consequences of original sin—concupiscence and bodily weakness—remain, and it is against these consequences that all human beings are to fight throughout their lives. Life thus necessarily involves struggle; this is the human condition.[2]

The Original Sin

The possibility for sin is found in the fact of free choice.[3] Bonaventure interestingly ties man's capacity for failing in the operation of his will to the fact that he is a being made out of nothingness. Man is imperfect in his nature by the very fact that he has been created, that is, made out of nothing, and an imperfect being, nevertheless capable of free choice, is able to act for an end other than God. Here lies the root of the great mystery of evil, for free choice entails the possibility of such a being choosing an end contrary to the good, while yet remaining good in its very being. The Supreme Good created a being with life, intelligence, and will, but this creature was to be conformed to the good in mode, species, and order, that is, "it was meant to act by the power of God, in accordance with God and for God as an end." However, because the human being has free choice, he is capable of acting for himself instead of for God, and thus not properly by the power of God, nor according to God, nor for God. "That precisely is sin: the vitiation of mode, species and order."[4]

In paradise, God gave us a twofold command, one of nature for our own good, and one of discipline for the sake of meriting the good that was promised but not yet attained. This disciplinary command was given purely for the sake of obedience, for "there is no better way of meriting than pure obedience." The command was obligatory just in itself, and not for some added reason. In this way, God intended that we should merit heaven by our willing obedience.

The human will of man was fallible or capable of failing to cling to God, even from the beginning before the first sin, because we are made out of nothing and had not yet been stabilized by glory. Since the human will was fallible, God gave us four aids, two natural and two gracious. The natural aids were right judgment (rectitude of conscience) and right will (synderesis). The aids of grace were actual and sanctifying grace. The actual grace helped man to know himself, his God, and the world; the sanctifying grace, which is charity, disposed man to love God above all else and his neighbor as himself.[5]

Bonaventure takes the Genesis story of the temptation and the Fall to be the report of an actual event and an illuminating paradigm of all subsequent sins. According to Bonaventure, Lucifer, the leader of the rebellious angels, took the form of a serpent in paradise in order to tempt the first woman, Eve. God permitted him to do so, but forced him to take the form of a serpent so that his cunning might be seen and so that all future human beings would know how shrewd Satan is in disguising himself.

Bonaventure gives Satan credit for his clever and carefully planned seduction. First, he attacked the very apex and citadel of the human being—the rational power. He did this by arousing doubt about the divinely given "precept of discipline." Satan began his seduction by cross-examining Eve about the very reason for the prohibition, thus suggesting that it is arbitrary and of no intrinsic value: "[The serpent] said to the woman, Did God say, 'You shall not eat of any tree of the garden?'" (Genesis 3:1). In this way, he awakened doubt about whether the supposed penalty of death would actually be incurred for transgressing the prohibition. Then, Satan aroused contempt in the irascible appetite for the penalty supposedly threatened by God: "You will not die" (Genesis 3:4). The fallen angel then aroused the concupiscible appetite by promising Eve that she would gain a knowledge of good and evil and be like God: "For God knows that when you eat of it your eyes will be opened, and you will be like God, knowing good and evil" (Genesis 3:5). Furthermore, Satan produced a distinct object for each power of the woman so aroused: knowledge for the rational power, Godlike eminence for the irascible, and the fruit of the tree for the concupiscible. By first arousing each power and then presenting each with a desired object, Satan seduced Eve into using her power of free choice to violate the explicit demands of the Good. And so, she consented to his advancements.

Eve "failed to read the internal book that was open and quite legible to the right judgment of reason." Instead, she kept her mind on the external book, the external good. "Because her mind was not upon the infallible truth, her desire soon began to lean toward the perishable good."[6] The sin of the first human being is thus a sin of the whole person, involving not just one power. The first sin involves a thought, a feeling, and a deed.

The sin of Adam was rooted in two things: (1) excessive love for what he had, namely, the friendship of the woman; and (2) selfish love for his own delight.[7] The woman was deceived; the man was not. In both cases, however, sin is the act of disordering God's universe, of turning away from the Good to grab hold of lesser goods. Both the man and the woman fell into disobedience and succumbed to greed; but at root, both had given in to pride. Both inordinately attempted to rise above where they were.

However, "the first Principle who governs all things with perfect foresight and presides over all with perfect justice, tolerates no disorder of any kind in the universe."[8] By forsaking the natural order, the human being becomes subject to the judicial order. As punishment for sin, God took away the special gifts given to the body; hence, it was afflicted with hard work and the defects of hunger and thirst. Furthermore, the body would no longer readily obey the soul, nor would it procreate without lust, grow without defect, or remain free from the corruption of death. God subjected the human soul to being separated from the body. The punishment of woman is twice as heavy because sin began in Eve; therefore, she incurred subjection, suffering, and the burden of multiplied distress.[9]

Bonaventure argues that sin is not a positive essence, but a corrupting tendency, which is a force that contaminates the will. It therefore has no being apart from the good in which it inheres, namely, the will. Moreover, the corruption of sin was to have lasting effects on all the posterity of Adam and Eve; such posterity would lack the righteousness of original justice. Henceforth, without this justice, human beings would suffer in both body and soul. Our souls would suffer the fourfold penalty of weakness (*infirmitas*), ignorance (*ignorantia*), malice (*malitia*), and concupiscence (*concupiscentia*).[10] Our bodies would suffer pain, imperfection, labor, disease, affliction, death, and corruption. In addition, we would be deprived of the beatific vision.

Bonaventure follows in a path marked out by Anselm, who came to hold that the first sin involved man's loss of "sanctifying" grace and a concomitant just or right relation between man and God. This state of injustice explains the necessity of a Savior. Thus, Bonaventure welds together Anselm's view that the first sin resulted in the loss of justice between human beings and God and Augustine's view that concupiscence is an effect of the original sin.

This set of punishments may seem exceedingly harsh, but Bonaventure does not think that any of us have a right to happiness. He believes that it is perfectly just of God to condemn us all. We are, after all, "children of wrath," as he says on numerous occasions, conceived with a privation of the very possession essential to attaining our end and to living without suffering, namely, the righteousness of original justice.

The transmission of original sin presents some difficulties. This sin cannot be passed down through the soul, because the rational soul is directly and immediately created by God. Nor can it be a straightforward matter of transmission through the body, because original sin has profound and deep-seated effects in the soul. Bonaventure tries to solve the problem of original sin's transmission by saying that it passes from the soul of Adam into the souls of descendents through the flesh, born of concupiscence. He speaks of the flesh being seeded with lust and carrying an infection that then taints and vitiates the soul. Hence, the spiritual originally corrupted the physical, but afterward, the physical infects the spiritual. The infected flesh then infects the soul so united with it by the creative act of God. God infuses the soul as he creates it out of nothing, but through this infusion, the soul unites with rebellious flesh. In this way, however, God cannot be blamed for the soul's infection.[11] Bonaventure remains consistent all the way through his discussion of sin: Sin entered the world not through the will of God, but through the will of man. And it is through that first sin that its effects are transmitted through the posterity of Adam.[12]

Sin

Augustine's corpus contains three definitions of sin. The first definition considers sin to be "anything done, said or desired against the natural law." The eternal law is "the divine order or will of God which requires the preservation of natural order and forbids its violation."[13] However, in an early work, Augustine defined sin as "a turning away from God and turning toward creatures."[14] In this view of sin, it is conceived primarily as an aversion to God and a conversion to creatures. In other words, sin involves turning from the Supreme Good to a lesser good. In the *City of God*, Augustine defines sin as the egoistic love of self, joined to an unwillingness to love. This view finds its inspiration in the biblical teaching that "Pride is the beginning of sin" (Sirach 10:13). Augustine writes: "The earthly by the love of self, even to the contempt of God; the heavenly by the love of God, even to the contempt of self. The former glories in itself, the latter in the Lord."[15] All three of these definitions find their place in Bonaventure's thought.

Bonaventure establishes the conditions under which a sin is venial and not mortal: (1) when a temporal good is merely loved too much, but without being actually chosen over the eternal; (2) when the useful is not actually chosen over the right; (3) when self-will is loved too much, but not actually preferred to the divine will; and (4) when the flesh is full of desires, but not actually preferred to the judgment of right reason. In these conditions, the sinner is outside the law, but not choosing directly against it. Indeed, Bonaventure does not think that sensual pleasure is ever actually preferred to right reason unless reason itself gives consent.

Every occurrence of actual sin recapitulates the dynamic involved in the original sin. "Every personal sin is in a way a copy of the first and original sin."[16] There are four steps to consummation of every sin: (1) the suggestion, (2) a subjective satisfaction with the suggestion, (3) consent to the suggestion, and (4) the act. All sin involves the will's withdrawal from the First Principle, and hence, "actual sin is an actual disorder of the will."[17] "When the disorder is slight and does not destroy, but merely disturbs the order of justice, it is called venial, or readily pardonable, for it does not result in total loss of grace or in God's enmity."[18] The order of justice still demands that the Good be preferred to any temporal good, as in the moment of the original sin. Mortal sin always involves some element of contempt, either for God himself or for his commands. Even so, the human being does not contemn the First Principle or his commands in themselves, but he either desires to have or fears losing something other than God. As a result, Bonaventure often says that sin has two roots: fear and love. And between these two, love is the ultimate and primordial root of sin, because fear arises from love. There is no fear of losing something unless some good is first loved. By this means, Bonaventure traces the root of all sin to the disordered love of perishable goods. By the same token, the root of all sin is sloth—the failure to love the Good enough, with diligence.

The City of Man

Man is by nature a social animal, who needs the help of other human beings and naturally loves their fellowship. There are three social orders— conjugal, domestic, and civil—each one a true society possessing its own proper authority: matrimonial (husband over wife), parental (parents over children), and civil (superior over subordinates). The proper authority of civil society gives rise to a coercive power of subjugation, but if man had remained in a state of innocence, this coercive power would not have been necessary;[19] it arose because civil authority needs to restrain man's propensity to evil and to inordinate desires.[20] Men could not live together in this fallen state if the sovereign did not repress the evil and defend the good.[21] Indeed, secular power may even employ lethal force against evildoers, provided that the intention is love of justice and not revenge.

The first question in such a political view is what ought subjects living under unjust rule or in an illegimiate regime to do? Bonaventure leaves little room for rebellion, but he does admit that when a ruler gains power either through violence or deceit, we may consider this power from two angles: that of the ruler or that of the subject. The ruler's power is clearly unjust from the perspective of the illicit ruler's will; but from the perspective of the merit that the subject may gain, this rule is just, because it is either for the trial of the good or the punishment of the bad.[22]

Though he does not approve, God permits the unjust ruler to rule. The subject should see this rule as part of the providence of God, whose judgment, while often hidden, is never ultimately unjust. Although unjust power may appear meaningless, we are to remember that it is part of a great order (*magna ordinatio*) in which evil is punished and the good advanced.[23]

Nevertheless, since the coercive power of political authority is postlapsarian and exists for the narrow purpose of restraining fallen man's propensity to evil and inordinate desires and of defending the good from harm, political authority is properly limited. In such an Augustinian conception, political power ought to respect the boundaries established by its limited domain of authority, circumscribed as it is within the legitimate societies of the family and marriage. The long recognized implication of such a conception is that the conjugal and domestic orders possess a inherent liberty that political authority ought to recognize. In short, Bonaventure's political theory is an Augustinian one of limited government that preserves the fundamental liberties of hearth and home.

The Incarnation of the Word

The Fittingness of the Incarnation

Out of sheer goodness and mercy, says Bonaventure, God chose to save the human race and his creation marred by sin. God could have done this in any number of ways, but, as Bonaventure neatly lays out, he chose the most fitting and the one most adapted to (1) the nature of redemption, (2) the redeemed, and (3) the redeemer. The restoration of the universe is no less a work than creation, and the key event in this restoration is the Incarnation, "the most perfect of all God's works." Discussions of the redeemer, of course, are usually referred to as Christology and, although Bonaventure does not use the term, he regards Christ to be the center of theology (as well as philosophy). The topic of the way in which Christ redeems the human race is often referred to soteriology, and here too, Bonaventure treats the subject at length without using this name.

As we have seen, Bonaventure holds that God does all things with power, wisdom, and goodness; so too in the case of the restoration. If we examine the Incarnation as a work of God in the light of power, wisdom, and goodness, we can see why it is the most perfect of all God's works, for there cannot be any greater act of power than to combine within a single person two natures as disparate as the human and divine. There is no wiser act than to perfect the universe by uniting the first and the last, that is, the origin of all things, the Word, and the last to be made, the human being. "For there is the consummation of perfection, as appears in a circle, the most perfect of figures, which is ended at the same point from which it begins."[1] There can be no greater act of benevolence than that the master redeem the slave by taking the very nature of the slave.[2]

While Bonaventure stresses the sheer gratuity of the redemption—that is, God was in no way obliged to save us—he is very clear that man could not have been saved by any healer other than God. To be healed of the malady of original sin and its effects, man needed to recover three things: purity of soul, the friendship of God, and that excellence proper to his nature whereby he had been subject to God. However, the human being could not recover his proper excellence if he had become subject to a mere creature, he could not have recovered the friendship of God except through a mediator who could "touch" God and man, and he could not have recovered purity of soul if his sin had not been blotted out in accord with divine justice after condign atonement had been made. All of these conditions for man's restoration—a supremely excellent restorer, a supremely friendly mediator, and superabundant satisfier—point to the appropriateness, indeed, conditioned necessity, of a God-man redeemer. Bonaventure follows Anselm in teaching that, although there was no absolute necessity for God to redeem man, it was necessary *if* he was going to complete the good he had begun in creating man and therefore restore him to happiness. In other words, because God has begun a good work, namely man, it was "necessary" for the honor of God and the happiness of the human being that he be saved. It was not necessary, however, that man be at all, nor was it strictly necessary that a good be completed. But if the good that is man was to be completed, it was necessary in this conditioned sense for God to save man.

Bonaventure argues against those who would say that only the Son could take on human nature and that the other persons of the Trinity could not be incarnate; in particular, he argues against those who would interpret Anselm in this way. Anselm, he says, did not say that it was impossible for any person but the Son to be incarnate, but that it was not as fitting for any person as for the Son.[3]

The Union of Natures

Bonaventure describes the Incarnation as the act by which God effected a union between himself and human nature, but the nature so assumed into the divine is not merely one of the flesh; it refers to an assumption of the rational spirit as well. In addition, this union was brought about not through a commingling of the divine and human natures into some third hybrid, but through a unity of person. The one divine person, the Son, truly united human nature to himself.[4] The union of the two natures could not have occurred in a human hypostasis, because the divine nature cannot subsist in any being other than its own hypostasis.

Bonaventure gives significant consideration to the type of union involved in the Incarnation.[5] After ruling out many types of union, there are four possibilities, for example, from the standpoint of the relationship between the two objects united: (1) the change of one into the other, (2) the change of the two into a third, (3) the constitution of a third object without a change in the two, and (4) the insertion of one object into the other without a change into or the constitution of a third. Bonaventure also considers the theories of union proposed by Al-Ghazali (1058–1111), Aristotle, and St. Bernard. He comes to the conclusion that the type of union involved in the Incarnation transcends all types of union found in the natural order or even in the supernatural order of grace.

There is no example of the type of union that must be involved in the Incarnation. This is not to say, however, that certain types of union cannot be ruled out. It is important to note that the "mystery" of the Incarnation consists in the nature of the union involved in a divine hypostasis assuming human nature. Hence, the scope of the mystery is significantly narrowed. The possibility of a Nestorian or subordinationist conception (that divine and human persons remained separate in the incarnate Christ) is rejected on the grounds that Nestorianism would commit us to a type of union that is not possible. Like other Scholastics, Bonaventure rules out Monophysitism (the doctrine that Christ has a single inseparable nature that is at once divine and human rather than having two distinct but unified natures) or Nestorianism on the philosophical grounds that both theories commit us to incoherent theories of unity.

The Incarnation proceeds from the whole Trinity such that God, the creative Principle, is also the restorative Principle. But in considering the restorative Principle, it is important to consider (1) the fullness of grace in the incarnate word, (2) the fullness of wisdom in his intellect, and (3) the fullness of merit in his actions.

The Fullness of Grace

With regard to the fullness of grace, Bonaventure believes that Christ possesses wholly all graces from the first moment of his conception. The incarnate Word is the restorative Principle. But since any perfection must exist more fully and completely in its source than in its effects, the restorative Principle of the human race must possess the fullness of all grace.

In particular, Christ possessed the grace of the particular person, the grace of headship, and the grace of union. By the grace of his particular person, the incarnate Word was immune from all sin, nor could he have sinned. By the grace of union, the incarnate Word merited not only the beatitude of glory, but also the adoration of *latria*, or the worship due God alone. By the grace of headship, the incarnate Word prompts and enlightens all those to turn to God in faith or through the sacraments of faith (by which he specifies that he means all the just, whether they lived before or after his coming).

The Fullness of Wisdom

Because the restorative Principle possesses the fullness of wisdom in his intellect, Bonaventure gives considerable attention—indeed, no fewer than three separate treatments—to the issue of Christ's knowledge: in his *Commentary on the Sentences*, in his *Breviloquium*, and in a set of disputed questions on the knowledge of Christ (*Quaestiones disputata de scientia Christi*). Just as he is free from all sin, so is Christ free from all ignorance. He was filled with the radiance of the divine wisdom itself. Hence, Bonaventure speaks of him enjoying perfect knowledge according to each nature in its proper cognitive powers.

This means that the incarnate Word not only knew all things, but also knew them in every possible way. This is because, as God, he knew eternally; as a sensitive being, he knew sensibly; and as a rational being, he knew intellectually. His intellectual knowledge was threefold: of nature, grace, and glory. Thus, Christ knew in a total of five distinct ways. By his divinity, he knew actually and comprehensively all things actual and possible, finite and infinite. By glory, he knew all things actual and finite, but the infinite he did not know (except perhaps by some sort of virtual knowledge). By grace, he knew everything related to the salvation of mankind. By integrity of nature (from Adam), he knew everything related to the structure of the universe. By sensible experience, he knew all that falls under the senses. It is only through this last experience that he can be said to have learned obedience from the things he suffered. And it is in this mode of knowing that he perceived things successively rather than simultaneously.[6]

The Fullness of Merit

Central to Bonaventure's Christology is the notion that Christ is the one who merited perfectly and completely for the human race. There are several reasons for this, but it is first important to understand the three ways in which a human being can gain merit: (1) by acquiring a claim he did not have before, (2) by increasing his right to what is his due, and (3) by acquiring a further claim to what he already has by right. No human being could gain merit before God apart from Christ, "for we are not worthy to be absolved from an offense against the supreme Good, nor do we deserve to be rewarded with the immensity of the eternal reward which is God himself."[7]

Insofar as Christ possessed the fullness of grace, he possessed the fullness and perfection of all merit. All the merits of the whole human race are based on his. To the extent that he possessed the grace of the particular person, he was established in charity and in virtue, both as habits and as acts. Insofar as he possessed the grace of headship, he acquired merit, not only for himself, but also for us. He is the root of all the merits for the human race. He could not merit the beatitude that he possessed in his soul. He merited only those things that could not coexist with the state of pilgrimage in this life.

The exalted knowledge of Christ and his meritorious life and action do not preclude his assuming certain defects of human nature. Bonaventure thinks that he clearly assumed certain penalties of the body incurred by the original sin—hunger, thirst, and fatigue—and certain penalties of the soul—sorrow, anguish, and fear. However, he did not assume all the penalties found in the body and soul. So, for example, Bonaventure does not think that the incarnate Word suffered any physical disease, ignorance, or concupiscence (disordered desire).[8] Four penalties incurred by original sin—ignorance, weakness, malice, and concupiscence—are incompatible with perfect innocence; it is for this reason that Christ simply could not be subject to them. He could be subject to the other penalties, though, because they served as the occasion for him to practice virtue and to testify to the authenticity of his humanity. No innocent person is morally obliged to suffer against his will, so Christ could only assume certain penalties in a qualified manner. He could not suffer in his rational will, since he lived in a state of beatitude and union with the Godhead and, what is more, possessed perfect innocence. He did not suffer any pain in his divine or rational will (even though in his passion, he suffered pain in his carnal will). He suffered only in his instinctive will. Quoting Hugh of St. Victor, Bonaventure says, " 'Each will acted in its field, tend-ing toward its proper object: divine will to justice, rational will to obedience, and sensible will to nature.' "[9]

In his discussion of Christ's sufferings, Bonaventure is ever mindful that in his divine nature, the incarnate Word could not suffer. It is only in his human nature that he could suffer, but even here one must be careful.

The Restorative Principle

As the mediator between God and man who was to lead man back to God, the incarnate Word had to share the state of righteousness and beatitude that he had with God. Christ is ever right with the Father and happy, while yet being subject to suffering and mortality.

In his passion, Christ suffered in his body and soul. In his soul, he grieved for the sins of the human race and suffered the shame of being associated with criminals. Furthermore, Christ's passion is a model of virtue in that he endured death for the sake of divine justice and obedience.

The passion of Christ is an offering of full satisfactory obedience to God. On this matter, Bonaventure quotes Anselm's definition of satisfaction, that it is the repayment of the honor due to God.[10] As man sinned through pride and disobedience, it was through humiliation and obedience that man was to be restored.

Our justification is attributed as much to the passion as to the resurrection. One must take care in saying this, however, for neither the causality of justification or the destruction of sin has properly been attributed to either the resurrection or the passion. Our justification is attributed to them in four ways: (1) by intervening merit, which can be reduced to the material cause; (2) by a provocative and prompting example, which can be reduced to the moving and efficient cause; (3) by regulating exemplar, which is the formal cause; and (4) by a quieting end, which is the final cause.

In his death, Christ suffered the separation of his soul from his body. Nevertheless, neither the body nor the soul was separated from the Godhead. However, since man is both body and soul, during the three days of separation, it cannot be said that Christ was a man, even though both body and soul remained united with the Word, because a man is a soul joined to a body.[11]

After his death on the cross, the soul of Christ descended among the dead, as the Apostles' Creed says. Bonaventure explains that this article of faith does not mean that Christ descended to be punished, only that he descended to the place of punishment (locus poenae), where the just (*iusti*) were. Within the lower world or hell (*infernus*), Bonaventure makes a distinction between a low place that includes only a punishment of the damned, and the lowest place, which includes both the punishment of the damned and of the senses. The former place Bonaventure calls "*limbus*." The name, "limbo," comes from the Latin word, *limbus*, meaning the border or outermost part. *Limbus* is further divided into the limbus of the children and the limbus of the fathers, also called the bosom of Abraham. The two must be distinguished, because the fathers, lacking the vision of God, nevertheless possessed great expectation of so attaining it; the children without baptism do not posses this expectation. It is into the limbus of the fathers that Christ descended, an event included in the Apostles' Creed: "he descended into hell."[12] In limbo, while suffering the deprivation of beholding God, they did not suffer the pains of the damned. Bonaventure distinguishes limbo (or "the bosom of Abraham" [*sinus Abrahae*], as he also calls it) from the part of hell where the damned suffer the punishments of the senses.[13] Christ descended to limbo, not out of necessity, but of his own will and power, to lead out the just. In this way, his personal presence consoled those bound, and confused his enemies, the demons.[14] He led out the souls of the elect, or the "holy fathers" ("*sancti Patres*"), those who were members of his body by their anticipatory faith. Bonaventure says that the passion of Christ saved those who either were members of his body when he suffered or would have been by a conversion to him.[15] The elect were those who had died as members of Christ through living faith or through the sacraments of faith. After the harrowing of hell, the just, although given immediately the eternal light and beatitude, then had to await the ascension of Christ before entering into heaven.[16]

One of the criticisms made of the ransom theory is that it elevates Satan too much. It implies that Satan is the near equal of God in that he can gain some right over man. In addition, God has to trick the devil into killing a sinless man in order for him to lose his power over human nature.

The satisfaction theory removes the devil from the picture. The atonement then becomes a matter between God and man alone, or more specifically, between the Father and the Son. The Son, united to human nature, satisfies the justice demanded by the offense against the Father. Anselm's exalted notion of that being than which nothing greater can be thought seems to require a different theory of atonement than the one provided by the ransom theory. God's honor is satisfied and justice is restored by the sacrificial death of the God-man.

Bonaventure has clearly appropriated Anselm's satisfaction theory of the atonement; it is this that has shaped his thinking. However, as is his custom, he does not deny long-standing traditions and so is also quite comfortable to present the ransom theory with rhetorical flourish in his devotional work, *The Tree of Life*:

> Now that the combat of the passion was over and the bloody dragon and raging lion thought he had secured a victory by killing the Lamb, the power of the divinity began to shine forth in his soul as it descended into hell. By this power our strong Lion of the tribe of Judah (Revelation 5:5) rising against the strong man who was fully armed (Luke 11:21) tore the prey away from him, broke down the gates of hell and bound the serpent. Disarming the Principalities and Powers, he led them away boldly, displaying them openly in triumph in himself (Col 2:15). Then the Leviathan was clad about with a hook (Job 40:25), his jaw pierced by Christ so that he who had no right over the Head, which he had attacked, also lost what he had seemed to have over the body. Then the true Samson, as he died, laid prostrate an army of the enemy (Jg 16:30). Then the Lamb without stain by the blood of his testament led forth the prisoners from the pit in which there was no water (Zach. 9:1). Then the long awaited brightness of a new light shone upon those that dwelt in the region of the shadow of death (Is 9:12).[17]

According to Bonaventure, however, Christ is the efficient cause of the restoration. And the restoration is a real process or series of interrelated events that take place in history. This process takes place by the action of Christ, and is described by Bonaventure as a hierarchization: Christ is the hierarch by whom this process transpires; Christ is the mediator through whom grace and merit flow into those who freely accept him in faith and love. This understanding of the restoration therefore highlights the importance of imitating Christ, even in the details of his life. In other words, the dominant way of conceiving how to be a Christian comes to be imitating the life of Christ.

To say that Bonaventure's spiritual theory centers on imitating Christ, however, is not to say that Bonaventure adopts a merely moral view of salvation. In other words, one way of conceiving this restoration would be to see Christ as providing a good example of the way human beings ought to live life. This view would see Christ as exercising his agency by persuasion or example. Bonaventure does not adopt this view; he believes that Christ brings about the restoration through the instrument of divine grace, which is itself a real cause in the natural order of things, and that grace effects the human intellect and will.

The Body of Christ: The Church

In the context of the Incarnation, Bonaventure most explicitly takes up the nature of the church. Indeed, he does not separate out his ecclesiology from his treatment of the Incarnation; the fundamental reason for this seems to be that the church is most properly the mystical body of Christ.

Bonaventure speaks of the church in the general context of his discussion of the fullness of grace that the incarnate Word possesses, and specifically, in his discussion of Christ's grace of headship. The Word made flesh is the font of all grace. He confers on those who turn to him the spiritual benefit of grace. The way to turn to Christ is through faith or through the sacrament of faith. "Yet faith in Christ is the same in all believers, past, present, and future."[18] By an inpouring of grace, the faithful of Christ are made members of his body and temples of the Holy Spirit, and thus also, sons of the Father. Indeed, these three modes of grace are conjoined, because baptism (or, for those before the coming of Christ, faith in the redeemer) confers a grace that makes the baptized (the faithful) a member of Christ's body, a temple of the Spirit, and a son of God by adoption. All the baptized are also at once joined to one another by "the unbreakable bond of love." "This bond is not destroyed by the passing of time any more than by distance in space: the just of all time and places constitute the one mystical body of Christ in that they receive both perception and motion from the one Head that influences them, through the fontal, radical, and original fullness of all grace that dwells in Christ the fountainhead."[19]

As detailed below, charity is the foundational bond of union for the church. This love is the force that Bonaventure thinks quite literally unites the lover with "the One most to be loved." Charity thus establishes a bond, a oneness, between lover and beloved. In this way, charity unites all those who love God above all else and forms them, through this force, into a single body with a single head. "Such oneness begins on earth, but is consummated in eternal glory."[20]

In the light of these bonds established by grace and love, it then makes sense when Bonaventure defines the church as "a union of rational beings (unio rationalium) living in harmony and uniformity through harmonious and uniform observance of divine Law, harmonious and uniform adherence to divine peace, harmonious and uniform celebration of divine praise."[21] A uniform law, uniform peace, and uniform praise define the church.

Church and State

Bonaventure seems to hold positions that modern historians of medieval thought have identified as "political Augustinianism," that is, the tendency to absorb the secular order into the sacred and to subordinate the political order to the church. This tendency receives considerable impetus from the view that coercive power is penal and part of the fallen human condition, and so lacking in complete justice and legitimacy apart from its relation to the church. Many found the warrant for such a view in a certain reading of Augustine's *City of God*, especially in those passages where Augustine seems to imply that no earthly political order possesses true justice, that is, loves God and neighbor as it ought: "Remove justice, and what are kingdoms but gangs of criminals on a large scale? What are criminal gangs but petty kingdoms?"[22] Although the tendency toward political Augustinianism is clearly present in Bonaventure's thought, it is significantly nuanced, since coercive power is still natural, even if only in the state of fallen nature, and authority itself is present in every state of human nature and throughout the hierarchically ordered universe.

Like many thinkers in the Middle Ages, Bonaventure identifies the church (*ecclesia*) with Christendom (*christianitas*). Unlike Aquinas, who adopts a dualistic conception of the relationship between church and society, Bonaventure remains firmly committed to the unitary conception of political Augustinianism, with its tendencies to hierocracy (a government ruled by priests or religious ministers).[23]

We find this tendency to hierocracy in his view that, for the sake of the unity of the human hierarchy, supreme authority must be vested in one person. Hence, Bonaventure follows Bernard of Clairvaux's hierocratic doctrine that the pope possesses both the spiritual and temporal swords or both royal and priestly power. He thinks that Peter was given a twofold power: the power of the keys (*potestas clavium*) for reconciling, and the power of the sword (*potestas gladii*) for compelling. And although Peter delegates the power of the sword to secular authority, the priestly power, rather than the royal, remains primordial.[24] Furthermore, Peter holds the power of the keys in its fullness[25] and thus rightfully exercises full jurisdiction over the church.[26] Citing Romans 13:1 ("Let every soul be subject to higher powers. For there is no power but from God and those that are ordained of God"), Bonaventure affirms the general Christian view that all power of ruling is from God. Not surprisingly then, Christians are obliged to obey their earthly rulers in all things not contrary to God.[27]

Aristotle's *Politics* presents an understanding of the political order as an entity that exists naturally. It is not a contractual arrangement made to restrain men merely from killing and harming each other. On the contrary, it possesses the dignity of being a natural institution, truly essential to the fulfillment of a rational animal. The political order is the arena where the human being flourishes and achieves his highest aspirations, for it makes possible the practice of the virtues. According to Aristotle, the only being that does not need human companionship is either a beast or a god.

There are two important implications of Aristotle's theory of the *polis*. First, as a natural institution, it does not need divine or ecclesiastical sanction for legitimacy, but possesses its own legitimacy from nature. Furthermore, the natural political order is worthy of one's allegiance in a way that an artificial (i.e., contractual) institution is not. To spend one's life in the service of the *polis* is a worthy and noble endeavor. These two implications of Aristotle's political theory transformed medieval society and government. Indeed, both of these premises fly in the face of long-held Augustinian views. With regard to the first, even though society may be natural, Augustine clearly does not regard coercive political power as such to be so. Regarding the second, it is Augustine who wrote, "What does it matter in what state we pass this mortal life?" It should surprise no one that the introduction of Aristotle's political theory coincides with the beginnings of the nation-state.

On the question of the value of the political order, we find important implications for the Bonaventurian view examined earlier that the natural moral virtues are imperfect. Under such a view, the political entity that claims to have the means to perfect the imperfect natural virtues has a claim on authority and political power. This is precisely what the papacy claimed in Bonaventure's day. The papalists claimed that the pope had authority over the means by which virtue is perfect, namely, supernatural grace. Hence, temporal authority ought to be subordinate to the spiritual.

On this issue, it may be helpful to consider the spectrum of positions on the question of how the natural and supernatural are related. For example, in the generation after Bonaventure, John of Paris (Jean Quidort, ca. 1255–1306) was to argue that the natural virtues are true and perfect virtues in themselves, without the need of grace for perfection. Hence, the pope does not possess political authority in the temporal sphere. Of course, John does not deny that the supernatural grace and virtues are superior to the natural virtues. This superiority, however, necessitates merely a proper *ordering* of the subordinate and natural good to the higher and supernatural good, not a perfecting and completion. Certain Augustinians of the day argued that the natural virtues are not true virtues at all. Hence, the temporal power must not only be subordinated to the spiritual, and thus properly ordered, but also, since it lacks the necessary power even to accomplish its task in its own sphere, must be fulfilled and legitimated by the authority of Christ given to Peter and his successors. Bonaventure seems to stop short of this extreme.

Grace

The effects of original sin are such that the human being cannot undo them by himself. It is only out of his sheer unfathomable goodness that God may choose to save certain human beings. But this salvation will always be a gift that the giver is not obliged to give. The very name for this divine gift, *gratia*, taken from Latin, simply means "gift."

Bonaventure distinguishes three meanings for grace. First, in a general sense, it is the assistance freely and liberally granted by God to creatures performing any of their acts. In its general sense, grace is the concurrence without which no created thing could do anything, even continue to exist. Bonaventure first defines grace as a gift given directly by God. It is worth noting that Bonaventure categorizes God's permitting the continued existence of the creature to be a grace. He regards even this most fundamental of acts as something to which the creature can lay no claim in justice. Here, again, Bonaventure stresses the contingency of creation. Indeed, his view on this matter parallels his stress on the nothingness out of which the creature is made and on the dependency of the creature on the divine will for continued existence. As he says in his discussion of grace, "of itself, therefore, the creature is nothing. Whatever it has it is indebted for. Thus it is that the creature, because of its deficiency, always remains dependent upon its Principle."[1] It is God's constant presence, clemency, and influence that maintains the creature in existence. "Such concurrence, although it applies to all creatures, is called a grace, for it derives, not from any obligation, but from the liberality of divine bounty."[2]

In a more proper sense, "grace" (*gratia*) is a term usually reserved for the gift from God by which the human soul is perfected and transformed. In this second sense, then, grace is the particular assistance that helps the soul and prepares it for receiving the gift of the Holy Spirit. This is "gratuitously given grace" (*gratia gratis data*) or actual grace, as it has come to be most commonly translated.

In its proper sense, however, grace is the divinely given aid for the actual acquiring of merit and thus for gaining eternal salvation. It is grace that makes us pleasing to God, or sanctifying grace (*gratia gratum faciens*).

The human soul is in need of transformation and perfecting, otherwise it cannot possess the supreme good, and it is precisely the possession of this supreme good that is man's beatitude. "No conceivable man is worthy to attain this supreme Good exceeding in every possible way the limits of human nature, unless he is lifted up above himself through the action of God coming down to him."[3]

God, however, does not come down in his immutable essence, but rather, through "an influence" that emanates from him. "This is the gift of sanctifying grace without which no one may acquire merit, advance in good, or attain eternal salvation."[4] In its proper sense, grace is this gift that makes the soul pleasing to God and able to attain beatitude, without which the human being can perform no action deserving of eternal reward. "Merit, therefore, is rooted exclusively in sanctifying grace."[5] Furthermore, sin defaces the image of God in the soul; grace is "a deiforming [God-forming] disposition" that restores that image.[6] The likeness of God in its deiformed perfection is "the image of the second creation (*imago recreationis*)."[7] Bonaventure speaks of grace as a gift that cleanses, enlightens, and perfects the soul; it reforms the soul and makes it like to God, while also at the same time uniting the human being with him.

What Bonaventure does not say, however, should be noted here. He does not speak of a deification or theosis (divinization) by the Holy Spirit, in the manner of discussing salvation in Eastern Christianity. East and West agree that salvation involves a transformation and not merely a juridical declaration, but they disagree about how this change comes about. The East's conception of salvation as a participation in the Divine Being through the work of the Holy Spirit in the soul, is absent from Bonaventure's thought. What Bonaventure does say places him solidly within the medieval Scholastic tradition in which salvation, although conceived as a process of transformation, is brought about through a divine gift or influence on the soul.[8] In the process of salvation, Bonaventure gives the central role to grace. Indeed, it is Bonaventure who, along with his fellow Scholastics of the 1250s, developed the concept of created grace as the means of justification and of this justification involving a change in being.

While justification was universally understood to involve the regeneration of man, the opinion that an ontological change is thereby effected with man is particularly associated with the period of High Scholasticism and the development of the concept of created grace. The earlier medieval theologians expressed the change effected in justification in terms of a particular presence of God in his creature, which did not necessarily effect an ontological change. Thus, the *Summa fratris Alexandri*, written after 1240, developed the Augustinian concept of the indwelling of God in his creatures by declaring that God is present in all his creatures, but only some (i.e., those who are justified) may be said to possess him.[9] Bonaventure explicitly discusses grace as a created gift.

The ontological view of grace stands in sharp contrast to the Pelagian view, which tended to see justification as a judgment, rendered by God, on a person's ability to follow the example of Christ. In this view, justification is thereby attributed to a person's own efforts to imitate the righteousness of God.[10]

One of the first questions that arises in this conception of grace is whether grace is a substance or an accident. Bonaventure argues that insofar as grace is a created gift, it must be in the genus of accident. Something is an accident if it refers to a subject and to a cause, as the blackness of a raven; accident can also refer to something related to a subject but not a cause, as a likeness in a mirror or light in air.[11] Saying that grace is an accident does not involve any derogation of its nobility, for the nobility and goodness of substance and accidents are not able to be compared.[12] As an accident, grace is not able to exist except in some subject. Furthermore, grace is not produced from something materially, but is simply a gift gratuitously and wholly given from above, since it is from nothing produced so into nothing it returns when corrupted.[13]

Restoring Godlikeness

Bonaventure speaks of the restoration of the human soul by grace as a process of deiformity, for this restoration involves a conforming of the soul to God. The image that is found in the human soul has been distorted and marred by sin. Grace restores and polishes the image, forming it and restoring its likeness to that of which it is an image, namely God.

Deiformity is thus closely bound up with Bonaventure's notion of rectitude and speaks of a "rectifying" of the soul.[14] In order to understand this notion, however, it is necessary to consider the relation of the human being to the divine will. Recall that for Bonaventure, God's will is perfectly righteous and effective, because in God, will, truth, and power are one. There cannot be the slightest deviation from the truth in the divine will; hence it is the very norm of righteousness.

The transformation of the human being involved in being "deformed" (or God-formed) includes living according to the standard found in human nature insofar as this human nature is an expression of the exemplar in the divine mind; but the transformation of the human being also involves, at one and the same time, living according to the standard found in Christ as the new man, or as the perfect expression of our humanity.

The East has tended to understand salvation in terms of theosis or divinization, the West in terms of justification. Bonaventure's doctrine of deiformity seems to be the middle ground between the two views. Our being reconciled to God, while consisting in the grace of justification, also involves being made Godlike. Thus, the ethical Christian life is never simply a question of external observance of extrinsic norms or laws, but always a question of who we are. The ultimate standard for the human being is found in God, specifically in the Word, where is found the plan of creation, or in metaphysical language, where is found all the exemplars of the things of this world.

It is important to note how far this understanding of the relation between divine will and righteousness or the moral law is from any sort of ethical voluntarism. In response to the ancient debate from Plato's *Euthyphro* about whether any particular action is good because the gods will it, or whether the gods will it because it is good, Bonaventure would answer unambiguously that this argument fails to appreciate the utterly indivisible unity between the divine will and intellect. As Bonaventure says on many occasions, there is no "indivision" in God.

The first implication of this view is that no one can be righteous without conforming to the divine will.[15] God's will is the very norm of righteousness. Hence, to be righteous is to be conformed to God, "deiformed."

God's will has been communicated to us through his law, but the law leads to a mere righteousness of law—the minimum that must be done. There is also a righteousness of perfection that concerns more than what must be done. As a result of this twofold righteousness, God has made his will known in different forms: commands, prohibitions, and counsels.[16] Nevertheless, Bonaventure's conception of grace and its deiforming power could hardly be farther away from a purely juridical notion of grace that sees it as a mere covering over of sin. The fractured image of God in man must be restored—it cannot be ignored or covered over if there is to be a return to communion between God and man. A purely juridical notion of grace would defeat the whole purpose of the Incarnation and redemption. To use an analogy that Bonaventure is fond of in discussing grace, if a man is sick, being made healthy again does not mean that the doctor comes to declare the patient healthy even when he is not. The doctor must provide the patient with the means—the medicine—to regain health. The doctrine of grace naturally leads to sacramental theology.

Bonaventure's frequent allusions and discussions of merit are rooted in his notion of sanctifying grace. In an absolute sense, a human being can merit nothing from God, for that, there can be no claim upon God in justice. God and man are infinitely far apart; God owes man nothing in an absolute sense. Any merit depends upon the order established by God; it is only in the context of that order that man can be said to merit any reward from God. In other words, merit is based on God's promise—a promise to remain faithful to an order that he has established as a sheer gift of his goodness. All merit, then, rests on sanctifying grace, which depends on the prevenient grace that prepares the human will for justification. When God crowns our merits, St. Paul says, he crowns nothing but his own gift.

Bonaventure follows in the path marked out by Anselm, who tended to equate the essence of original sin to the loss of sanctifying grace in the sin of the first parents. Bonaventure sees concupiscence as one of the effects of this loss. Like other Scholastic theologians, he speaks of the Spirit's influence in the soul as *gratia gratum faciens*, or "sanctifying grace," as it is usually translated. In this way, he can explain how baptism restores what was lost (a gift that makes us friends with God and confers the right to enter heaven) while explaining how the effects of that loss remain (namely, concupiscence and ignorance).

"Actual grace" is the gift required for the performance of good moral acts, that is, acts that are both externally righteous and right intentioned. Rightly intentioned acts are those done not with merely the good of the agent in view, but also for the supreme good. However, this nobility of action is accessible to the "naturally self-centered spirit" only if first moved by God through actual grace.

It is important to understand that this deiforming of the soul is also a reordering, or as Bonaventure puts it, the soul must be hierarchized (*hierarchizata*). One of the principal tasks of grace is this hierarchization of the soul, or "total reorganization" as Gilson translates it.[17] Bonaventure draws on a notion of hierarchy that came to him through Pseudo-Dionysius, who defines hierarchy in the following way: "In my opinion hierarchy is a sacred order."[18] A sacred order must be brought to the human soul; the process by which this is done is a hierarchization.

There must be a twofold hierarchization of the human being, one without, and one within. The external hierarchization must resituate man within his place in the hierarchy of creation. The internal hierarchization must reorder the human soul so that it loves God above all things, and the neighbor as itself. This interior hierarchization is equivalent to the threefold operation of grace in justifying the human soul: purification, illumination, and perfection. This corresponds to the threefold practice of the spiritual life through purgation, illumination, and perfection. Bonaventure's *Itinerarium* provides a presentation of the threefold operation of grace in the soul. "Then [grace] descends into the heart when through the reformation of the image, through the theological virtues, and through the delights of the spiritual senses and the ecstatic upliftings, our spirit is made hierarchical, that is to say, purified, illuminated, and perfected."[19]

The soul's hierarchization allows it to ascend to God: "In as much as it is in conformity with that heavenly Jerusalem, our spirit is hierarchical in order that it may ascend above."[20] The hierarchized soul resembles the heavenly Jerusalem.[21]

If grace reorders the human will so that it clings to the Supreme Good and in this way transforms the human soul by hierarchizing it, so too does grace transform human society through its effects on individual human souls. One of the fruits of grace is a society of hierarchized souls, a society that in turn will be hierarchized, that is, ordered. Bonaventure's term for this deiformed and hierarchized society is "the Church."

Since the first sin, the human will no longer possesses the liberty of doing what it ought. It is now left with simply the power of free choice (*liberum arbitrium*), but even this free choice is limited; it is in a sense captive to sin (*liberum arbitrium captivatum*). Only God's grace can heal this power of its proclivity to choose the wrong. Only grace frees the power of free choice (*liberum arbitrium liberatum*).

Bonaventure clearly attempts to preserve a balance between grace and free will. At one point, he borrows from Augustine the analogy for grace and free will of a rider and his mount. Grace directs and leads the will on to its goal, as does the rider the horse.[22] While it is certainly the case that he stresses the latitude of grace's role (as we have seen in his teaching that God's mere concurrence in creation's continued existence is itself a grace), he also gives considerable weight to the action of the will, for God effects no transformation in the human being without the consent of the free will. Four things must concur, then, for the justification of the sinner: the infusion of grace, the expulsion of sin, contrition, and an act of free will. But even the expulsion of sin does not occur without the consent of free will—a consent that finds fulfillment in the detestation of sin referred to as contrition. "Actual grace arouses free will, and free will must either give or refuse consent to such arousal."[23] It is only after this consent that sanctifying grace is conferred. Bonaventure quotes Augustine in support of his view that "He who created you without your assistance will not justify you without your consent."[24] God crowns nothing within us except his own gifts, but the gift must be accepted.

Grace branches out into three distinct forms of gifts: the theological virtues, the gifts of the Holy Spirit, and the beatitudes. Each of these different forms of grace is a *habitus* of the soul. On this point, Bonaventure differs from Aquinas, who saw the beatitudes as acts, produced by the individual person as fruits of grace.[25] This notion requires some explanation.

The Virtues from Above

In his discussion of the "habit" of grace, Bonaventure is speaking of a disposition given by God to the soul that prompts its recipient to think and act in certain ways. As the creating Principle confers the first perfection of life on creatures, so the restoring Principle confers this second perfection that is act. Grace is this act or second perfection completing the grace-filled recipient.

Vivifying grace branches out into various habits for the sake of different activities. Bonaventure explains that certain acts are foundational and set the soul aright, such as believing; some intermediate and prompt the soul onward, such as understanding what is believed; and some final and definitively perfecting, such as attaining the vision of what is understood. "Hence, sanctifying grace [*gratia gratum faciens*] branches out into habits of virtue, that set the soul aright [purgation], those of the gifts, that urge it on [illumination], and those of the beatitudes, that perfect it."[26]

Since grace is a rectification of the soul, when the gratuitous virtues are infused by God into a soul, made virtuous by acquired habits, the rectitude that they bring "supervenes" on the rectitude of nature (*naturae rectitudinem*), enlarging and confirming it.[27] This supervenient grace concurs with the acquired virtues and leads them to perfection. As an analogy, Bonaventure offers a horse with an aptitude for carrying and walking, and a rider. The aptitude for particular motions of such a horse is able to be brought to its full development in three ways: through habituation, through the hard work of a knowledgeable horseman, or through both.

The horse, in its relation to such a horseman, is like our free decision (*liberum arbitrium*) in relation to grace: Grace and habit can be concurrent causes. In short, grace builds on nature. As Bonaventure says a little later in the same article, "Our action (*opus*) does not exclude a divine action and gift; on the contrary it presupposes and necessarily requires it."[28]

In his *Collations on the Six Days of Creation*, Bonaventure uses light imagery to speak about the infused virtues. The exemplar of all the virtues (as of all things) is the eternal light. He quotes Plotinus in support of this view: "It is absurd that the exemplars of other things be in God, and not the exemplars of the virtues."[29] He quotes Wisdom 8, in which the speaker, after expressing a passionate love of wisdom in nuptial imagery ("Her I loved and sought after from my youth: I sought to take her for my bride and was enamored of her beauty," Wisdom 8:1), then claims that Wisdom is the teacher of the cardinal virtues: "For she teaches moderation and prudence, justice and fortitude, and nothing in life is more useful than these" (Wisdom 8:7). Bonaventure proceeds to explain that the exemplary light impresses these on the soul, where they infuse the cognitive, affective, and operative powers.[30] Having reached down into the depths of the human soul, the cardinal virtues are then to lead the soul back to its origin: "These virtues flow from eternal light in the hemisphere of our mind and they retrace the soul to its origin."[31] These virtues are not only for our life in community, and hence political; they are also for the cleansing of the soul, and therefore purgative; finally, they are for the soul already cleansed, and thus unitive. Bonaventure makes much of the political, purgative, and unitive nature of the virtues in this work. The four cardinal virtues can be classified in each of these categories depending on their function in a particular soul. Following Plotinus, Bonaventure adds a fourth category of virtues, namely, the exemplary.

These exemplar virtues exist in the mind of God: Prudence is the very mind of God; temperance is the fact that this mind is perpetually turned upon itself; fortitude, that this mind is unchanging; and justice, that by an eternal law it is never deflected from its sempiternal operation.[32]

The purgative virtues are for the person who has decided to enter into nothing but the things of God and so to flee human matters. "These virtues belong to free individuals who have cut themselves away from political activities."[33]

The unitive virtues are for the soul already purged, cleansed, and washed of every stain of this world. Unitive prudence prompts the soul not only to prefer divine things as a result of choice, but also to know nothing else. Unitive temperance is not only to repress earthly desires, but to forget them completely. Unitive fortitude leads the soul to ignore the passions so as to become incapable of anger and desirous of nothing. Unitive justice is to contemplate the higher things and so imitate them.[34]

Like many of his fellow Scholastic theologians, Bonaventure posits three fundamental habits that are the basis of the whole Christian life: faith, hope, and charity. These habits are foundational, because they rectify the soul, that is, set it right with God, and thereby provide the basis for all further graces.

However, the task of rectifying the soul is complex and requires a thorough reformation of the human soul in all its various activities. Hence, the first task of these infused virtues is to expunge and correct vice. As a result, Bonaventure thinks that the four cardinal virtues can be infused directly by God into the soul for the purpose of rectifying it. So, for example, prudence rectifies the rational power; fortitude, the irascible appetite; temperance, the concupiscible appetite; and justice redirects all these powers insofar as they are related to one's self, to any given person, or to God. Justice includes every power and therefore involves the rectitude of the whole soul. In this regard, justice may be defined as simply "rectitude of the will," since the will is involved either in choosing the acquired cardinal virtues or in consenting to the infused cardinal virtues. Bonaventure is here following Anselm's definition of justice, as found in De veritate.[35]

As we have seen, Bonaventure maintains that charity is the form of all the virtues; in other words, that all other virtues are related to charity as matter to form. This relation so obtains because the other virtues are inchoate and potential until properly ordered to man's true final end. It is only by being so ordered by charity that all other virtues become actual and true virtues. Virtues are able to subsist without charity, but in such a formless state that they cannot be a means of acquiring merit, for their rectitude is proportioned to charity, and charity is their origin, form, and end. Bonaventure uses the analogy of color: Without light a color may subsist, but it remains invisible.

Gifts of the Holy Spirit

Bonaventure follows the enumeration of the gifts of the Spirit as found in Isaiah 11:2–3: "The Spirit of the Lord shall rest upon him: the spirit of wisdom and of understanding, the spirit of counsel and of fortitude, the spirit of knowledge and of godliness. He shall be filled with the spirit of the fear of the Lord." The first task of these gifts is to deliver us from the difficulties of the aftereffects of the vices. Since there are seven capital or major vices, so there are seven gifts. There are six further tasks enumerated for these gifts; among these are assisting the natural powers and the virtues, helping the Christian to suffer in the same spirit as Christ, helping the contemplative life, and facilitating both action and contemplation.[36]

Beatitudes

The beatitudes are special graces and habits infused into the soul for the sake of bringing it to perfection. Bonaventure takes the enumeration of these graces from the beatitudes of the Sermon on the Mount (Matthew 5:1–11), but reduces the traditional eight beatitudes to seven in order to preserve the symmetry of the numbers: poverty of spirit, meekness, mourning, thirst for justice, mercy, cleanness of heart, and peacefulness.

No one can deserve sanctifying grace, but once having possessed it, one can deserve to have it increased by God until it is one day perfect "in the fatherland." It is important to note that the free will can acquire not only a legitimate promise to growth in grace, but can also "fittingly merit" its perfecting in heaven. Thus, this grace is not only a pledge of a future gift; it is the foundation for saying that the soul rightly merits a reward, not as a matter of absolute justice, but as a matter of what is congruous, given the promises of God and the order of grace that he has established.[37]

Bonaventure gives considerable attention to the relation of grace to meritorious practices, for grace prompts the believer to the whole of the Christian life. Indeed, the Christian is to be so filled with grace that his whole life flows from grace, in what is believed, in what is loved, in what is done or not done, and in what is prayed. This life of grace has external aids: What is to be believed is found in the articles of faith; what is to be loved is found in the single habit of charity; what is to be done is found in the divine law; what is to be prayed for is found in the Lord's prayer. Hence, the creed, charity, the divine law, and the "Our Father" form a summary of the whole Christian life. All of these prompt the human being back to the First Principle, as the supreme truth, the supreme good, the supreme justice, and the supreme mercy. "To supreme Truth is due firm assent; to supreme Good, fervent love; to supreme Justice, total submission; to supreme Mercy, trusting prayer."[38]

Bonaventure regards the creed as a summary of what is found in sacred scripture. He thus understands scripture as an authoritative guide to faith and to what is to be believed. But the content of sacred scripture may be summarized in the Apostles' Creed. The articles of faith contain the "depths" of scripture.[39]

What is to be done is found in the divine law. Bonaventure thus interprets the law as the external guide to action. He divides the law of Moses into three categories of precepts: the judicial, the figurative, and the moral. The Ten Commandments are among the moral.

The Gospel fulfills the Old Law, but in different ways: It voided the judicial precepts; abrogated the figurative by fulfilling them, and perfected the moral by adding to them. The Gospel adds to the moral precepts in three ways: by providing instructive lessons, incentive promises, and perfective counsels.

Since God is supremely just and since justice consists in complying with the rule of law, divine justice promulgates judicial norms by impressing them on human minds, and by expressing them in declarations of truth and in decrees of the will. There are two principal incentives for obeying divine commands: fear of punishment and love of justice.

What is to be prayed for is found in the "Our Father." Bonaventure follows a traditional division of the prayer into seven petitions, three concerning the glory of God and the reward of heaven, and four concerning life in this world. It summarizes the whole life of grace and purpose of human life.

What is to be loved in the life of grace flows from the habit of charity, which leads us to love (1) God, (2) that which we are, (3) our neighbor, and (4) our body.[40] Moreover, this order is the proper one that must be observed if a person is to be truly charitable. In fact, Christ summarizes the demands of the *habitus* of charity in his "great" commandment: "You shall love the Lord your God with all your heart, and with all your soul, and with all your mind.... You shall love your neighbor as yourself" (Matthew 11:20). Bonaventure understands this second commandment quite literally, such that the Christian must love not only his neighbor but also his self, which includes both soul and body. Hence, Bonaventure says that there are four things properly loved with charity. "Charity, therefore, loves him above all else as being the Beatifier, and loves as a consequence all other beings which through him are made fit for beatitude." This point significantly narrows the range of charity since only rational beings are destined for beatitude, but insofar as the body is to be beatified together with the soul, then it too must be the object of charity. As a result of original sin, the practical intellect has been damaged; its judgments about the sense appetites are disordered.[41] The cardinal virtues, especially as infused graces, are meant to counter the four "inflictions" of original sin. Prudence is to counter ignorance; temperance, concupiscence; fortitude, weakness; and justice, malice.[42]

The order of charity is particularly important. The righteous and well-ordered love that is charity has the good as its principal object:

> The proper order of loving is to love God first, more than all else and for His own sake; soul second, less than God but more than any temporal good; the neighbor third, as much as ourselves, as a good of the same degree; our body fourth, less than our soul, as a good of lesser degree. It is here also that we should place our neighbor's body that, like our own, is a less good than our soul.[43]

Love is the "gravitational force" of the soul. Bonaventure thus defines charity as "the force of properly ordered attraction (*pondus inclinationis ordinatae*) and the bond of perfect union."[44] Charity is the force that restores creation, for it sets all things in order and unites all things to each other, each in its proper place. It is this force that brings about the "oneness" that is the church, in fulfillment of Christ's priestly prayer to the Father, which Bonaventure quotes: "that they may be one, as we also are one: I in them and Thou in me; that they may be made perfect in one" (John 17:22–23). The oneness established by charity is the true consummation and end of all reality. "With this unity fully completed through the bond of love, God shall be 'all in all' (1 Corinthians 15:28) throughout an assured eternity and in perfect peace."

The Sacramental Cure

The twelfth and thirteenth centuries saw a renaissance of interest in the sacramental system of Christianity. Part of this renewed interest was prompted by severe criticisms of the system, especially as these came from two groups: (1) latter-day Donatists, who thought that sacraments performed by unworthy priests were invalid; and (2) the Cathars of southern France, who regarded the material world as evil.[1] The decrees of the Fourth Lateran Council (1215) reflect this concern for safeguarding the sacramental system.

The Diversity of "Sacrament"

It is important to be aware that Bonaventure uses "sacrament" to refer to all signs of faith in the Redeemer, even those that are not explicitly focused on Jesus of Nazareth. He refers to this as the "diversity" of the sacraments. "Sacraments" in this sense were instituted from the very beginning, but they have enjoyed a diversity through three different ages and their concomitant laws: the law of nature, the law of scripture, and the law of grace. This division of the sacraments is borrowed from Hugh of St. Victor.[2] It is the Word, as the restoring Principle, who has been at work in all these different sacraments, "making use" of "diverse and various medicines" as the various circumstances in succeeding ages dictate.

Under the law of nature, which prevailed until the covenant with

Abraham, the sacraments consisted of oblations, sacrifices, and tithes. The sacraments were instituted as signs in which God is honored as creator, as redeemer, and as judge. The sacraments were signs manifesting faith in the redeemer, but they did not have in themselves the power of curing or justifying. At the time of the natural law, faith illumined the faithful that they might believe that God was creator, redeemer, and remunerator. The oblations honored God as the creator of all things, the sacrifices honored God as redeemer, and the tithes honored God as the perfect remunerator. The first reason that God instituted the sacraments of the natural law was that he might be honored, for no one can be saved without faith.[3]

The second reason for instituting the sacraments of the natural law was so that man might profess faith in the redeemer, for no one is able to rise from sin without faith in the mediator. The third reason was for the founding of the active life of justice. As someone is not able to please God without faith, or rise from sin without faith in the redeemer, so neither is someone able to be in good standing before God without good works. Hence, signs were added to faith to signify those things that are necessary with faith. In the tithe is a recognition of sin and the dismissal of it, because what is perfect and good is given to God and what is imperfect remains for us. This is signified because all good things are from God, but bad things are only from us.

Under the law of scripture, which prevailed from the covenant with Abraham until Christ, circumcision and expiation were introduced to stand along with the sacrifices, the various oblations, and the tithes. Under the law of grace, the sacraments became fewer in number but greater in effect, and more powerful in virtue.[4] These sacraments of grace supersede all "ancient sacraments" by fulfilling and abolishing them.[5] The ancient sacraments were a price promised; the new sacraments, a price paid. The old were preparations and guides on the way to the new; indeed, they were signs pointing to the things signified.

The Sacraments of the New Law

Long before Bonaventure began his study of theology, the underlying premise of sacramental theology was that the visible is a vehicle or instrument for the invisible, or to put it in the terms commonly used in Western Christianity, the sensible communicates a divine gift, usually referred to by the Latin name for "gift," *gratia*. It had become common practice to say that the sacraments were instituted in words and elements (*in verbis et elementis*) for the purpose of sanctifying. In Bonaventure's view, the sacraments are sensible signs instituted by God as remedies through which God's power operates beneath the veil of material species. The sacraments are truly "mysteries," as the Greek name for them suggests, because God works in a hidden manner in them.

Throughout his sacramental theology, Bonaventure emphasizes the medicinal purpose and character of the sacraments. To put it simply, they are the cure for a disease, namely, sin. They are the means of conferring a certain spiritual grace by which the human soul is to be healed of its weaknesses due to sin and vice. Christ is the physician, man, the patient, original sin, the disease; and ignorance and concupiscence are the major symptoms of the disease in the soul. As a result of the symptoms of this disease, we can no longer read the book of God's creation; so God gives us medicines that alleviate the symptoms and cure the disease. Since the whole world consists of signs that speak of the uncreated Word of God, it should not be surprising that the incarnate Word has established a system of signs for the purpose of sanctifying and restoring souls to health. The world came forth from God in signs; the way back is by means of signs.

The Institution of the Sacraments

Christ instituted seven sacraments, but he instituted them in diverse ways and not all explicitly. Bonaventure follows Lombard in the reckoning of the number of the sacraments, but there was considerable discussion among the Scholastics about how this number was determined and the different ways Christ employed in instituting the sacraments. Bonaventure thinks that he established, brought to full perfection, and received in person three sacraments: baptism, holy Eucharist, and orders. He confirmed, approved, and brought to full perfection matrimony and penance. He established, confirmation and extreme unction, only implicitly.[6] Bonaventure finds the implicit institution of confirmation in the imposition of hands upon the children (Matthew 19:13) and in foretelling his disciples that they would be baptized with the Holy Spirit (Acts 1:5). Extreme unction finds its implicit institution in Christ's sending the disciples to care for the sick and anoint them with oil (Mark 6:13).

Since the sensible or material things involved in the sacraments cannot produce any effect in the order of grace in themselves as material things, it was necessary that the Principle and source of grace institute them and bless them for the purpose of sanctifying. This "institution" and "benediction," however, does not deny that each of the sacraments bears a certain natural likeness through which it represents and signifies a particular grace; but the efficacy of the sacraments (i.e., their effectiveness in an objective sense) derives from their original "institution" and "benediction." Furthermore, the sacraments are meant to produce a threefold effect: prompting, teaching, and humbling. They teach through their signification, humble in being received, and prompt to action through their diversity.

Bonaventure analyzes the causes that brought the sacraments to be. The efficient cause of the sacraments is their institution by God; their material cause, their representation through sensible signs; their formal cause, the sanctification through grace; and their final cause, the healing of the human being through a proper medicine.

The Nature and Integrity of the Sacraments

Since a medicine must be suited to the patient and the disease, it was necessary for the medicine of the sacraments to be both spiritual and physical. Since the disease involves our concupiscence and ignorance, it was important to have sacraments that are not only gratuitous, but also "mystical," that is, "figurative" and "significative"[7] to alleviate the symptoms. They are nonetheless the cure. Indeed, there is a fitting irony in the sacramental system: Since it was by means of the sensible (the apple) that man fell, it is by means of the sensible that man shall rise.

Bonaventure follows in the long-established view that the sacraments are signs; indeed, a sacrament is most essentially a sign.[8] A sacrament thus involves a corporeal element (the sign), as well as a spiritual element (thing signified). Furthermore, a sacrament is a specific type of sign, namely a voluntary one (as opposed to a natural one, such as smoke from a fire), since the sacrament comes from the will of God.[9] Bonaventure, however, thinks that the sign of any sacrament builds on a natural symbolism found in the physical object or act involved.

According to Bonaventure, a sign has a twofold relation—to that which it signifies and to that for whom it signifies. The former is essential and always in act; the latter is in disposition. So, for example, the circle over the tavern is always a sign, even if no one ever sees it. This view might seem strange at first, since one might say that the circle over a tavern is merely a circle until a sign reader sees it and recognizes it as a sign. Nevertheless, there is a great deal at stake in Bonaventure's contention about the actuality of the sign, for if the sign did not possess an intrinsic referent, then the baby would not receive the sacrament in baptism, because the sacramental sign of water means nothing to the infant.

The Causality of the Sacraments

The somewhat surprising teaching behind the medieval Scholastic understanding of the sacraments is not only that the physical confers a spiritual gift, but that it does so necessarily as a cause. The medieval Scholastics, using Aristotle's theory of causality, set about trying to understand how the sacraments were real causes of divine grace. Bonaventure also took up this endeavor, but with caution and hesitancy, careful not to attribute what he would regard as too much power to the creature.

It is important to notice the force of the claim: It is not simply that the sacraments are occasions when God confers grace on the believer. An occasionalist theory of the sacraments balks at the notion that there could be any cause of grace other than, or even working in conjunction with, God. The occasionalist view regards it as going too far to posit any secondary cause, because this would give too much power to the sensible thing, the action, or the agent involved in the sacrament. While this view denies that the sacraments are real causes, it stops short of an even more extreme position, what we might call a subjectivist theory. In the latter view, the sacrament is not necessarily even an occasion for God's conferring grace, but simply a means of arousing the proper beliefs and sentiments within the believer, so that this believer could better receive grace whenever or however God confers it.

As "demonstrative signs," Bonaventure says, the sacraments give what they signify. As a result, they have twofold signification: proper and allegorical. Their proper signification refers to the present; their allegorical to what will be. Furthermore, the sacraments have a twofold reality (*veritatem*): one from their institution (which cannot be changed), another from their use (which can be changed). Hence, the sacraments can be "badly used" in the sense of impeded in their signification by their recipients.[10]

The recipient of the sacrament must be properly disposed if the grace is to be efficacious in bringing about any change. Bonaventure appeals to an argument by analogy to physical medicine: Just as a medicine is not able to heal the body unless the patient is prepared for it and able to receive it, so too is the case of the sacraments. In addition, since it is faith that disposes the recipient to receive the healing grace, the sign is essential to arousing and moving the faith (*motus fidei*) of the recipient. A sensible sign is thus crucial for disposing the human being to the cure. If the sacrament is to be an efficacious and sufficient medicine, it must possess a signification in its own integrity.[11] Nevertheless, Bonaventure argues a number of times that the power of the sacraments is dispositive, not effective, because God communicates the effective power on no one.[12] To effect belongs to God alone. Bonaventure says explicitly that the sacrament and grace are not related as (effective or efficient) cause and effect.[13]

Bonaventure resists saying that the sacraments are real, efficient causes in themselves. The sacraments are causes in that God really does confer grace as a result of their having been performed (*ex opere operato*); but not because they are themselves efficient causes. God is the sole efficient cause of grace. Admittedly, Bonaventure is not entirely clear about the nature of sacramental causality. But it is inaccurate to say that the sacraments are mere occasions for the conferral of divine grace in Bonaventure's theory, as Pierre Pourrat says[14] because of the dispositive power of signification. Bonaventure does think the sacraments are causes in a certain sense, for they are "vessels of grace." By this, he does not mean that grace is "substantially" present in them (*substantialiter contineatur*) or "causally effected by them (*causaliter efficiatur*)."[15] They simply do not contain grace as a vase does water or a box medicine.[16] Grace is only in the soul, not in the visible signs, and is infused only by God; grace is not a substance. But the grace of the sacraments comes from "Christ the divine Physician through and by these sensible signs."[17] The "through" and "by" of this statement should be taken seriously and given its proper importance because of Bonaventure's robust theory of signification. In Bonaventure's view, the sacraments seem to be dispositive instrumental causes, even if not efficacious instrumental causes, because as signs, they really do bring about change, specifically in the soul of the believer. But like any tool or instrument, they cannot function apart from an agent. They are not magic. The sacraments are instrumental causes because God is the agent who wields them and who has willed them to be so and who has fashioned them to be so. God abides by his sacramental order. In this regard, Bonaventure's understanding of sacramental causality reflects the original meaning of the Latin word, *sacramentum*, "oath."

Bonaventure follows Augustine's strong anti-Donatist view that the validity of the sacraments does not depend on the moral condition or faith of the minister. "And so, if the administration of the sacraments were reserved to the virtuous, no one would be certain of having received them validly. . . . Neither would there be any stability in the hierarchical degrees of the Church militant."[18] Thus, the sacraments depend not on the holiness of the minister, but on his authority, which is constant, and may be present in the good and the bad alike, or even to those within the church or to those without. Since no one may be saved who is outside the "communion of faith and love which makes us children and members of the Church," when the sacraments are received outside of it, they have no efficacy toward salvation.[19] If the recipient returns to "Holy Mother Church," the effectiveness of the sacraments returns. Quoting an anti-Donatist passage from Augustine, Bonaventure is unambiguous that "no one outside the Church may receive or possess beatific salvation,"[20] but he uses an analogy from Genesis to explain how the sacraments can be real without being efficacious: "The waters of paradise, then, are found outside it, but beatitude only within."[21] The sacrament of baptism helps grace absolve the punishment for sin.[22]

The Necessity of the Sacraments

Bonaventure thinks that the sacraments are necessary for salvation, and the necessary is what must be. However, this necessity can be imposed from an intrinsic or extrinsic cause, so there can be a necessity imposed by the final cause, such that, unless one employs a particular means, one cannot achieve a desired end. For example, an airplane is necessary as a means of transportation if one is going to travel from New York to San Francisco in a single day. There can also be a necessity imposed by an efficient cause, a necessity of coaction, as well as a necessity of congruity, which is a high degree of fittingness or congruity.[23] According to Bonaventure, it was a necessity of congruity that was involved in the institution of the sacraments.[24]

In other words, the sacraments are necessary in the sense that they are particularly fitting to the mercy, justice, and wisdom of God. They fit the mercy of God because man badly needs grace on account of the vertibility of his will. God therefore instituted the sacrament so that man might recover grace, not only for the remission of sin, but also for the remission of the penalty. The sacraments fit God's justice in being the form of humiliation found in begging for divine grace. The sacraments befit God's wisdom in that as man fell through a tree (lignum), so he finds the remedy of the fall in the tree.[25]

One of the more interesting objections that Bonaventure treats in his discussion of the sacraments is the nature of their necessity. It could be objected, he points out, that no sacraments are necessary, because faith and the virtues are sufficient to restore or justify the human being. One might argue, therefore, that the sacraments are superfluous—that there is no need to multiply causes of our justification. To this argument, Bonaventure responds that justification is not simply a question of the power of the agent, but also a question about fitting the remedy to the one in need. Hence, the infused virtues are not enough for justification; there should be a preparation for these virtues, and these are the sacraments.[26] The sacraments aid grace in the justification of the soul. Indeed, as a result of the sacramental order established by Christ, Bonaventure thinks that certain sacraments not only aid, but are, in fact, necessary for salvation, such that without their reception, one cannot be saved. Baptism is such a sacrament. The other sacraments are necessary in that salvation is not easily attained without them. Furthermore, the grace of the sacraments makes obeying the Commandments easier.[27]

Baptism

The first sacrament is that of expiation and justification. Under the law of nature, it was an offering; under the law of scripture, circumcision; and under grace, baptism. One of the reasons for the change is that "the form and symbol of purification" are somewhat hidden in an offering, more clearly expressed in circumcision, and manifestly revealed in baptism.

Certain sacraments involve the imposition of an indelible sign. Bonaventure refers to this kind of sign as a "character," and such characters, because they are indelible, cannot be repeated. Furthermore, because these indelible signs are impressed upon an incorruptible and spiritual substance—namely, the rational soul—they fall in the category of quality; indeed, they are indelible spiritual qualities. Baptism, confirmation, and holy orders are the sacraments that confer these indelible spiritual signs upon the soul.[28]

Bonaventure holds the notion that infants who die without baptism are not punished with any positive pain. Although they are not subject to positive punishments, they are, nonetheless, deprived of the beatific vision.[29] The reason for not receiving this punishment is that God is just: The absence of justice in them is not caused by any personal act of their will. This deprivation of the beatific vision, however, is not unjust, because the vision is a gift not owed to man. In his goodness, God intended the first parents to enjoy eternal beatitude after their probationary life in the garden; even then, however, the vision of God was a gift, superadded to the gifts of existence, life, and spirit. Admission to the beatific vision always remains a gift not owed in justice to man; in fact, after the Fall, it would be an injustice to admit him. It is only after the redemption of man by Jesus Christ that a few good people may once again hope for this gift.

Yet, this answer may not be wholly satisfying, especially in the light of the thoroughly teleological account of nature found in Aristotle's philosophy. "Nature does nothing in vain." However, a being that cannot achieve its end is vain, that is, without a goal and so objectively purposeless. The beatific vision is the only good that can truly satisfy the human being, and therefore the only true good for man. It therefore seems unjust of God to make creatures who in fact cannot achieve their true end, through no fault of their own, and despite whatever endless striving they may do. Such a view seems to imply that nature does quite a lot in vain, and such vanity is presided over by God.

The Eucharist

The Eucharist is the central act of public worship in Christianity and from the beginning has consisted of a commemorative meal of Christ's last supper with his apostles on the night before he died. The Eucharist had become a topic of increased speculation in the century before Bonaventure. No issue was more central than Christ's presence in the Eucharist, specifically in the bread and wine. This medieval discussion focused on the nature of Christ's presence: how is he present in the Eucharist. What is of particular interest is that Bonaventure insists upon the real presence as essential in two regards: both to the sacrificial nature of the Eucharist and to the reality of the union between Christ and the believer in communion. In other words, if Christ is not truly present, the Eucharist is not a real sacrifice, offering, to the Father, and the union between Christ and the soul is not real. The identification of the Eucharist with the Passion is further reinforced by the centrality of the crucifixion in Bonaventure's whole theology and spirituality. All of the sacraments, in Bonaventure's view, are memorials of the Passion, but the Eucharist above all. In short, Bonaventure's Eucharistic theology summarizes the main themes of his whole theology. The Eucharist is to be a sort of compendium of the Christian life and of the history of the redemption, which finds its center in the cross.

Berengarius of Tours (ca. 999–1088) had taught that the bread and wine remain after the consecration as before, since appearance marks the presence of form. Berengarius is an interesting case, because his teaching on the Eucharist reflects John Scottus Eriugena's (ca. 800–877) Neoplatonism. Berengarius argued that the Eucharist is substantially both bread and wine, as well as, in some sense, the body and blood of Christ. In other words, the real presence does not entail the destruction of the substance of bread: "The material Bread and Wine could co-exist with the spiritual Body and Blood."[30] Lanfranc (ca. 1005–1089) attacked Berengarius's position, and argued that the two substances cannot occupy the same space simultaneously. The change in the Eucharist involves the replacement of one substance by another.[31] It is of particular interest that Lanfranc analyzed the Eucharist according to an explanation drawn from Aristotle's *Categories*. "The use of the sciences and logic to clarify theological problems was to have many triumphs in the next two centuries, and the success of Lanfranc's argument was one of the first."[32] Berengarius's view was condemned by a synod at Rome under Gregory VII.

There are different terms that have been used in the course of Christianity to describe the change that takes place in the Eucharist. Gregory of Nyssa speaks of the bread and wine being transformed; Ambrose speaks of them being transfigured. In the late eleventh century, various theologians began to use the term "transubstantiation" to describe the change.[33]

Bonaventure unambiguously affirms transubstantiation as the means of explaining the presence of Christ in the sacrament of the Eucharist: "When the words are said by the priest with the intention of consecrating, the substance of the elements is transubstantiated into the body and blood of Christ."[34] Bonaventure explains that even though the species (or likenesses) remain unchanged in their sensible form, "both contain the whole Christ." He speaks of "a change of substance" of the bread and wine into the body and blood of Christ that involves the accidents remaining as signs containing and expressing the body and blood.[35] Furthermore, there is a twofold reality (*res*), namely, the true body of Christ and the mystical body of Christ. Bread and wine fittingly express this twofold reality of the sacrament of the Eucharist.[36]

Bonaventure affirms that the whole bread as substance—that is, matter and form—is converted into the body of Christ, the accidents alone remaining, but he does not describe this change as involving an annihilation of the bread.[37] "Therefore this sacrament contains the true body and immaculate flesh of Christ in such a way that it penetrates our being, unites us to one another, and transforms us into Him through that burning love by which He gave Himself to us, offered himself up for us, and now gives himself back to us to remain with us until the end of the world."[38]

In receiving Christ, however, there is no change in him. He does not become us; rather, he transforms us into him. We "pass over" into the mystical body of Christ.[39]

The Eucharist is a sacrificial offering, a sacramental union, and a sustaining food for the way. Christ is the one acceptable offering or victim. Furthermore, the Eucharist is the continuation of the offering on the cross. Indeed, because the Eucharist is an offering and specifically, the offering of the cross, it was necessary that the body and blood of Christ be present, "not only figuratively but in reality (*non tantum figurative, verum etiam veraciter*)."[40] Furthermore, any portion of the species represents the body of Christ: He is as fully present in part as in the whole. If Christ's presence is so important, one may well ask why he remains hidden behind the veil of bread and wine. The reason is simple in Bonaventure's view: It is necessary for Christ to remain veiled for us in order that we may merit by our faith. "He is hidden in every sense so that faith may have its field and acquire merit."[41]

Bonaventure carefully develops the notion that the elements of the sacraments are chosen with great care and specifically because of the natural signification present within them. For example, bread and wine were chosen for the Eucharist because "nothing is better suited for refection than bread for food and wine for drink." Nor is anything better suited for symbolizing the unity of the body of Christ than the one bread made from many grains, and the one wine pressed from many grapes.

> Wherefore also it is commanded that this sacrament be surrounded with great solemnity, of place as well as time, of words and prayer as well as of vestments, in the celebration of masses; so that both the celebrating priests and the communicants may realize the gift of grace through which they are cleansed, enlightened, perfected, restored, vivified, and most ardently transformed into Christ by rapturous love.[42]

Penance, Orders, and Matrimony

The sacrament of penance, says Bonaventure, is like a life-saving plank after a shipwreck. It is specifically a plank for the human being drowning in mortal sin. There are three parts to this sacrament: contrition in the soul, confession in words, and satisfaction in deed.[43]

Bonaventure understands orders to be a certain sign through which a spiritual power is conferred upon the ordained. (Of course, he reads significance into the fact that there are seven orders; the sixth and seventh are the deaconate and priesthood.) He regards orders as the sacrament that imparts order, distinction, and power. The one who receives orders is to be totally consecrated to the worship of God.

Bonaventure regards matrimony as a legitimate union of a man and a woman forming an indissoluble communion of life.[44] He follows Augustine's teaching in his *Literal Commentary on Genesis* that sexual intercourse and marriage existed both before the Fall. Augustine is unique among the church fathers in teaching that sexual intercourse and marriage were part of the human condition before the original sin. Adam and Eve were married and would have had children by sexual intercourse in paradise, even though they did not. Other church fathers maintain that Adam and Eve were not married and would not have had intercourse. These are all part of the lapsarian condition.[45]

Hence, according to Bonaventure, marriage is not merely a remedial state, but was to function even before the Fall, as the sacrament of union. After the Fall, of course, it took on a new role, namely, as the remedy against "the disease" of lust. In this regard, then, lust is excused by matrimony, but marriage does not erase the effects of the disease. Also, it was originally a symbol of the union of God with the soul; now it further signifies the union of Christ with the church and the hypostatic union of the divine and human natures in one divine person.[46]

"Matrimony is effected by free consent of the mind on the part of two persons of opposite sex, expressed externally through a certain sensible sign and consummated by physical union."[47] Matrimony is thus brought about by the will's consent, and since the will is not visible in itself, there must be some external sign indicating the act and intention of the will.

Bonaventure follows Augustine in positing that there are three benefits to the sacrament: fidelity (*fides*), offspring (*proles*), and sacrament (*sacramentum*).[48] He understands the sacrament to refer to the indissoluble bond; fidelity as the fulfillment of conjugal intercourse; and offspring as the principal effect proceeding from both. One of the most important implications from this is that the marriage and the family are part of man's created nature. The family is a natural society. It is appropriate to end this brief examination of Bonaventure's sacramental theology with marriage, for he sees in it the symbol of the divine.

The Last Things

A Theology of History

The question of time and of history (as the order of events through time), took on tremendous urgency in Bonaventure's day. Bonaventure found himself enmeshed in acrimonious debates about time and history both in the university and in the Franciscan order. As we have already seen, Bonaventure has philosophical reasons to reject the notion of an eternal universe, defended by the Averroists. Bonaventure thinks that creation necessarily involves having a beginning in time, i.e., having being at some point after not having being. Time is thus necessarily lineal, not cyclical. But as Bonaventure thinks it clear in the light of sound philosophy that creation has a beginning in time, so in the light of scripture he thinks it clear that it will have an end. And it is also scripture that makes clear the order of events in between the beginning and the end.

Bonaventure's reflection on history was prompted, in part, by the necessity of defending a proper understanding of the phenomenon of Francis and of the movement he inspired. In Bonaventure's day the Franciscan movement became enmeshed in the apocalyptic theory of Joachim of Fiore.[1] Joachim of Fiore tends to regard Christ as merely a turning point in history and not at the definitive moment, for there will be a seventh age of the Spirit, which has often been understood to supersede the age of the Son and to involve an abolition of the Gospel.[2] Joachim takes over the patristic and Augustinian division of history into seven ages corresponding to the seven days of creation. (But he thinks that the seventh and final age will take place in history before the final judgment, not beyond history in eternity, as Augustine believed.)[3]

There has been some dispute among scholars as to what degree Bonaventure was influenced by Joachim. Joseph Ratzinger has argued that Bonaventure, in his later work, was significantly so influenced but without going to Joachim's extreme;[4] others have been more sanguine about this.[5] There is clearly a development in Bonaventure's view: in his early work, the *Sentences*, he is dismissive of Joachim, referring to the latter's "ignorant" criticism of the Lombard on the topic of the Trinity.[6] Indeed, given the dearth of Joachite influence on the early Bonaventure, he might have agreed with the remark later attributed to Pope Boniface VIII about the Joachites (ca. 1234–1303; r. 1294–1303), "Why are these fools awaiting the end of the world?"[7] As Bernard McGinn says, "Bonaventure's academic period seems strangely free of influences from Joachim's visions of history."[8] In any case, Bonaventure as minister general worked to rescue the Franciscans from a more extreme apocalypticism, inspired by the reading of Joachim among some of his brother friars, above all, in his predecessor as minister general, John of Parma. John envisioned a subsequent age of the spirit, which he thought inaugurated by St. Francis. In attempting to correct this heretical view, "Bonaventure does not accept the notion of an age of the Holy Spirit which destroyed the central position of Christ in the Joachimite view."[9] Instead, he develops a moderating position that avoids Aristotle's secular view of time on the one hand and a Joachite charismatic apocalypticism on the other.

Christianity sees history in general, as a coherent narrative and the movement of events as part of a larger plot. For Bonaventure, however, creation is a particular type of story—the story of a journey, an odyssey, of how all things come forth from God and will return back to their source. It has a beginning in creation, a climax in the coming of Christ, and will have an end with a final judgment. In the dominant patristic understanding of history, there are seven ages that parallel the seven days of creation. The coming of Christ marks the sixth day and thus the beginning of the end of time. With the coming of Christ, the world is over; the last age is a dénouement. Bonaventure tends to follow this schema in his *Commentary*; but in the *Breviloquium*, his doctrine acquires a new tone in which Christ's coming is the "fullness of time." By the writing of the *Hexaemeron* Christ is clearly presented as the center, the midpoint of history, and not merely as a turning point. "For Bonaventure, Christ is the axis of world history."[10] But unlike in the patristic configuration presented in the *Commentary*, the time of the church will occupy a longer and distinct age of its own. In the *Hexaemeron*, Bonaventure will adapt Joachim's conception of spirit-inspired contemplatives, and which Joachite Franciscans tended to identify with the Order itself, to be those members of the church who attain a mystical union with God.

The first implication of this Christocentric view is that time is never the neutral measure of motion, as it is for Aristotle, but one of the structural elements of the universe. Indeed, time is not merely a measurement of motion relative to an observer at any given moment; it is an objectively reckoned measurement of proximity to the event of Christ's incarnation. All time is saving time, for all time belongs to Christ. That is to say, time is a measurement of the duration from Christ, either in anticipation of him or looking back to him. Time is, in short, the reckoning of a narrative, and Christ is the climax from which all event are reckoned. In Bonaventure's view, the history of Christ is not a tale imposed on events. The story of Christ is the history of the universe, and time. therefore, is the duration from the center of history. As Gilson puts it very succinctly, "The root of the matter is that St. Bonaventure's Christian universe differs from the pagan universe of Aristotle in that it has a history."[11]

The Final Judgment

Philosophers and religious thinkers have long conjectured that the world will end in some kind of judgment. Plato is perhaps the most famous example among philosophers, but even Heraclitus, the Presocratic philosopher, hypothesized that the world would end in a vast conflagration. For both of these Greek thinkers, it seemed the nature of reality was such that definitive justice must be restored to human events. It does not seem quite right, their reasoning seems to run, that good people go unrewarded and evil unpunished. Goodness, such philosophers maintain, requires that the good be rewarded and evil punished; otherwise, the goodness of reality is strictly limited and provisional. To hold that such could be the case involves maintaining that there is no general plan or providence for the course of human events. Such a view further involves holding the premise that reality is not just, it just is. On the contrary, the human story is not a tale told by an idiot, in which the good suffer and the wicked prosper. Without a judgment, the view that providence ultimately guides events is very difficult, if not impossible, to argue, since there are massive amounts of evidence that evil goes unpunished and good unrewarded. Without a definitive judgment and righting of all evils, it seems a dubious thesis that reality is fundamentally good.

The Christian, taking a definite stand on this issue, believes that "Christ will come to judge the living and the dead," as Christ himself seems to claim (Matthew 24:27; 25:31) and as the Apostles' Creed says. (The Christian view is admittedly inspired by Christ's own words, not the philosophers.) The Christian thus believes that Christ revealed how the world will end, at least in some sense. The end will involve three events: a second coming of Christ, a general judgment, and the resurrection of the dead.

The world will end with a judgment in which God will judge the living and the dead, treating each according to his merits. Bonaventure thinks that the hour of this judgment is known only to the Trinity and to Christ's assumed humanity. It may also be known to certain angels and to the blessed, but it is certainly unknown to all pilgrims.[12] This judgment will involve an "opening" or examination of the consciences of every human being who has ever lived.

In Bonaventure's day it was not defined doctrine what would happen to souls immediately after their death but before the end of time. By the second Council of Lyon's profession of faith in 1274, it is clear that the Western church had come to believe the doctrine that there would be a judgment of each individual immediately after death, "a particular judgment" as it is called, followed at once by the reward of heaven, the temporary purification of purgatory, or the punishment of hell. The Eastern church did not possess doctrinal uniformity on this matter.

Bonaventure explains that the rectitude of truth imposes on human beings a law that obligates them to righteousness, but not in such a way that their wills are forced. As he puts it, quoting Augustine, God "so governs his creatures as to let them act by their own power."[13] Thus, in order to preserve and to manifest the rectitude of truth, there must be a recognition of merit; in order to manifest the plenitude of power, there must appear a just distribution of rewards; and to manifest the loftiness of might and power, there must be a passing of sentence.

The mystery of evil, says Bonaventure, finds its roots in the free will. Nothing can come to be apart from the divine will, but the very condition for the possibility of there being a creature with a free will (and thus for a creature that can truly love) is a will that can turn away from the good. "And so, if He suffers free will to fall, He does so in all justice, since by the very law of its nature free will is able to turn either way."[14] God is simply being just when he so administers creation that he does not infringe upon the laws he himself has established for it and he cooperates with the things he has made such that he lets them move by their own inner powers.[15]

The nature of man is such that it must have will. That is to say, the free and rational being can be perfected (completed) only in loving the good or in being punished for this failure. For the good to be forced upon the free rational being would itself be an injustice. In possessing free will, however, the human being can turn away from the good; and in so turning away, a free, rational being must receive justice, for otherwise an injustice would be committed. Hence, all human beings must be completed either through God's justice or his mercy. All human beings will come to their proper end and the fulfillment of their nature, whether among the elect or the reprobate. In justice, all human beings deserve condemnation; it is by nothing but the sheer, unfathomable benevolence of God that anyone is saved. Bonaventure thinks that God has chosen from all eternity those whom he will save. These are the elect, or the "pre-elected" as he also refers to them. Those who will not be saved are the reprobates. "When therefore, He condemns and reproves, He acts according to justice; when He pre-elects, he acts according to grace and love, which do not preclude justice."[16] Bonaventure thus holds what would later be called a monergistic theory of salvation in which God preelects or predestines certain human beings for salvation without consideration of their merits. He does not think that God positively reprobates the damned—these he merely permits to turn away. In short, Bonaventure's theory of predestination is one that includes positive election and negative or permissive reprobation. He thinks that more souls are reproved than elected, in order "to show that salvation is a special grace, while condemnation is ordinary justice."[17] If God helps or sustains anyone through grace, he does no injustice to anyone else.

Bonaventure defends what was to become one of the most controversial, yet most distinctly medieval, doctrines, namely, purgatory. Purgatory is a state of purification for souls who have repented of all mortal sins, but (1) have not been freed from their attachment to sin, or (2) have not satisfied the temporal punishment due for their sins. "As supreme goodness suffers no good to remain unrewarded, so also it cannot suffer any evil to remain unpunished."[18]

As a result of this fundamental principle, sin demands three things: a punitive penalty, a due reparation, and a proper cleansing. All three of these elements necessitate the existence of purgatory for those souls who have repented of their mortal sins. With regard to the penalty, Bonaventure quotes Augustine: " 'the pain must burn as fiercely as love had clung.' "[19] As a reparation, the story is more complex. Since there can be no meriting in purgatory, the element of atonement is necessarily lacking. Hence, Bonaventure thinks that the lack of freedom in the will must be made up for by the bitterness of the pain itself. Finally, the fires of purgatory must have a cleansing effect in the soul.

The Resurrection of the Body

Bonaventure believes that the bodies of all human beings will rise at the end of the world. In order to understand Bonaventure's teaching on this matter, it is necessary to return to his anthropological doctrines, and specifically, to this view that the human being is a rational animal, that the rational soul is the substantial form of the body, and that the soul and body possess a unibility for each other. Indeed, the matter and form will need and seek each other. Nature is not complete unless man be reconstituted body and soul, as matter and form, for without such reconstitution, one does not have man. This unibility of soul and body is accurately described as an appetite of each for the other, and more properly, of the appetite of the soul for the matter of the body. The rational soul retains an appetite for a particular body, and Bonaventure understands the resurrection to be such that it will entail the reunion of the soul with the same flesh it possessed in this life.

From a philosophical viewpoint one of the most difficult aspects of the doctrine of the resurrection to defend is the identity of the individual at the time of death and the individual who rises again. It would seem that in order for both moments to involve the same individual, it is necessary that every body return to the soul to which it belonged and which had been its original principle of life and growth. "Therefore the same individual body (*idem corpus numero*) must be raised from the dead, or else there would be no true resurrection."[20] Of course, Bonaventure admits that nature, in its seminal or natural causes, has not the power to bring all this about. Such an occurrence depends on the intervention of the prime cause. "Everything born of nature is doomed to die."

Like other Scholastics, Bonaventure speculates about who will possess the flesh consumed by cannibals. Will it belong to the cannibals or the original owner? Admittedly, a strange question to our ears, but a common Scholastic one nonetheless. Bonaventure argues that it will belong to the one to whom it first belonged.[21] What is at stake in this seemingly strange line of speculation is the nature of identity. In other words, does identity of substance between the individual human being who lived on earth and the resurrected human being require the same body for there to be an identity of substance across the two instances? Like certain other Scholastics, Bonaventure thinks it does. Granted of course, that the resurrected person cannot possibly possess all of the molecules or parts that she ever possessed throughout her life, since then she would be humongous and no longer a well-proportioned human being.

While the wicked shall rise to misery and pain, the just will rise to eternal happiness. But the bodies of the wicked shall rise with all of the distortion and defects that they had in life. "But in the good, 'nature will be safeguarded and all imperfection removed,' and they will rise with a body complete, in the prime of life, and well-proportioned."[22]

The fullness of grace demands that every imperfection be removed and that the just receive the fulfillment of their natural integrity, any missing portion being restored, any excess growth eliminated, and any malfunctioning corrected. All the just are to receive bodies in the prime of life, which the tradition took to be the age at which Christ died.

A Consuming Fire

In his eschatology Bonaventure adds one more event to the end: he thinks that the world will end in a consuming fire, which will not involve the total destruction of the sensible world, but will entail all the things of the world being set aflame, all animals and plants being consumed, and the elements cleansed and renewed.[23] Fire will cleanse the elect and punish the damned.[24] On this point, Bonaventure's teaching interestingly resembles Stoic doctrine, originally derived from the teaching of the Presocratic philosopher, Heraclitus. After the cleansing of fire, the motion of the heavens shall cease, and with all the elect completed, the bodies of the universe shall be renewed and rewarded.[25]

Of particular interest in Bonaventure's discussion of the final judgment is the implicit view that the universe rises or falls with man. Man is the microcosm who sums up the macrocosm. All of physical creation is ordered to the best thing that is within it, namely, the human rational soul. As the Fall of man involved a fall of creation, so the restoration of man must involve the restoration of the whole universe. When the human being is cleansed, so too is the whole universe. "Finally, this world must be consummated once man is consummated,"[26] but man is not consummated until the number of the elect is filled up.

Therefore, as soon as this number is completed, the motion of the heavenly bodies must end and cease, as likewise the transmutations of elements; and consequently the process of generation in animals and plants; for since all these creatures were ordained toward the more noble form, the rational soul, once souls have attained their final state of rest, all other things beside must come to completion and repose.[27]

Furthermore, this punishment must be eternal, "for a sin which a man commits and never repents remains forever in the soul, and separates it from eternal life, that is, from God."[28] As man sinned against the infinite, so he must suffer an infinite penalty.

All the just shall receive the vision of God, bodily glory, and a special additional honor called an aureole. Any reward less than God would not satisfy such a creature as man. "Hence, it receives as reward a God-conforming glory: it becomes like unto God and sees Him clearly through the intellect, loves him through the will, and retains him forever through the memory."[29]

Formless (Nulliform) Wisdom: Peace and Ecstatic Love

As discussed earlier, the purpose of theology is nothing less than salvation. That is to say, theology's task is to lead the human being to eternal life with God, and this, in turn, involves leading the soul to virtue. Theology thus has a practical end. And the end of scripture, as synonymous with theology, is "the superabundance of overflowing happiness," and is thus the same as the end of the human being.[30] Theology as a science ultimately aims at a loving union with God. In this sense, Bonaventure tends to regard theology as a practical science. Indeed, it has as its most profound aim nothing less than human salvation and beatitude found in eternal union with God. Not surprisingly, then, it aims at a foretaste or anticipatory experience of that eternal union through the believer's mystical, ecstatic union with God even in this life, in via, as Bonaventure often says. In this conception, life is a pilgrimage, and part of theology's ordinary task is to dispose the pilgrim to catch a glimpse of the lasting city to strengthen him on the way.

Before the day of judgment, then, whether the general or particular, Bonaventure thinks that there is already available to the devout soul some cognition of God in this life. In order to understand this mystical knowledge of God, recall the different senses of the word "wisdom," and that in a strict sense, it refers to the mind's ecstatic union with God. This final type of wisdom is a "formless wisdom" (*sapientia nulliformis*) that transcends the categories of thought, and so, it should not be surprising that Bonaventure draws on the apophatic tradition. As mentioned, Bonaventure speaks of this wisdom as formless, because the mind is unable to grasp it in any concept or to express it in any proposition. In this way, it is beyond form; it is no-form. This wisdom is ineffable.

It is particularly noteworthy that this wisdom is not merely a distant goal for eternity, but is already the goal of human life on earth. There exists on earth a knowledge of the divine essence that is possible.[31] This formless wisdom can be found in this life by the contemplative in the interior knowledge of God; it involves a cognition of God by experience (*cognitonem Dei experimentalem*). This formless cognition is a mystical state that, while beginning in cognition, ends in affection and an ecstatic outpouring of one's self toward God.[32]

Insofar as union with God involves the perfect tranquility of order, peace (*status*) can also be said to be the final end of man.[33] This peace can begin in this life with the attainment of formless wisdom. We see this in Bonaventure's discussion of the Beatitudes, where he speaks of a special grace, called "peacefulness." He regards this as a grace meant to perfect the soul that is already rectified by the infused virtues and that has grown in holiness through the gifts of the Holy Spirit. It is not surprising that peace arises in such a soul, since the soul is also supremely ordered or hierarchized (*anima hierarchizata*).[34] (Francis is an example of such a soul, "a hierarchic man" [*vir hierarchus*].)[35] Peacefulness is a certain spiritual grace that perfects and crowns these other graces. It is a grace meant for a "holy soul," who loves the good alone. The good is the one single good in which all goods are found, and this alone will suffice to make man happy. If one desires the supreme good, nothing else is necessary. "Why, then, servant of God do you wander so far, seeking delights for your body and mind? Love one single Good in which all goods are found, and that will suffice; desire one simple Good which is all good and that will be enough."[36] This solitary good is the beatitude of the human being.

Bonaventure consistently uses two types of language when discussing peace of soul: ecstatic and nuptial. He describes the union with the good as like inebriation; it is only in such repose that there will be peace. It is important to point out that this wise unknowing (or learned ignorance) is not based on a denial of reason and rationality. The mystic is not one who denies the principle of contradiction, but rather one who has come to an ecstatic knowledge that the rationality of God is infinite and thus beyond what the finite mind can comprehend.

Bonaventure's mysticism does not belong to the tradition developed much later among the Rhineland mystics. For them, God is the being of all that is, and the nonbeing of all that is not; God is beyond the principle of contradiction. According to Bonaventure the principle of contradiction seems to be one with God. This point follows from his doctrine on the divine word: The divine Word is the perfect expression of the First Principle, but there can be no expression without coherence and no coherence with contradiction. The rational and mystical are not opposed, rather reason and mysticism are related as operation and end.[37] Being does not yield its intelligibility readily, and we are greatly hampered in grasping this intelligibility (above all, because matter as the mark of all finite things having come from nothing, is unintelligible, a "darkness"); nevertheless, once we have grasped this intelligibility of being, we find it leads to an inexhaustible source, that wells upon eternally, "a fontal plenitude."

Bonaventure explains that these spiritual senses express mental perceptions of the truth being contemplated. Indeed, the infused virtues and the gifts of the Spirit are all ordered to lead the soul to the repose of contemplation and the habits of the beatitudes that bring about its perfection. The prophets received contemplation through revelation, while other just souls receive contemplation through "speculation." This speculation starts in the senses, but proceeds to the intellect and the attainment of wisdom. This wisdom is the ecstatic knowledge that begins in this life, but reaches fulfillment in eternal glory.[38]

When the soul attains this wisdom, "it transcends itself, entering mystical darkness and ecstasy through a certain wise unknowing (*ignorantia docta*)."[39] The self-transcendence or passing over (*transitus*) is a theme to which Bonaventure frequently averts in his writings.[40] While no one may acquire this contemplation of wisdom by one's own efforts, for "divine grace alone can procure such experience," only those who strive for it may receive such grace.[41] Near the end of his *Journey of the Mind to God*, Bonaventure quotes Pseudo-Dionysius on these themes:

> We can say with Dionysius, "And you, my friend, in this matter of mystical visions, redouble your efforts, abandon your senses, intellectual activities, visible and invisible things—everything that is not and that is—and, oblivious of yourself, let yourself be brought back, in so far as it is possible, to unity with Him Who is above all essence and all knowledge. And transcending yourself and all things, ascend to the superessential gleam of the divine darkness by an incommensurable and absolute transport of a pure mind."[42]

Notes

Preface

1. Étienne Gilson, *Christian Philosophy: An Introduction*, trans. Armand Maurer (Toronto: Pontifical Institute of Medieval Studies, 1993). See also John Marenbon, *Later Medieval Philosophy (1150–1350): An Introduction* (New York: Routledge & Kegan Paul, 1987), 85. Marenbon presents current approaches to medieval philosophy: (1) separationism, (2) Christian philosophy; and (3) modern analytic. The Christian philosophy approach agrees with separationism that the history of medieval philosophy is rightly considered a separate subject from the history of medieval theology, but disagrees in holding that "it is a philosophy which depends on Christian revelation and cannot be understood in abstraction from certain fundamental tenets of the faith" (85).

2. Jan A. Aertsen, *Medieval Philosophy and the Transcendentals: The Case of Thomas Aquinas*, ed. Josef Koch, vol. LII, *Studien und Texte zur Geistesgeschichte des Mittelalters* (Leiden: E. J. Brill, 1996), 8.

3. Zachary Hayes, OFM, "Bonaventure: Mystery of the Triune God," in *The History of Franciscan Theology*, ed. Kenan B. Osborne, OFM (St. Bonaventure, N.Y.: The Franciscan Institute, 1994), 50; Philipp Rosemann, *Peter Lombard*, Great Medieval Thinkers (New York: Oxford University Press, 2004).

4. Étienne Gilson, *The Philosophy of St. Bonaventure*, trans. Dom Illtyd Trethowan and Frank J. Sheed (Paterson, N.J.: St. Anthony Guild Press, 1965); originally published as *La philosophie de Saint Bonaventure*, Études de philosophie médiévale, IV (Paris: J Vrin, 1924).

5. Rufin Silic, *Christus und die kirche: ihr verhaltnis nach der lehre des heiligen Bonaventura*, Breslauer studien zur historischen theologie, vol. 3 (Beslau: Muller

& Seiffert, 1938). For a summary of the dispute between the developmental and chronological approaches, see Zachary Hayes, OFM, *The Hidden Center: Spirituality and Speculative Christology in St. Bonaventure* (St. Bonaventure, N.Y.: The Franciscan Institute, 1992), 7, n. 7.

6. Bernard McGinn, *The Flowering of Mysticism*, vol. III of *The Presence of God: A History of Western Christian Mysticism* (New York: The Crossroad Publishing Company, 1998), 87. See also Zachary Hayes, OFM, *Bonaventure: Mystical Writings*, The Crossroad Spiritual Legacy Series (New York: The Crossroad Publishing Co., 1999).

Chapter 1

1. See Edward Grant, *God & Reason in the Middle Ages* (New York: Cambridge University Press, 2001), 25–29.

2. See R. W. Southern, *Scholastic Humanism and the Unification of Europe*, vol. 2, *The Heroic Age* (Malden, Mass.: Blackwell Publishers, 2001), 4, 36–48.

3. Augustine, *Teaching Christianity: De Doctrina Christiana*, trans. Edmund Hill, OP. Part I, vol. 11 of *The Works of Saint Augustine: A Translation for the 21st Century*, ed. John E. Rotelle, OSA (Hyde Park, N.Y.: New City Press, 1996).

4. Hugh of St. Victor, *Didascalicon*, trans. Jerome Taylor (New York: Columbia University Press, 1961), bk. I, ch. 8.

5. Hugh of St. Victor, *Didascalicon*, bk. II, ch. 1: "This, then, is what the arts are concerned with, this is what they intend, namely, to restore within us the divine likeness, a likeness which to us is a form but to God is his nature."

6. Southern, 2:4.

7. H. Denifle and E. Chatelain, eds., *Chartularium Universitatis Parisiensis* (Paris: Delalain, 1889–1897).

8. Southern, 2:135.

9. The first order traces its origin back to the primitive rule of 1209 approved by Innocent III. (The Friars Minor were later given a second rule, rewritten by the saint, and confirmed by Pope Honorius III in 1223.) There were eventually three branches of the First Order: the Order of Friars Minor (1209), the Friars Minor Conventual (1517), and the Friars Minor Capuchins (1619). The Second Order was for women, and dates from 1212. The Third Order was for those unable to embrace Francis's way of life in one of the other two orders, and includes the Third Order regular and Third Order secular (for devout persons of both sexes who live in the world).

10. Along with the Order of Friars Minor or Franciscans, the mendicant orders in the thirteenth century were the following: the Order of Preachers or Dominicans; the Order of the Blessed Virgin of Mt. Carmel or Carmelites, which began in the twelfth century, but was included among the mendicant orders by Innocent IV in 1247; and the Order of Hermits of Saint Augustine (started in the thirteenth century), which was not declared a mendicant order until 1318.

11. Lazaro Iriarte, OFM Cap., *Historia Franciscana*, Nueva Edicion (Valencia: Editorial Asis, 1979), 123.

12. Badin Gratien, Mariano d'Alatri, and Servus Gieben, *Histoire de la fondation et de l'évolution de l'ordre des Frères Mineurs au XIII siècle*, Bibliotheca Seraphico—Capuccina 29 (Rome: Istituto Storico dei Cappuccini, 1982), 516, 520, 526.

13. Hans Wolter, "The Papacy at the Height of Its Power, 1198 to 1216," in *Handbook of Church History: From the High Middle Ages to the Eve of the Reformation*, ed. Hubert Jedin and John Dolan; trans. Anselm Biggs (New York: Herder and Herder, 1970), 4:181.

14. Williell R. Thomson, *Friars in the Cathedral: The First Franciscan Bishops 1226–1261* (Toronto: Pontifical Institute of Medieval Studies, 1975), 13.

15. Thomson, 20. Thomson discusses some of the problems of reconciling the Franciscan rule with the office of bishop (10–16).

16. Fourth Lateran Council, in *Decrees of the Ecumenical Councils*, ed. Norman Tanner, SJ (Washington, D.C.: Georgetown University Press, 1990), vol. 1, chap. 21, 245.

17. Michael Robson, OFM Conv., *St. Francis of Assisi: The Legend and the Life* (London: Geoffrey Chapman, 1997), 158–186.

18. St. Francis of Assisi, "The Admonitions," in *The Saint*, vol. 1 of *Francis of Assisi: Early Documents*, ed. Regis J. Armstrong, OFM Cap., J. A. Wayne Hellman, OFM Conv., and William J. Short, OFM (New York: New City Press, 1999), 132.

19. Although Portuguese by birth, Anthony became associated with Padua because it was there that he worked in his later life, and there that he is buried.

20. St. Francis, "A Letter to Brother Anthony of Padua" in *The Saint*, vol. 1 of *Francis of Assisi: Early Documents*, ed. Regis J. Armstrong, OFM Cap., J. A. Wayne Hellman, OFM Conv., and William J. Short, OFM (New York: New City Press, 1999), 107.

21. Bert Roest, "*Studia*, Students, Lectors, and Programs," in *A History of Franciscan Education (c. 1210–1517)*. Education and Society in the Middle Ages and Renaissance, vol. 11 (Boston: Brill, 2000), 1–117.

22. Étienne Gilson, *The Philosophy of St. Bonaventure*, trans. Illtyd Trethowan and Frank J. Sheed (Paterson, N.J.: St. Anthony Guild Press, 1965).

23. Paschal Robinson, "Bonaventure," *Catholic Encyclopedia* (New York: Robert Appleton Company, 1907).

24. Dominic Monti, OFM, Introduction to vol. 5 of *The Works of Bonaventure: Saint Bonaventure's Writings Concerning the Franciscan Order* (St. Bonaventure, N.Y.: Franciscan Institute, 1994), 6, n. 12. For the *Chronicles*, see *Chronica XXIV generalium O.F.M.*, *Analecta franciscana* 3 (1897).

25. In 1950, Giuseppe Abate argued for the 1217 date of birth: Giuseppe Abate, "Per la storia e la cronologia de S. Bonaventura, O. Min.," *Miscellanea francescana* 49 (1949): 534–568; 50 (1950): 97–130. In 1974, Theodore Crowley, OFM, argued vigorously against Abate's dating: T. Crowley, "St. Bonaventure Chronology Reappraisal," *Franziskanische Studien* (1974): 310–322. Scholars are divided; some have accepted Abate's argument, while other writers hold to the traditional date (e.g., John Moorman, *A History of the Franciscan Order: From Its*

Origins to the Year 1517 [Oxford: Clarendon Press, 1968], 140). For the chronology of Bonaventure's works and the many disputed dates, see Jacques G. Bougerol, vol. 2, S. *Bonaventura 1274–1974* (Grottaferrata: Collegio S. Bonaventure, 1973), 2:11–16; J. Bougerol, *Introduction to the Works of Bonaventure*, trans. J. de Vinck; J. F. Quinn, "Chronology of St. Bonaventure," *Franciscan Studies* 32 (1972) 168–186; Zachary Hayes, OFM, Introduction to *Disputed Questions on the Knowledge of Christ*, vol. IV of *The Works of Bonaventure* (St. Bonaventure, N.Y.: The Franciscan Institute, 1992), ch. 3. The Quarrachi editors give the date of 1221 (Disertatio de eius vita, *Operum omnium complementum* [X, 39b]).

26. "A seventeenth-century legislative enactment is a poor guide to thirteenth century practice. . . . One has only to keep in mind the ever-changing pattern of thirteenth century university regulations to realize that one cannot argue from what was laid down in 1215 to what might be permitted in 1250" (Crowley, 311).

27. Crowley, 322.

28. Today, it is referred to as the "Città di Bagnoregio," or "Città" for short, in order to distinguish it from the "new" Bagnoregio, which arose nearby after earthquakes in various centuries damaged the old town.

29. Maria Luisi Polidori, *Città and Bagnoregio* (Florence: Bonechi, 1999), 6.

30. Bonaventure, *Legenda minor sancti Francisci*, in vol. 8 of *Doctoris seraphici S. Bonaventurae opera omnia: opuscula varia theologica*, ed. the Fathers of the Collegium S. Bonaventurae (Ad Claras Aquas [Quaracchi]: Collegium S. Bonaventurae, 1898), VIII, 579.

31. Polidori, 22.

32. Brief of October 14, 1482; Sixtus IV to the Franciscan convent at Bagnoregio, *Bullarium Franciscanum*, vol. III (1471–1484) Qiaraccjo, 1949 (838).

33. For an introduction to the life and works of Alexander of Hales, see Gedeon Gál, "Alexander of Hales," in *The Routledge Encyclopedia of Philosophy*, ed. Edward Craig, vol. 1 (New York: Routledge, 1998).

34. Bonaventure, *Commentaria in quatuor libros sententiarum*, vol. 2 of *Doctoris seraphici S. Bonaventurae opera omnia*, ed. the Fathers of the Collegium S. Bonaventurae (Ad Claras Aquas [Quaracchi]: Collegium S. Bonaventurae, 1885), II, 1a.

35. Bonaventure, *II Sent.*, 2, 3, 23 (II, 547b) and *II Sent.*, Praelocutio (II, 1a).

36. John Moorman, *Medieval Franciscan Houses*, Franciscan Institute Publications, History Series, no. 4, ed. George Marcil, OFM (St. Bonaventure, N.Y.: Franciscan Institute, 1983), 371. The friars arrived in Paris in 1217, and soon thereafter, the Benedictines of St. Denis gave them quarters on their land. It was not until 1230 that the Franciscans had their own settlement. Also, see Laure Beaumont-Maillet, *Le Grand Couvent des Cordeliers de Paris: Etude historique et archéologique du XIIIe siècle à nos jours*, Bibliothèque de l'École des Hautes Études, 4th sec., vol. 325 (Paris: Librairie Honoré Champion, 1975); Christian Eugène, "Saint Bonaventure et le grand couvent des cordeliers de Paris," *Études franciscaines* 18 (Supplément annuel, 1968): 167–182.

37. There has been some debate about just how well Alexander knew the

teachings of Aristotle. Van Steenberghen does not think that Alexander's knowledge of Aristotle goes beyond a surface level; some scholars have argued otherwise.

38. Léon Veuthey, "Les divers courants de la philosophie augustino-franciscaine au moyen age," in *Scholastica ratione historico-critica instauranda,* Acta Congressus Scholastici Internationalis Rome, 1950 (Rome: 1951), 629. For a more recent discussion of these schools, see Steven P. Marrone, *The Light of Thy Countenance: Science and Knowledge of God in the Thirteenth Century,* Studies in the History of Christian Thought, vol. 98, ed. Heiko A. Oberman (Boston: Brill, 2001), 1:1–25. Marrone's work helps to show the difficulty of defining schools of thought by doctrine.

39. J. De Ghellinck, *Le mouvement théologique du XII siècle* (Bruges: Éditons de Tempel, 1948), 85–86. Michael Robson, OFM, makes the case that Grosseteste also should receive credit for introducing Anselm's writings into the Franciscan school: Michael Robson, OFM, "Saint Anselm and the Franciscan Tradition," in *Robert Grosseteste: New Perspectives on His Thought and Scholarship,* ed. James McEvoy, Instrumenta Patristica XXVII (Turnhout: Brepols Publishers, 1995), 233–256.

40. Wadding and the Bollandists hold that Bonaventure entered the order in 1243; Sbaraglea Bonelli, Panfilo da Magliano, and Jeiler argue for 1238. L. Wadding, *Annales Minorum,* III, 83; *Acta Sanctorum,* July 14; Sbaraglea, *Bullarium Franciscanum* III, 12, n. B. The secondary literature on this chronology is considerable.

41. There is evidence for boys entering the order before age eighteen, which is the minimum stipulated by the Constitutions of Narbonne (even these make an exception for boys of special merit, who could enter down to age fifteen) (Moorman, *A History of the Franciscan Order,* 148); Bihl, "The Constitutions of Narbonne" *Archivum Franciscanum Historicum* (1941).

42. M. D. Lambert, *Franciscan Poverty: The Doctrine of the Absolute Poverty of Christ and the Apostles in the Franciscan Order 1210–1323* (London: Society for the Promotion of Christian Knowledge, 1961), 116.

43. Lambert, 110.

44. Lambert, 59.

45. Bonaventure, *Quaestiones disputatae de perfectione evangelica,* in vol. 5 of *Doctoris seraphici S. Bonaventurae opera omnia: opuscula varia theologica,* ed. the Fathers of the Collegium S. Bonaventurae (Ad Claras Aquas [Quaracchi]: Ex typographia Collegii S. Bonaventurae, 1891), q. 1, a. 1 (V, 120b).

46. Bonaventure, *De perfectione evangelica,* in *Opera omnia,* q. 1, a. 1 (V, 120b).

47. Lambert, 111. Lambert points to F. Ehrle as the best representative of this view: Ehrle, "Der heilige Bonaventura, seine Eigenart und seine drei Lebensaufgaben," *Franziskanische Studien* VIII (1921): 109–124; but others are mentioned as well: L. Lemmens, *Der heilige Bonaventura Kardinal und Kirchenlehrer aus dem Franziskanerorden (1221–1274)* (Kempten and Munich: Jus Köselschen, 1909); Gratien, *Histoire de la Fondation et de l'Évolution de l'Ordre des Frères Mineurs au XIII siècle.*

48. David Burr, *Olivi and Franciscan Poverty: The Origins of the Usus Pauper*

Controversy (Philadelphia: University of Pennsylvania Press, 1989). It was, to a large extent, Pope John XXII's repudiation of Bonaventure's moderate approach on the poverty issue that brought the issue to a head. Pope Nicholas III ratified the "Bonaventurian settlement" on poverty in his papal bull of 1279, *Exiit qui seminat* (Conal Condren, "Rhetoric, Historiography and Political Theory: Some Aspects of the Poverty Controversy Reconsidered," *Journal of Religious History* 13, no. 1 [1984], 20ff.).

49. Three Franciscans presided over this council at one time or another: Bonaventure, Odo Rigaud (archbishop of Rouen), and Paolo de' Conti da Segni (titular bishop of Tripoli). For the role of various mendicants at this council, see Moorman, *A History of the Franciscan Order*, 177ff.

50. Wolter, 89.

51. Wolter, 90.

52. Wolter, 91.

53. Ignatius Brady provides a history of this edition: I. Brady, "The *Opera Omnia* of Saint Bonaventure Revisited," in *Proceedings of the Seventh Centenary Celebration of the Death of St. Bonaventure*, ed. Pascal F. Foley (St. Bonaventure, N.Y.: The Franciscan Institute, 1975), 47–59; also, Brady, "The Edition of the 'Opera Omnia' of St. Bonaventure (1882–1902)," *Archivum Franciscanum Historicum* 70 (1977): 352–376. Also, "Brevis relatio de collegio S. Bonaventurae ad Claras Aquas," in *Acta Ordinis Fratrum Minorum* 23 (1904): 27–29.

54. For a complete life and study of the Lombard, see the two-volume work: Marcia Colish, *Peter Lombard*, Brill's Studies in Intellectual History, ed. A. J. Vanderjagt, vol. 41 (New York: E. J. Brill, 1994). See also, Southern, *Scholastic Humanism and the Unification of Europe*, 2:133–47; Rosemann, *Peter Lombard*.

55. Josef Pieper comments on the Lombard's *Sentences*: "Peter Lombard's *Sentences* became one of the most successful textbooks in European intellectual history precisely because it 'lacked every trace of genius' " (Josef Pieper, *Scholasticism* [New York: Pantheon Books, 1967], 97). Grosseteste began lecturing at the friars' school about 1230, and continued to do so until he was made bishop of Lincoln in 1235. As a result, although not himself a Franciscan, he exercised considerable influence on the early Franciscan school. Grosseteste does not seem to have shared Alexander's enthusiasm for the Lombard; he was concerned that priority be given to the scriptures over the *Sentences* in the schools (Robinson, 248).

56. Colish, *Peter Lombard*, 1:34.

57. Colish, *Peter Lombard*, 1:25.

58. Richard McKeon, *Selections from Medieval Philosophers*, vol. 1, *Augustine to Albert the Great* (New York: Charles Scribner's Sons, 1929), 187.

59. Colish, *Peter Lombard*, 1:25.

60. Alister E. McGrath, *Iustitia Dei: A History of the Christian Doctrine of Justification*. 2d ed. New York: Cambridge University Press, 1998), 39.

61. Cf. Anselm, *Monologion*, prologue (I7, 5–11); I (I13, 5–11).

62. P. Glorieux, "Le date des collations de Saint Bonaventure," *Archivum franciscanum historicum* 22 (1929): 257–272.

63. Glorieux.

64. Ferdinand Delorme, OFM, *Collationes in hexaemeron*, Bibliotheca Franciscana Scholatica, vol. 8 (Ad Claras Aquas [Florence]: Collegium S. Bonaventurae, 1934).

65. Bonaventure, *Hexaemeron* (Delorme), VI, 2–5.

66. Bonaventure, *Comm. In Eccl.*, 1, 11, q. 2 (VI, 16b): "Verbum divinum est omnis creatura, quia Deum loquitur."

67. Paul Sabatier, *Vie de Saint François d'Assise* (Paris: Fischbacker, 1894). Also, see A. G. Little, "Guide to Franciscan Studies," *Études franciscaines* 41 (1929): 64–78; John Moorman, *The Sources for the Life of St. Francis of Assisi* (Manchester: University Press, 1940); Rosalind B. Brooke, "St. Bonaventure as Minister General," in *S. Bonaventura Francescana: Convegni del Centro di Studi sulla Spiritualità Medievale* XIV (Todi: Presso L'Accademia Tudertina, 1974), 75–105. Moorman even goes so far as to say that Bonaventure never really understood the Franciscan ideal.

68. A reedited version of this text is found in Renato Russo, *La metodologia del sapere nel sermone di S. Bonaventura "Unus est magister vester Christus"* (Grottaferrata: Editiones Collegii S. Bonaventurae, 1982), 100–132.

69. Since then, considerable debate has transpired. See Gerald McCool, *The Neo-Thomists* (Milwaukee, Wis.: Marquette University Press, 1994), 39; Fernand Van Steenberghen, *The Philosophical Movement in the Thirteenth Century* (Edinburgh: Nelson, 1955), 5.

70. Marrone has defended the use of "school" to describe thinkers who share certain doctrinal views.

71. Gordon Leff points to Alexander's *Summa* as evidence for the existence of an Augustinian philosophical school before the controversies of the 1260s. On two major historical controversies, Leff takes definite sides. He clearly sides with the Gilsonian position in the Gilson-Van Steenberghen dispute over whether there was an Augustinian school before the 1260s: "The *Summa* [of Alexander of Hales et al.] hardly leaves us in doubt that there was an Augustinian outlook before 1250 and that it was very largely in response to Aristotle and Islam" (Gordon Leff, *Medieval Thought: St. Augustine to Ockham* [Chicago: Quadrangle Books, 1958], 196). Leff also suggests that there is much in the Augustinian school that goes back to Augustine himself, though he does caution, "Much that was not pure St. Augustine came to be included [in Augustinianism]: it could not have failed to be, if Augustinianism was to survive" (Leff, 192). Hence, Leff consistently refers to the "Augustinians" and "Augustinianism," rather than "pre-Thomism" or "eclectic Aristotelianism" (Leff, 198). "He [Bonaventure], rather, gives greater point to the common outlook of his school, which goes back through thinkers like William of Auvergne, the Victorines, St. Bernard, St. Anselm, to St. Augustine himself" (Leff, 198). Maurice de Wulf argues that certain doctrines of "Augustinianism" are foreign to Augustine himself. See Maurice de Wulf, "Augustinisme et aristotélisme au XIII siècle," *Revue néoscolastique* (1901).

72. Ignatius Brady, OFM, "St. Bonaventure's Doctrine of Illumination: Reac-

tions Medieval and Modern," in *Bonaventure and Aquinas: Enduring Philosophers*, ed. Robert W. Shahan and Francis J. Kovach (Norman: University of Oklahoma Press, 1976), 62.

73. For a discussion of these "schools" or groups of disciples, see Roest, 187–188.

74. Peter Trigoso de Calatayud, *Sancti Bonaventurae Summa Theologica* (Roma: Ex typographia Vaticana, 1593), cited in George Marcil, OFM, "The Franciscan School," in *The History of Franciscan Theology*, ed. Kenan Osborne, OFM (St. Bonaventure, N.Y.: The Franciscan Institute, 1994), 319–320. See also, Colman Majchrzak, OFM, *A Brief History of Bonaventurianism* (Pulaski, WI: Franciscan Publishers, 1957).

75. Jacques G. Bougerol, OFM, "Dossier pour l'étude des rapports entre Bonaventure et Aristote," *Archives d'histoire doctrinale et littéraire du moyen age* (1973): 218. This study supersedes the earlier work on this matter by Bougerol in which he presents the number of quotations from each of the Aristotelian texts: Bougerol, *Introduction to the Works of Bonaventure*, 27.

76. Bonaventure, however, refuses to accept the Aristotelian *Organon* as the sole criterion of truth in philosophy (Andreas Speer, "Bonaventure and the Question of a Medieval Philosophy," *Medieval Philosophy and Theology* 6 [1997]: 27).

77. Bonaventure, *Epistola de tribus quaestionibus*, in vol. 8 of *Doctoris seraphici S. Bonaventurae opera omnia*, ed. the Fathers of the Collegium S. Bonaventurae (Ad Claras Aquas [Quaracchi]: Ex typographia Collegii S. Bonaventurae, 1891) (VIII, 335b).

78. See Joseph Ratzinger's *The Theology of History of Saint Bonaventure* (Chicago: Franciscan Herald Press, 1989) for a discussion of Bonaventure's relationship to Aristotle and Augustine, also in the context of Bonaventure's use of the thought of Joachim of Fiore. Ratzinger's study does not make a sharp distinction between Aristotelianism and Averroism.

Chapter 2

1. Bonaventure, *Itinerarium mentis in Deum*, in vol. 5 of *Doctoris seraphici S. Bonaventurae opera omnia: opuscula varia theologica*, ed. the Fathers of the Collegium S. Bonaventurae (Ad Claras Aquas [Quaracchi]: Ex typographia Collegii S. Bonaventurae, 1891), I, 9 (V, 298b).

2. Bonaventure, *I Sent.*, prooem., q. 3 con. (I, 13a). Charles Carpenter, *Theology as the Road to Holiness in St. Bonaventure* (New York: Paulist Press, 1999), 24–37.

3. Bonaventure, *Brevil.*, trans. Erwin Esse Nemmers (St. Louis, MO: B. Herder Book Co., 1946), I, 2, 5 (V, 211b).

4. For a brief, clear presentation of these four senses, see Philotheus Boehner, Notes and Commentary to *Itinerarium mentis in Deum*, 131–32, n. 3; also see, J.-G. Bougerol, s. v. Sapientia, *Lexique Saint Bonaventure* (Paris: Éditions Franciscaines, 1969).

5. "Sapiens est qui omnia novit, secundum quod convenit" (Aristotle, *Metaphysics* I, c. 2, quoted in Bonaventure, *In III Sent.*, d. 35, a. 1, con. [III, 774a]).

6. Bonaventure, *In III Sent.*, d. 35, a. 1, con. (III, 774a).

7. Augustine, *De vera religione*.

8. Bonaventure, *In III Sent.*, d. 35, u. 1 (III, 774).

9. Bonaventure, *Itin.*, 7.1 (V, 312a).

10. Bonaventure, *Itin.*, Prol., 3 (V, 295b); also 1.4 (V, 297b).

11. Bonaventure, *In II Sent.* (II, 320b).

12. Bonaventure, *Hexaemeron*, II, 8 (V, 337b).

13. Bonaventure, *Collations on the Six Days (Hexaemeron)*, trans. José de Vink, vol. 5 of *Works of Saint Bonaventure* (Paterson, N.J.: St. Anthony Guild Press, 1970), V, 24 (V, 358a).

14. Bonaventure, *Hexaemeron*, II, 20 (V, 340a).

15. Cf. Augustine, *Confessions*, Book IX, 10, 24.

16. Bonaventure, *In III Sent.*, d. 16, a. 1, q. 1 sed contra 1 (III, 296a).

17. Ratzinger, 132.

18. M.-D. Chenu, OP, *La théologie comme science au XIIIe siècle* (Paris: Librairie philosophique J. Vrin, 1957).

19. Augustine, *De utilitate credendi*, 2, n. 25, quoted in Bonaventure, *Brevil.*, p. 1, c. 1, n. 4 (V, 210b).

20. Bonaventure, *In I Sent.*, prooemiun, q. 2 (I, 10b).

21. Bonaventure, *In IV Sent.*, in vol. 4 of *S. Bonaventuae opera omnia*, Quaracchi Edition (Florence, 1882) d. 18, a. 2, q. 1, ad 6.

22. Gilson, *The Philosophy of St. Bonaventure*, 438–439.

23. Bonaventure, *Christus Mag.*, n. 18 (V, 572a).

24. Bonaventure, *Hexaemeron*, 6, 6 (V, 361b).

25. Bonaventure, *De reductione*, 26 (V, 325b).

26. Bonaventure presents this division of philosophy not only in *The Reduction of the Arts to Theology*, but also in his *Itin.*, III, 6 (V, 305b).

27. Grant, *God & Reason in the Middle Ages*, 14.

28. Grant, *God & Reason in the Middle Ages*, 32. Clement of Alexandria, *Stromata*.

29. Bonaventure, *Hexaemeron*, I, 11 (V, 331a).

30. Étienne Gilson, *The Spirit of Mediaeval Philosophy (Gifford Lectures 1931–1932)*, trans. A.H.C. Downes (New York: Charles Scribner's Sons, 1940), 37. John Marenbon presents Gilson's approach as one of four current and major approaches to medieval philosophy; the other three are the "separationist" approach (exemplified in the work of Van Steenberghen, below), the "modern analytical" (exemplified by the work found in *The Cambridge History of Later Medieval Philosophy: From the Rediscovery of Aristotle to the Disintegration of Scholasticism 1100–1600*, ed. Norman Kretzman et al. (New York: Cambridge University Press, 1988), and the "historical analysis" approach, which "tries to explain the ideas and arguments of medieval thinkers, so far as possible, in terms accessible to readers today" (John Marenbon, *Later Medieval Philosophy (1150–1350): An Introduction* [New York: Routledge & Kegan Paul, 1987], 83–90).

31. Gilson, *The Philosophy of St. Bonaventure*, 437: "Looked at from the rationalist point of view of modern philosophy, St. Bonaventure's doctrine does undoubtedly appear as the most mediaeval of mediaeval philosophies; and so, in certain respects, it is."

32. Fernand Van Steenberghen, *La philosophie au XIII siècle*, 2d ed. (Paris, Institut supérieur de philosophie, 1991), ch. 5; see also Speer, "Bonaventure and the Question of a Medieval Philosophy," 27.

33. Fernand Van Steenberghen, *Aristotle in the West: The Origins of Latin Aristotelianism* (Louvain: E. Nauwelaerts, Publisher, 1955), 159.

34. Van Steenberghen, *Aristotle in the West*, 160.

35. Van Steenberghen, *Aristotle in the West*, 28.

36. Van Steenberghen, *Aristotle in the West*, 26; see also Van Steenberghen, *Siger of Brabant d'après ses oevres inédites* (Louvain: Édtions de l'Institute supérieur de philosophie, 1931), 378–381.

37. Van Steenberghen, *Aristotle in the West*, 36; see *Siger of Brabant*, 381–389.

38. Van Steenberghen, *Aristotle in the West*, 130.

39. Van Steenberghen, *Aristotle in the West*, 154.

40. Van Steenberghen, *Aristotle in the West*, 159.

41. Van Steenberghen, *Aristotle in the West*, 162.

42. Bonaventure, *Hexaemeron*, I, 11 (V, 331a).

43. Gilson, *The Philosophy of St. Bonaventure*, 28.

44. Bonaventure, *Itin.* I, 9 (V, 298a–b).

Chapter 3

1. Augustine, *Soliloquies*, ii, 7.

2. The twelfth century's renewed interest in the natural order has been studied and well discussed. The most important study of this intellectual development is Marie-Dominique Chenu's *Nature, Man, and Society in the Twelfth Century: Essays on NewTheological Perspectives in the Latin West*, ed. and trans. Jerome Taylor and Lester Little (Chicago: University of Chicago Press, 1968); this is an edited version of *Le théologie au douzième siècle*, Études de philosophie médiévale, 45 (Paris: J. Vrin, 1957). See also Andreas Speer, "The Discovery of Nature: The Contribution of the Chartrians to Twelfth Century Attempts to Found a *Scientia Naturalis*," *Traditio* 52 (1997):135–151.

3. Plato, *Timaeus* 30d, 2–5.

4. This text came to the Latin West thanks to a translation by the Neoplatonist, Chalcidius. See J.C.M. Van Winden, OFM, *Chalcidius on Matter: His Doctrine and Sources: A Chapter in the History of Platonism*, Philosophia Antiqua, vol. 9 (Leiden: E. J. Brill, 1959).

5. William Wallace, OP, *The Modeling of Nature* (Washington, D.C.: The Catholic University of America Press, 1998), xi.

6. Grant, *God & Reason in the Middle Ages*, 149–150.

7. Grant, *God & Reason in the Middle Ages*, 15.

8. *Chartularium Universitatis Parisiensis*, I, ed. H. Denifle and A. Chatelain (Paris: Delalain, 1889), 70, no. 11.

9. *Chartularium*, 143–144, no. 87.

10. Wallace, xi.

11. For a discussion of this worldview, see Edward Grant, *Planets, Stars and Orbs: The Medieval Cosmos 1200–1684* (New York: Cambridge University Press, 1994); Edward Grant, *Science and Religion, 400 B.C.–A.D. 1550: From Aristotle to Copernicus*, Greenwood Guides to Science and Religion (Westport, CT: Greenwood Press, 2004); Edward Grant, *The Foundations of Modern Science in the Middle Ages: Their Religious, Institutional, and Intellectual Contexts*, Cambridge History of Science (New York: Cambridge University Press, 1996).

12. Bonaventure, *In II Sent.*, d. 2, p. 2, a. 1, q. 1 (II, 70–75).

13. Bonaventure, *In II Sent.*, d. 14, p. 1, a. 1, q. 1 (II, 335–338).

14. Bonaventure, *In II Sent.*, d. 14, p. 1, a. 1, q. 2 (II, 338–341).

15. Philotheus Boehner, OFM, *John of Rupella—Saint Bonaventure*, in part II of *The History of the Franciscan School* (St. Bonaventure, NY: St. Bonaventure University, 1944), 62.

16. Bonaventure, *Epistola de tribus quaestionibus*, n. 12 (VIII, 335b).

17. There has been considerable discussion in the secondary literature about whether Bonaventure regards his arguments on this matter as demonstrative. See Stephen Baldner, "St. Bonaventure on the Temporal Beginning of the World," *New Scholasticism* 63 (1989): 206–228; "St. Bonaventure and the Demonstrability of a Temporal Beginning: A Reply to Richard Davis," *American Catholic Philosophical Quarterly* 71 (1997): 225–236; Richard Davis, "Bonaventure and the Arguments for the Impossibility of an Infinite Temporal Regression," *American Catholic Philosophical Quarterly* 70 (1996): 361–380; Matthew D. Walz, "Theological and Philosophical Dependences in St. Bonaventure's Argument against an Eternal World and a Brief Thomistic Reply,"*American Catholic Philosophical Quarterly* 72 (1998): 75–98; Francis Kovach, "The Question of the Eternity of the World in St. Bonaventure and St. Thomas: A Critical Analysis," *Southwestern Journal of Philosophy* 5 (1974): 141–172; Fernand Van Steenberghen, "Saint Bonaventure contre l'éternité du monde," in *S. Bonaventura: 1224–1974* (Rome: Collegio S. Bonaventura, 1974), 259–278; Antonius Coccia, OFM Conv., "De Aeternitate Mundi apud S. Bonaventuram et Recentiores," in *S. Bonaventura: 1274–1974* (Rome: Collegio S. Bonaventura, 1974) 279–306; Bernardino Bonansea, OFM, "The Question of an Eternal World in the Teaching of St. Bonaventure," *Franciscan Studies* 34 (1974): 7–33; Stephen Brown, "The Eternity of the World Discussion in Early Oxford," in *Mensch und Natur im Mittelalter, Miscellanea Mediaevalia*, vol. 21.1 (New York: Walter de Gruyter, 1991): 259–280.

18. For the sources of these arguments and a discussion of them, see Richard Sorabji, "Infinity and the Creation," in *Philoponus and the Rejection of Aristotelian Science*, ed. Richard Sorabji (Ithaca, N.Y.: Cornell University Press, 1987), 164–178.

19. Bonaventure, *In II Sent.*, d. 1, p. 1, a. 1, q. 2, arg. 1 (II, 20b).

20. Bonaventure, *In II Sent.*, d. 1, p. 1, a. 1, q. 2, arg. 3 (II, 21a–b).

21. Philotheus Boehner, OFM, *John of Rupella — Saint Bonaventure*, 54.

22. Boehner, *John of Rupella — Saint Bonaventure*, 55.

23. Bonaventure, *In II Sent.*, d. 1, p. 1, a. 1, q. 2, 5 (II, 21b–22a).

24. Bonaventure, *Hexaemeron*, 6, 4 (V, 361a).

25. Bonaventure, *In II Sent.*, d. 1, p. 1, a. 1, q. 2, 6 (II, 22a).

26. Heraclitus: "Upon those that step into the same rivers different and different waters flow." In *The Presocratic Philosophers*, ed. G. S. Kirk, J. E. Raven, and M. Schofiled, 2d ed. (New York: Cambridge University Press, 1983), 195, fr. 214.

27. Bonaventure, *In II Sent.*, d. 3, p. 1, a. 1, q. 2 (II, 96b).

28. Bonaventure, *In II Sent.*, d. 3, p. 1, q. 2 (II, 97b).

29. Bonaventure, *In II Sent.*, d. 12, a. 1, q. 1 con (II, 294a).

30. Bonaventure, *In II Sent.*, d. 12, a. 1, q. 1 con (II, 294a).

31. Bonaventure, *In II Sent.*, d. 12, a. 1, q. 1 con. (II, 294a).

32. John F. Quinn, *The Historical Constitution of Saint Bonaventure's Philosophy* (Toronto: Pontifical Institute of Mediaeval Studies, 1973), 149.

33. Quinn, *Historical Constitution*, 318.

34. Augustine, *Confessions*, XII, 15.22.

35. Augustine, *De Genesi ad literram*, I, ch. 15, n. 29.

36. Bonaventure, *In II Sent.*, 18. 1. 3, conclusion (II, 441a–442b).

37. Bonaventure, *In II Sent.*, d. 13, a. 2, q. 2 fund. 2 (II, 319a). See also Robert Grosseteste, *De luce seu de inchoatione formarum*, where he teaches that light is the first corporeal form. He also maintains that God is pure, eternal, incorporeal light, and the angels are incorporeal lights. See also J. T. Muckle, "Robert Grosseteste's Use of Greek Sources," *Medievalia et Humanistica* 3 (1945); J. J. McEvoy, *Robert Grosseteste*, Great Medieval Thinkers (New York: Oxford University Press, 2000). See Pseudo-Dionysius: *De divinis nominibus* ch. 4, sections 1, 4, 5.

38. Pseudo-Dionysius, ch. 4, sec. 4.

39. See in particular, *De reductione*, where all human knowledge is spoken of in terms of illuminations.

40. Quinn, *Historical Constitution*, 317.

41. Gilson, *The Philosophy of St. Bonaventure*, 253. Anton Pegis also thinks Bonaventure holds to a plurality of forms: "In fact, the theory of matter and form as interpreted here has as its natural complement the doctrine of the plurality of forms and is connected also with the old Stoic doctrine of seminal reasons" (A. Pegis, *St. Thomas and the Problem of the Soul in the Thirteenth Century* [Toronto: Pontifical Institute of Medieval Studies, 1978], 39).

42. Pierre Duhem discusses Avicebron's influence on Alexander of Hales in *Le Système du monde*, vol. V (Paris: A. Hermann, 1917), 326–338; for the influence of Avicebron on Bonaventure, see vol. VI (Paris: A. Hermann, 1954), 100–105. Also see Daniel Callus, "The Origins of the Problem of the Unity of Form," *The Thomist* 24 (1961): 257–285; J. Weisheipl, "Albertus Magnus and Universal Hylomorphism: Avicebron," in F. Kovach and R. Shahan, eds., *Albert the Great* (Norman: University of Oklahoma Press, 1980), 239–260; O. Lottin, "La com-

position hylémorphique des substances spirituelles. Les débuts de la controversie," *Revue neo-scholastique de philosophie* 33 (1932): 21–41.

43. Bonaventure, *In II Sent.*, d. 17, a. 1, q. 2, ad 6 (II, 415b–16b); also see Pegis, *The Problem of the Soul*, 40.

44. Bonaventure, *In II Sent.*, d. 19, a. 2, q. 1, fund. 3 (II, 465a).

45. J. F. Quinn, *The Historical Constitution*, 277. Also see Osborne (240), who takes a similar line.

46. Bonaventure, *Itin.*, II, 2 (V, 300a).

47. Bonaventure, *Itin.*, trans. Philotheus Boehner, OFM, vol. 2 of *Works of Saint Bonaventure*, ed. Philotheus Boehner and Sr. M. Frances Laughlin, SMIC (St. Bonaventure, N.Y.: The Franciscan Institute, 1956), II, 10 (V, 302b).

48. Bonaventure, *Brevil.*, II, 9 (V, 226b).

49. Bonaventure, *Brevil.*, II, 9 (V, 226b).

50. See the study by Eduard Lutz, *Die Psychologie Bonaventuras* (Münster: Aschendorf, 1909).

51. Bonaventure, *In II Sent.*, d. 18, a. 2, q. 1, fund. 1 (II, 445a).

52. Bonaventure, *In II Sent.*, d. 18, a. 2, q. 1, fund. 1 (II, 445a).

53. Aristotle, *On the Soul (De anima)*, ed. Barnes, 2.412a17–22.

54. Aristotle, *On the Soul (De anima)*, ed. Barnes, 2.412b6–8.

55. Bonaventure, *In III Sent.*, d. 22, a. un, q. 1, resp. (III, 451a–b).

56. C. O'Leary, *The Substantial Composition of Man according to St. Bonaventure* (Washington, D.C.: The Catholic University of America Press, 1931), 70–81). Bonaventure, *Brevil.*, II, 9, 5. For Bonaventure's discussion of the body's composition from the four elements, see *In II Sent.*, d. 17, a. 2, q. 1, resp. (II, 419b).

57. Quinn, 133.

58. Thomas Osborne, Jr., "*Unibilitas*: The Key to Bonaventure's Understanding of Human Nature," *Journal of the History of Philosophy* 37 (1999): 227–251.

59. Bonaventure, *In II Sent.*, d. 1., p. 2, a. 3, q. 2, ad 2, 3 (II, 50b–51a).

60. Bonaventure, *Brevil.*, II, 9 (V, 227a).

61. T. Osborne, 235.

62. Bonaventure, *In II Sent.*, d. 8, p. 1, a. 3, q. 2 (II, 221b–222a); also, Bonaventure, *Brevil.*, II, 9, 5.

63. Bonaventure, *Brevil.*, II, 9 (V, 227b).

64. Bonaventure, *Brevil.*, V, 3 (V, 254b).

65. Bonaventure, *Brevil.*, II, 9 (V, 227b).

66. Bonaventure, *Itin.*, II, 3 (V, 300b).

67. Bonaventure, *Itin.*, II, 6 (V, 301a).

68. Bonaventure, *Itin.*, III, 2 (V, 303b).

69. Bonaventure, *Itin.*, III, 2 (V, 303b).

70. Bonaventure, *Itin.*, II, 8 (V, 301b).

71. Bonaventure, *Itin.*, II, 6 (V, 301a).

72. Bonaventure, *Itin.*, II, 6 (V, 301a).

73. Bonaventure, *In II Sent.*, d. 24, p. 1, a. 2, q. 4 (II, 569b); *In II Sent.*, d. 17, a. 1, q. 1, ad 6 (II, 412b–413a). Marrone points to Averroes as the source of the notion that the agent intellect generates knowledge of the principles of sci-

ence (Marrone, 1:174). Marrone points out that Bernard Rosenmöller, in *Religiöse Erkenntnis nach Bonaventura*, 29, argues that Bonaventure held that God is the agent intellect. Luyckx in *Die Erkenntnislehre Bonaventuras*, 66–72, argues that God functions like a second agent intellect in human knowing (Marrone, 1:179, n. 98).

74. Bonaventure, *In II Sent.*, d. 24, p. 1, q. 4 ad 5–6 (II, 570b).
75. Gendreau, 167.
76. Gendreau, 167.
77. Bonaventure, *In II Sent.*, d. 39, a. 1., q. 2 (II, 903a) (Marrone, 1:153, n. 4).
78. Bonaventure, *In II Sent.*, d. 39, a. 1., q. 2 (II, 904b).
79. Bonaventure, *In II Sent.*, d. 18, a. 2, q. 1 resp. (II, 446a).
80. Bonaventure, *In II Sent.*, d. 18, a. 2, q. 1 resp. (II, 446b).
81. Kent, 99.
82. Bonaventure, *In II Sent.*, d. 25, p. 1, a. 1, q. 6 (II, 605b).
83. Augustine, quoted in Bonaventure, *Brevil.*, II, 9 (V, 227b).
84. Bonaventure, *Itin.*, III, 4 (V, 305a).
85. Bonaventure, *Hexaemeron*, 22, 24 (V, 441a). Cf. James McEvoy, "Microcosm and Macrocosm in the Writings of St. Bonaventure," in *S. Bonaventura 1274–1974*, 2:309–343.
86. McEvoy, "Microcosm and Macrocosm in the Writings of St. Bonaventure," 2:309–343.

Chapter 4

1. Bonaventure, *Hexaem.*, 1, 17 (V, 332b): "Hoc est medium metaphysicum reducens, et haec est tota nostra metaphysica: de emanatione, de exemplaritate, de consummatione, scilicet illuminari per radios spirituales et reduci ad summum. Et sic eris verus metaphysicus."
2. Bonaventure, *Hexaem.*, 3, 5 (V, 344a).
3. Editors, introitus to *Magistri Alexandri de Hales Glossa in quattuor libros sententiarum Petri Lombardi*, Bibliotheca Franciscana Scholastica Medii Aevi, vol. 12 (Quaracchi [Florentia]: Collegium S. Bonaventura, 1951) I:4, n. 8.
4. Bonaventure, *In I Sent.*, d. 28, dub. 1 (I, 504), quoted in Philotheus Boehner, OFM, *John of Rupella—Saint Bonaventure*, part II of *The History of the Franciscan School* (St. Bonaventure, NY: St. Bonaventure University, 1944), 102.
5. Aertsen, 163.
6. Bonaventure, *Itin.*, III, 3 (V, 304a).
7. Bonaventure, *Itin.* V, 2 (V, 308b).
8. Bonaventure, *Itin.*, III, 3 (V, 304a).
9. Cf. Thomas Aquinas, *Commentary on Boethius's De trinitate*, 1, 3; also Aertsen, 164ff.
10. Bonaventure, *Itin.*, V, 2 (V, 308b).
11. Thomas Aquinas, *Summa theologiae*, I–II, q. 44, art. 4, ad 1. Cf. *De veritate*, 21.4, ad 4.

12. Efrem Bettoni, *Saint Bonaventure*, trans. Angelus Gambatese, OFM (Westport, Conn.: Greenwood Press, 1981; originally published, Notre Dame, Ind.: University of Notre Dame, 1964), 103.

13. Carol Harrison, *Augustine: Christian Truth and Fractured Humanity*, Christian Theology in Context (New York: Oxford University Press, 2000), 91, n. 21.

14. Bonaventure, *Disputed Questions on the Mystery of the Trinity* (M. Trin.), trans. Zachary Hayes, OFM, vol. 3 of *Works of Saint Bonaventure*, ed. George Marcil, OFM (St. Bonaventure, N.Y.: The Franciscan Institute, 1979), q. 1, a. 1, 28 (V, 48a).

15. Bonaventure, *M. Trin.*, q. 1, a. 1 con. (V, 49a).

16. Bonaventure, *M Trin.*, q. 1, a. 1 con. (V, 49a).

17. Bonaventure, *M Trin.*, q. 1, a. 1 con. (V, 49b).

18. Bonaventure, *M. Trin*, q. 1, a. 1 con. (V, 49b).

19. Bermardino M. Bonasea, OFM, *God and Atheism: A Philosophical Approach to the Existence of God* (Washington, D.C.: The Catholic University of America Press, 1979), 71–106.

20. Bonaventure, *M. Trin.*, q. 1, a. 1, n. 3 (V, 45b).

21. Bonaventure, *M. Trin.*, q. 1, a. 1, n. 6 (V, 46a).

22. Bonaventure, *M Trin.*, q. 1, a. 1, n. 10 (V, 46b). Cf. Bonaventure, *Brevil.*, I, 2, 5 (V, 211a): "The proof of God's existence is founded not only upon the authority of the divine book, but also upon the entire natural universe around us to which we ourselves belong and which proclaims a transcendent Creator."

23. Bonaventure, *M. Trin.*, q. 1, a. 1, n. 13 (V, 46b).

24. Bonaventure, *M Trin.*, q. 1, a. 1, n. 20 (V, 47a).

25. Bonaventure, *M. Trin.*, q. 1, a. 1, n. 26 (V, 47b).

26. Bonaventure, *In I Sent.*, 8, 1, 2 con (I, 154–155).

27. Bonaventure, *M. Trin.*, q. 1, a. 1, n. 22 (V, 47b).

28. Bonaventure, *M. Trin.*, q. 1, a. 1, ad 6 (V, 50b).

29. Philip L. Reynolds, "Analogy of Names in Bonaventure," *Medieval Studies* 65 (2003): 117–162.

30. Bonaventure, *In I Sent.*, d. 1, dub 5 (I, 43); *In I Sent.*, d. 14, a. 1, q. 2 resp. (I, 248a); *II Sent.*, d. 25, p. 2, dub. 3 (2:626b); *In II Sent.*, d. 35, dub. 3, resp. (II, 837b); *In IV Sent.*, d. 24, p. 1, a. 2, q. 4, ad 2 (IV, 619b), cited in Philip L. Reynolds, "Bonaventure's Theory of Resemblance," *Traditio* 49 (2003): 226, n. 30.

31. Aristotle, *Categories* 1a1–12, cited in Reynolds, "Bonaventure's Theory of Resemblance," 226.

32. Reynolds, "Analogy of Names in Bonaventure," *Medieval Studies* 65 (2003): 119.

33. Bonaventure, *In I Sent.*, d. 1, a. 3, q. 1 ad 1 (I, 38b–39a), cited in Reynolds, "Analogy of Names in Bonaventure," *Medieval Studies* 65 (2003): 119.

34. Bonaventure, *M. Trin.*, q. 4, a. 1 con. (V, 81a).

35. Bonaventure, *M. Trin.*, q. 5, a. 1 con. (V, 89b–90a).

36. Bonaventure, *Brevil.*, I, 2 (V, 271b).

37. Anselm, *Cur Deus Homo*, I, 20; *De fide Trinitatis* 5; cf. Bonaventure, *In I Sent.*, d. 42 and 43.

38. Bonaventure, *Brevil.*, I, 7 (V, 216a).

39. Bonaventure, *Brevil.*, I, 8 (V, 217a).

40. Bonaventure, *Brevil.*, I, 8 (V, 217a).

41. Bonaventure, *Brevil.*, I, 9 (V, 218a).

42. Bonaventure, *Brevil.*, I, 9 (V, 218a).

43. Bonaventure, *In I Sent.*, d. 8, p. 1, a. 2, q. 2 ad 7–8 (I, 161a–b).

44. Bonaventure, *In I Sent.*, d. 37, p. 1, a. 1, q. 1 con. (I, 639a).

45. Bonaventure, *Brevil.*, V, 1, 3.

46. Bonaventure, *Brevil.*, V, 1, 3.

47. Bonaventure, *In I Sent.*, d. 37, p. 1, a. 1, q. 1 con. (I, 639a).

48. Bonaventure, *In I Sent.*, d. 37, p. 1, a. 1, q. 1 con. (I, 639a).

49. Bonaventure, *Brevil.*, I, 9 (V, 218a–b).

50. Bonaventure, *Brevil.*, I, 9 (V, 217b).

51. Augustine, *De Trinitate* III, 4, 9, quoted in *Brevil.*, I, 9 (V, 217b). This divine will is manifested through five different types of signs: commands, prohibitions, counsels, fulfillment, and sufferance.

52. Bonaventure is very clear that things have a twofold existence—in themselves and in the divine mind as exemplars: "To the third point which was objected, that from eternity there was only one being, it should be said that there is a twofold being of the thing, namely, in itself and in its cause, i.e., in its proper genus and in its exemplar. And its existence in its cause (or in its exemplar) suffices for the cognition of the thing; and because it is represented through the exemplar as it will be in its proper genus, therefore it is known as it will be completely by its existence in the exemplar" (Bonaventure, *In I Sent.*, d. 39, a. 1, q. 1 ad 3 [I, 686b]).

53. Bonaventure, "Christ the One Teacher of All," in *What Manner of Man: Sermons on Christ by St. Bonaventure*, trans. Zachary Hayes, OFM (Chicago: Franciscan Herald Press, 1989), n. 18 (V, 572a).

54. Bonaventure, *Disputed Questions on the Knowledge of Christ*, trans. Zachary Hayes, OFM, vol. 4, *Works of Saint Bonaventure*, ed. George Marcil, OFM (Saint Bonaventure, N.Y.: The Franciscan Institute, 1992), q. 2 (V, 6).

55. Bonaventure, *Sc. Chr.*, 2 con. (V, 8b).

56. Bonaventure, *Sc. Chr.*, 2 con. (V, 9a).

57. Likenesses (*Similitudines*): One being resembles another: (1) a likeness of imitation, for example, creature of Creator } expressing, and (2) an exemplary likeness, for example, Idea of creature } expressive.

58. "Such a likeness is received from outside and therefore involves a sort of composition or addition in the knowing intellect" (Bonaventure, *Sc. Chr.*, 2 con. (V, 9a).

59. Two Ways of Knowing: (1) Knowledge that causes things to be: requires an exemplary likeness; and (2) Knowledge that is caused by things: requires likeness of imitation.

60. Bonaventure, *Sc. Chr.*, 2 con. (V, 9a).

61. Bonaventure, *Sc. Chr.*, 2 ad 5 (V, 9b).

62. Bonaventure, *Sc. Chr.*, 2 ad 6 (V, 9b).

63. Bonaventure, *Sc. Chr.*, 2 ad 7 (V, 9b).

64. Truth Understood in Two Ways: (1) Identical with the entity of a being: remote principle of knowledge, (2) the expressive light in intellectual knowledge: proximate and immediate principle of knowledge.

65. Bonaventure, *Sc. Chr.*, 2 ad 9 (V, 10a).

66. Bonaventure, *Christus mag.*, nn. 8–10.

67. Also see, Bonaventure, *Hexaem.*, 6.6 (V, 361b).

68. Bonaventure, *Hexaem.*, 3.4 (V, 344b).

69. Tavard, 25, 583; Klaus Hemmerle, *Theologie als Nachfolge: Bonaventura, ein Weg für heute* (Freiburg im Breisgau: Herder, 1975).

70. Bonaventure, *In I Sent.*, d. 27, p. 2, a. 1, q. 1c (I, 482b): "Loqui ad se nihil aliud est quam aliquid mente concipere. Mens autem concipit intelligendo, et intelligendo aliud concipit simile alii, intelligendo se concipit simile sibi, quia intelligentia assimilatur intellecto. Mens igitur dicendo se apud se concipit per omnia simile sibi; et hoc est verbum conceptum."

71. Bonaventure, *In I Sent.*, d. 27, p. 2, a. 1, q. 1 conclusio (I, 482b): "Alio modo dicere ad alterum est conceptum mentis exprimere; et huic dicere respondet verbum prolatum." Trans., "In another way to speak to another is to express a concept of the mind; and to this speaking corresponds a spoken word."

72. Bonaventure, *Hexaem.*, I, 1 (V, 331b).

73. Bonaventure, *Hexaem.*, 6, 2–4 (V, 360b–361a).

74. Bonaventure, *Hexaem.*, 3, n. 8 (V, 344b): "Omnis creatura mendacium est." Trans., "Every creature is a lie."

75. This is why Bonaventure entitles one of his major works *Itinerarium*.

76. Marrone, 1:112.

77. Marrone, 1:111.

78. Brady, "Illumination," 32.

79. Marrone, 1:114.

80. Brady, "Illumination," 34.

81. Brady, "Illumination," 27. Among these Capuchins, there was Bartholomaeus de Barberis, *Flores et Fructus Philosophici ex Seraphico Paradiso excerpti seu Cursus Philosophici ad Mentem Sancti Bonaventurae Seraphici Doctoris*, Lyons, 1677.

82. Bonaventure, *De donis*, 8, 12 (5, 496a). For a discussion of the importance of the light of sensible things, see John White, *Fides Quaerens Intellectum*, 2001.

83. Two works are considered classic to Bonaventurean illuminationism: Ignatius Brady calls these "the *loci classici* of Bonaventure's theory of illumination" (Brady, OFM, "St. Bonaventure's Doctrine of Illumination," 61, 76).

84. Brady, OFM, "St. Bonaventure's Doctrine of Illumination," 27.

85. Luyckx.

86. Scholars such as Schwendinger and Gilson have advanced this theory. According to Gendreau, Father Schwendinger "holds that in the domain of sense perception and of simple apprehension as well as of definition, the role of the

immediate contact and direct influence of the eternal ideas do not enter into play (175). See also F. Schwendinger, "Die Erkenntnis in den ewigen Ideen nach der Lehre des hl. Bonaventura," *Franziskanische Studien* 15 (1928): 69–95, 193–244; 16 (1929): 29–64.

87. A. Fonck, "Ontologisme," in *Dictionnaire de Théologie Catholique*, XI (Paris: Letouzey et Ané, 1931), 1002f, 1008f.

88. Vicenzo Gioberti, *Introduzione allo studio della filosofia*, 2 vols. (Milan: Fratelli Bocca, 1849), I: 140 (in French translation of first edition [Paris: 1847], 137).

89. G. C. Ubaghs, *De mente S. Bonaventurae circa modum quo Deus ab homine cognoscitur* (Louvain: Typographie de Vanlinthout, 1859); also *Essai d'idéologie ontologique* (Louvain: Typographie de Vanlinthout, 1860).

90. G. Ortoleva, *L'Ontologismo e la Questione già inedita del serafico Dottore San Bonaventura su la cognizione certitudinale della verità* (Acireale: V. Strano, 1876).

91. Bonaventure, *S. Bonaventurae opera omnia* (Quaracchi: Ex typographia Collegii S. Bonaventurae, 1890), V: 313–316.

92. Bernard Gendreau, "The Quest for Certainty in Bonaventure," *Franciscan Studies* 21 (1961): 150, 170.

93. Gendreau, 174.

94. Marrone, 1.

95. Bonaventure, *Itin.*, II, 9 (V, 302a); Augustine, *De libero arbitrio*, 2.14.38.

96. Bonaventure, *Itin.*, II, 9 (V, 302a).

97. Bonaventure, *Sc. Chr.*, 4 con. (V, 23b).

98. Bonaventure, *Sc. Chr.*, 4 con. (V, 23a).

99. Bonaventure, *Sc. Chr.*, 4 con. (V, 23b).

100. Bonaventure, *Sc. Chr.*, 4 con. (V, 23b).

101. Bonaventure, *Sc. Chr.*, 4 con. (V, 23b).

102. Bonaventure, *Sc. Chr.*, 4 con. (V, 23b).

103. Bonaventure, *Sc. Chr.*, 4 con. (V, 24a).

104. Marrone, 1:129.

105. Bonaventure, *Itin.*, 2, n. 6, cited in Marrone, 1:129.

106. Bonaventure, *Sc. Chr.*, 4 ad 21 (V, 26a).

107. Augustine, *The Trinity*, trans. Edmund Hill, OP. The Works of Saint Augustine, vol. 5 (Brooklyn, N.Y.: New City Press, 1991) XIV, 21.

108. Bonaventure, *Sc. Chr.*, 4 ad 23–26 (V, 26b): "Quia omnis creatura incipit a non-esse et est vertibilis in non-esse." Trans., "Because every creature comes from non-being and can return to non-being."

109. Bonaventure, *Sc. Chr.*, 4 ad 23–26 (V, 26b).

110. Bonaventure, *Sc. Chr.*, 4 ad 23–26 (V, 27b).

111. Augustine, *De libero arbitrio* 2.82.

112. Augustine, *De libero arbitrio* 12.136: "Therefore, if truth is neither inferior nor equal to our minds, it follows that it is superior to them and more excellent."

113. "Before St. Thomas Aquinas the agreement was almost unanimous for maintaining the Augustinian doctrine of illumination; after St. Thomas Aquinas, this agreement ceased to exist, at which point the Franciscan doctor, John Duns Scotus, himself abandoned the Augustinian tradition on the essential point of

which his order had remained the most faithful supporter until then" (Étienne Gilson, "Pourquoi saint Thomas a critiqué saint Augustin." *Archives d'histoire doctrinale et littéraire* 1 [1926–1927]: 5).

114. Bonaventure, "*Christus mag.*"

115. Bonaventure, *Hexaemeron*, 4.1 (V, 349a): "This light never fails. Indeed, it shines so powerfully upon the soul that this soul cannot possibly believe it to be non-existing, or abstain from expressing it, without an inner contradiction. For if truth does not exist, it is true that truth does not exist: and so something is true. And if something is true, it is true that truth exists. Hence if truth does not exist, truth exists."

116. Gilson, *The Philosophy of St. Bonaventure*, 363.

117. Bonaventure, "*Christus mag.*," n. 16. Also see, Marrone, 1:137–140.

118. Bonaventure, "*Christus mag.*," n. 18.

119. Bonaventure, *Itin.*, 1.4 (V, 297a–b).

120. Bonaventure, *Brevil.*, II, 1 (V, 219b).

121. Bonaventure, *In I Sent.*, d. 24, a. 1, q. 1 con. (I, 421b).

122. Bonaventure, *Brevil.*, I, 6 (V, 215a).

123. Aertsen, *Medieval Philosophy and the Transcendentals: The Case of Thomas Aquinas*.

124. Bonaventure, *Itin.*, 6.1 (V, 310b).

125. Adrian Pattin, OMI, ed., "Le *Liber de causis* Édition établie à l'aide de 90 manuscrits avec introduction et notes," *Tijdschrift voor Filosofie* 28 (1966): 90–203.

126. Bonaventure, *In I Sent.*, d. 27, p. 1, a. 1, q. 2 ad 3 (I, 471a). It is important to note that Bonaventure and his contemporaries thought the *Liber de causis* to be by Aristotle. Aquinas was the first to realize the mistake of this attribution.

Chapter 5

1. Bonaventure, *In IV Sent.*, d. 49, p. 1, a. 1, q. 2 (IV, 1003b).

2. Aristotle, *Nicomachean Ethics*, 1101a, 1177a.

3. Bonaventure, *Brevil.*, II, 9 (V, 227a).

4. Bonaventure, *Brevil.*, II, 9 (V, 227a).

5. Bonaventure, M. *Trin.*, q. 1, a.1 fa 3, 7 [V, 45, 46]; Boethius *De consolatione* 3, pr. 2 [PL 63, 724]; Augustine, *De Trinitate* 4. 7 [PL 42, 1018–1019]; 20.25 [PL 42, 1034].

6. Bonaventure, *Brevil.*, 5, 8, 4 (V, 262a). Cf. Augustine, *Confessions* 13, 9, 10: "Pondus meum, amor meus." Trans., "My love is my weight (destiny)."

7. Bonaventure, *De reductione*, n. 24 (V, 325a).

8. Bonaventure, *De reductione*, n. 25 (V, 325b).

9. Bonaventure, *In II Sent.*, d. 25, p. 1, a. 1, q. 3 (II, 598).

10. There are four conditions for the will to achieve rectitude: two with regard to the object intended, and two with regard to the end. It must be a good in itself and a good in its being an object of choice; the act which is directed to this end

is objectively good in itself in its aptitude to be ordered to the end intended; and the will actually wills the end and makes it its own (Bonaventure, *In II Sent.*, d. 38, a. 1, q. 1 conc [II, 882]).

11. Bonaventure, *Sc. Ch*, 7, nn. 5–12 (V, 37b–38a).

12. Bonaventure, *In III Sent.*, d. 33, a. 1, q. 5 con. (III, 723a–b).

13. Bonaventure, *Perf. Ev.*, q. 1, a. 1 (V, 120b).

14. Aristotle, *De caelo et mundo*, Bk. 1, c. 11, quoted in Bonaventure, *In II Sent.*, d. 27, dub. 3 resp.

15. Aristotle, *Physics*, ch. 3, quoted in Bonaventure, *In II Sent.*, d. 27, dub. 3 resp.

16. Aristotle, *Nicomachean Ethics*, II, 6, quoted in Bonaventure, *In II Sent.*, d. 27, dub. 3 resp. (II, 671).

17. Aristotle, *Nicomachean Ethics*, II, 6, quoted in Bonaventure, *In II Sent.*, d. 27, dub. 3 resp. (II, 671):

18. Bonaventure, *Hexaemeron*, VI, 12 (V, 362b).

19. Cicero, *De rhetorica*, II, 54; Augustine, *De spiritu et anima*, 4 (PL 40, 782); Augustine *De quantitate animae*, ch. 16, n. 27 (PL 32, 1050), quoted in Bonaventure, *In II Sent.*, d. 27, dub. 3 resp.

20. "Virtus est bonus usus voluntatis." Trans., "Virtue is good use of the will," Bonaventure, *In II Sent.*, d. 27, dub. 2, (II, 672a).

21. Bonaventure, *In III Sent.*, d. 33, a. 1, q. 2 ad 5 (III, 715b).

22. Bonaventure, *In III Sent.*, d. 33, a. 1, q. 5 resp. (III, 722b).

23. Augustine, *Soliloquies*, I, ch. 6, n. 13 (PL 32, 876), quoted in Bonaventure, *In II Sent.*, d. 27, dub. 3 resp. (II, 672b).

24. Augustine, *The City of God*, XIV, ch. 6 (PL 41, 409ff.), quoted in Bonaventure, *In II Sent.*, d. 27, dub. 3 resp. (II, 672b).

25. Augustine, *De moribus ecclesiae*, I, ch. 15, n. 25 (PL 32, 1322), quoted in Bonaventure, *In II Sent.*, d. 27, dub. 3, resp. (II, 672b).

26. Augustine, *De magistro*, quoted in Bonaventure, *In II Sent.*, d. 27, dub. 3 (II, 672a).

27. Bonaventure, *Hexaemeron*, coll. 7, nn. 5–12 (V, 366a–367a).

28. Bonaventure, *In III Sent.*, d. 33, a. 1, q. 1 resp. (III, 712a).

29. Bonaventure, *In III Sent.*, d. 33, a. 1, q. 1 ad 3 (III, 712b).

30. Bonaventure, *In III Sent.*, d. 33, dub. 5 (III, 730a).

31. Bonaventure, *In III Sent.*, d. 33, a. 1, q. 3 resp. (III, 717a).

32. Bonaventure, *In III Sent.*, d. 33, a. 1, q. 3 ad 4 (III, 718a–b).

33. Bonaventure, *In III Sent.*, d. 33, a. 1, q. 3 resp. (III, 717a–b).

34. "Since moral philosophy is concerned principally with rectitude, it treats of general justice which St. Anselm calls 'the rectitude of the will' " (Bonaventure, *De reductione*, n. 23 [V, 325a]).

35. Also, see Bonaventure, *In III Sent.*, d. 33, dub. 1 (III, 728a–b).

36. Bonaventure, *Decem praec.*, coll. 1, n. 21 (V, 510a).

37. Cicero, *De rhetorica*, II, 54, quoted in Bonaventure, *Hexaem.*, c.VI, n. 15 (V, 363a).

38. Bonaventure, *Hexaem.*, c.V, n. 3 (V, 354b).
39. Bonaventure, *Hexaem.*, c.V, n. 4 (V, 354b).
40. Bonaventure, *Hexaem.*, c.V, n. 4 (V, 354b).
41. Bonaventure, *Hexaem.*, c.V, n. 4 (V, 354b).
42. Bonaventure, *Hexaem.*, c.V, n. 8 (V, 355a–b).
43. Bonaventure, *Hexaem.*, c.VI, n. 18 (V, 363a).
44. Bonaventure, *Hexaem.*, c.VI, n. 29 (V, 364a–b).
45. Bonaventure, *Hexaem.*, c.VI, n. 12 (V, 362b).
46. Bonaventure, *Hexaem.*, c.VI, n. 12 (V, 362b).
47. Bonaventure, *De donis*, coll. IV, n. 10 (V, 475b).
48. Bonaventure, *Hexaem.*, V, n. 12 (V, 356a).
49. Bonaventure, *Hexaem.*, V, n. 12 (V, 356a).
50. René Gauthier, "Trois commentaires 'averroistes' sur l'*Éthique à Nicomaque*," *Archives d'histoire doctrinale et littéraire du Moyen age* 16 (1947–1948): 187–346.
51. Franciscan scholar Patrice Robert thought that there were significant problems with the Quaracchi edition; John Quinn thought that the Delorme edition was closer to Bonaventure's thought. See Patrice Robert, "Le problème de la philosophique bonaventureienne: Discipline autonome ou heteronome?" *Laval théologique et philosophique* 7 (1951): 36–43.
52. Kent, 49.
53. Harrison, 92.
54. Aristotle, *Topic*, II, 3.110a23–111a7.
55. Bonaventure, *Hexaem.*, V, 9 (V, 355b).
56. Bonaventure, *In II Sent.*, d. 34, a. 2, q. 3, con. et ad 2 (II, 815a–b).
57. Augustine, *De libero arbitrio*, I (PL 32, 1229).
58. Bonaventure, *In IV Sent.*, d. 33, a. 1, q. 1 con. (IV, 748).
59. Bonaventure, *In II Sent.*, d. 39, a. 1, q. 2 (II, 901a).
60. Bonaventure, *De perf. ev.*, q. 4, a. 1, con. (V, 181), quoted in Matthew M. De Benedictis, OFM, *The Social Thought of Saint Bonaventure: A Study in Social Philosophy* (Washington, D.C.: The Catholic University of America Press, 1946), 92.
61. Bonaventure, *Comm. Lc.*, ch. 19, no. 34 (VII, 484), quoted in De Benedictis, 93.
62. Bonaventure, *In II Sent.*, d. 39, a. 1, q. 1 con. (II, 899b).
63. Bonaventure, *In II Sent.*, d. 39, a. 2, q. 1 ad 4 (II, 911a–b).
64. Quinn, "The Moral Philosophy of St. Bonaventure," *Southwestern Journal of Philosophy* 5 (1974): 51.
65. Bonaventure, *In IV Sent.*, d. 50, p. 2, a. 2, q. 2, ad 4 (IV, 1052b).
66. Bonaventure, *Comm. Eccl.*, Prooemium, q. 1 resp. (VI, 6b): "Amor castus est quo diligit anulum in memoriam sponsie propter amorem sponsi; adulterius quo diligit anulum plus quam sponsum."
67. It is this proper contempt that Bonaventure claims is the concern of the book of Ecclesiastes.

68. Bonaventure, *Comm. Eccl.*, Prooemium, q. 2 (VI, 7a).

69. Bonaventure, *Comm. Eccl.*, Prooemium, q. 2 (VI, 7a): "Alio modo dicitur verum secundum quod addit supra esse impermixtionem ad non-esse; quod nullo modo habet potentiam ad illud; et sic dicitur habere verum esse, quod habet esse immutabile; et hoc modo vanum oppositum vero est illud quod est mutabile et transmutabile. Et sic omnis creatura vana est, quia subiecta vanitati, id est mutabilitati."

70. J.-G. Bougerol, s.v., "Vanitas," *Lexique Saint Bonaventure*, Bibliothèque Bonaventurienne (Paris: Éditions Franciscaines, 1969), 131.

71. Bonaventure, *Comm. Eccl.*, Prooemium, q. 2 (VI, 7b).

72. Bonaventure, *Comm. Eccl.*, c. 1, p. 1, a. 1 (VI, 11b).

73. Bonaventure, *Comm. Eccl.*, (VI, 16b). Cf. Hugh of St. Victor, *In Salomanis Ecclesiasten Homiliae XIX*, Hom. 2, p. 142, quoted in notes by the Quarrachi editors: "The creation of God is his word through which he speaks to us and our eyes are as instruments through which, by contemplation, are perceived the words of God. For just as the ear is an instrument for perceiving the word of a man, so the eye is an instrument for perceiving this word."

74. Bonaventure, *Sermones de tempore: Feria sexta in parasceve*, serm 1 (IX, 262a), quoted in De Benedictis, 102.

75. Bonaventure, *Sermones de sanctis: de S. patre nostro Francisco*, serm. 5 (IX, 594b), quoted in De Benedictis, 102.

76. Bonaventure, *In I Sent.*, I, 650.

77. Bonaventure (IX, 724).

78. Bonaventure, *Apol. paup.*, xii, n. 14 (VIII, 321a); *De perf. evan.*, q. 2, a. 3, f. 12 (V, 159b).

79. For the development of this view, see Georges Duby, *The Three Orders: Feudal Society Imagined*, trans. Arthur Goldhammer (Chicago: University of Chicago Press, 1980).

80. Bonaventure, *Hexaem.*, VI, 28 (V, 364a).

81. Bonaventure, *M. Trin.*, q. 11, a. 2 ad 1 (V, 57a).

Chapter 6

1. Bonaventure, *Brevil.*, prologue, n. 1 (V, 201a): "Sacred Scripture which is called theology" ("Sacra Sciptura quae theologia dicitur"). See also, Bonaventure, *In I Sent.*, Prooem. (I, 6–13); *In II* Sent. d. 3, a. 1, q. 2 con. (II, 97); Bougerol, *Lexique Saint Bonaventure*, 127: "With the great medieval scholastics, Saint Bonaventure identifies theology and sacred scripture. This identification, however, is not total but partial. For the two disiciplines are distinguished by their formal object: both have the same material object: the *credibile*."

2. "Theologia quae sacra Scriptura dicitur" (Thomas Aquinas, *In Boet. De Trinitate*, q. 5, a. 4), quoted in Henri de Lubac, *Medieval Exegesis: The Four Senses of Scripture*, trans. Mark Sebanc, *Retrieval & Renewal: Ressourcement in Catholic Thought* (Grand Rapids, Mich.: William B. Eerdmans Pub. Co., 1998), 1:27. Orig-

inally published as *Exégèse médiévale: Les quatre sens de l'écriture* (Paris: Éditions Montaigne, 1959).

3. Ratzinger, *Theology of History*, 57–94; see also Ratzinger, *Milestones: Memoirs 1927–1977*, trans. Erasmo Leiva-Merikakis (San Francisco: Ignatius Press, 1998), 108–109.

4. Ratzinger, *Theology of History*, 57–58.

5. Ratzinger, *Theology of History*, 58.

6. Ratzinger, 67–68.

7. Bonaventure, *Brevil.*, prologue, 1.1 (V, 202b).

8. Bonaventure, *Brevil.*, prologue, n. 3 (V, 201b).

9. Bonaventure, *Brevil.*, prologue, 2.4 (V, 204b).

10. Bonaventure, *Brevil.*, prologue, n. 2 (V, 201a).

11. Bonaventure, *De anunc.*, s. 4 (IX, 671), quoted in De Lubac, 2:198.

12. Bonaventure, *Brevil.*, prologue, 4.4.

13. Bonaventure, *Brevil.*, prologue, 5.2.

14. Bonaventure, *M. Trin.*, q. 1, a. 2 con. (V, 54b).

15. Richard of St. Victor, Book Three of the Trinity in *Richard of St. Victor: Selections*, trans. Grover Zinn, *Classics of Western Spirituality* (New York: Paulist Press, 1979), 317.

16. Augustine, *De Trinitate*, 8.8.12; also, 5, 11–12.

17. Bonaventure, *Itin.*, 5.2 (V, 308b).

18. Bonaventure, *Itin.*, 6.1 (V, 310b).

19. Bonaventure, *In I Sent.*, d. 3, p. 1., q. 4 (I, 75–77).

20. Bonaventure, *M. Trin.*, q. 1, a. 2 con. (V, 55a).

21. Théodore de Régnon, SJ, *Études de théologie positive sur la sainte Trinité*, 3 vols. (Paris: Victor Retaux et Fils, 1892–1898).

22. In the early twentieth century, a study by A. Stohr accepted the main points of De Regnon's study: A. Stohr, *Die Trinitätslehre des hl. Bonaventura: Eine systematische Darstellung und historiche Würdigung* (Münster: Aschendorf, 1923).

23. O. Gonzalez, *Mistério Trinitário y existencia humana: estudio histórico teológico en torno a san Buenaventura* (Madrid: Ediciones Rialp, 1966).

24. Leonard Hodgson, *The Doctrine of the Trinity* (New York: Charles Scribner's Sons, 1944).

25. "Richard is a pure Latin, an Augustinian, whose theology has emerged at root from his fascination with Augustinian, and who, if not exclusively, is fundamentally an Augustinian" (Gonzalez, 337–338, quoted in Hayes, 19, n. 26).

26. Anselm, *Monologion*, 9.

27. Bonaventure, *Itin.*, 6. 2 (V, 310b): "in which the diffusing good communicates to another his whole substance and nature."

28. Bonaventure, *Itin.*, 6.2 (V, 310b): "For the diffusion that occurred in time in the creation of the world is no more than a pivot or point in comparison with the immense sweep of the eternal goodness."

29. Bonaventure, *Brevil.*, I, 2 (V, 211a).

30. Bonaventure, *Brevil.*, I, 3 (V, 212a).

31. Bonaventure, *In I Sent.*, Prooemium.
32. Bonaventure, *Brevil.*, I, 4 (V, 212b).
33. Bonaventure, *Brevil.*, I, 6 (V, 215a).
34. Bonaventure, *Brevil.*, I,6 (V, 215a).
35. Augustine *De doctrina christiana*, I, 5, 5, quoted in Bonaventure, *Brevil.*, I, 6 (V, 215a).

Chapter 7

1. For a discussion of Francis's relation to the world of nature, see Walter Nigg, *Great Saints*, trans. William Stirling (Hinsdale, Ill.: H. Regnery Co., 1948); also, Edward A. Armstrong, *Saint Francis: Nature Mystic: The Derivation and Significance of the Nature Stories in the Franciscan Legend*, Hermeneutics: Studies in the History of Religion, ed. Kees W. Bolle (Berkeley: University of California Press, 1973); Roger D. Sorrell, *St. Francis of Assisi and Nature: Tradition and Innovation in Western Christian Attitudes toward the Environment* (New York: Oxford University Press, 1988).
2. Thomas of Celano, *The Remembrance of the Desire of a Soul*, in *The Founder*, vol. 2 of *Francis of Assisi: The Early Documents*, ed. Regis J. Armstrong, OFM Cap. et al. (New York: New City Press, 2000), Bk. 2, ch. 124, p. 353.
3. Augustine, *De Trinitate*.
4. Bonaventure, *Brevil.*, III, 11 (V, 24a).
5. Bonaventure, *M. Trin.*, q. 1, a. 2 con.
6. Bonaventure, *Brevil.*, II, 1 (V, 219a).
7. Bonaventure, *Brevil.*, II, 1 (V, 219b).
8. Bonaventure, *Brevil.*, II, 2 (V, 220a).
9. Bonaventure, *Brevil.*, II, 7 (V, 225a).
10. Pseudo-Dionysius, *De caelesti hierarchia*, VI, VII.
11. St. Gregory, *Hom 34, In evan.*
12. Bonaventure, *Itin.*, II, 2 (V, 300a).
13. G. R. Evans, *Philosophy and Theology in the Middle Ages* (New York, Routledge, 1993), 94.
14. Bonaventure, *In II Sent.*, d. 18, a. 2, q. 3 (II).
15. Bonaventure, *In II Sent.*, d. 17, a. 1, q. 3, resp.
16. Bonaventure, *Brevil*, II, 9 (V, 227a).
17. Bonaventure, *In II Sent.*, d. 18, a. 2, q. 3, fund. 2.
18. Bonaventure, *M. Trin.*, q. 1, a. 2 ad 1 (V, 57a).
19. Bonaventure, *Brevil.*, II, 11 (V, 229a).

Chapter 8

1. Bonaventure, *Brevil.*, III, 1 (V, 231a).
2. No human being is exempt from this struggle save the Virgin Mary, whom Bonaventure singles out as one who receives "an extraordinary grace" by which concupiscence is extinguished, for it is fitting that she be pure to bear the Word

of God. "She received a privilege that radically frees her from concupiscence, so that her conception of the Son of God would be all-pure and perfect" (Bonaventure, *Brevil.*, III, 7 [V, 236b]). Bonaventure quotes Anselm to support this view (Anselm, *De conceptu virginali et originali peccato*, 18, quoted in *Breviloquium*, III, 7, 5 [V, 236b]).

3. Bonaventure, *Brevil.*, III, 1 (V, 232a).
4. Bonaventure, *Brevil.*, III, 1 (V, 231b).
5. Bonaventure, *Brevil.*, II, 11 (V, 229b).
6. Bonaventure, *Brevil.*, III, 3 (V, 232b).
7. Bonaventure, *Brevil.*, III, 3 (V, 233a).
8. Bonaventure, *Brevil.*, III, 4 (V, 233b).
9. Bonaventure, *Brevil.*, III, 4 (V, 234a).
10. Bonaventure, *In III Sent.*, d. 33, a. 1, q. 4 resp. (III, 720a); also see *Hex.*, 14, 8 (V, 394b); *II Sent.*, d. 22, dub. 2 (II, 528a).
11. Bonaventure, *Brevil.*, III, 6 (V, 235a).
12. Bonaventure, *Brevil.*, III, 6 (V, 235b). Bonaventure quotes Augustine to support this view: "It is not generation but lust, that transmits original sin to posterity" (Augustine, *Fulgentius*, "De fide ad Petrum," 2:16).
13. Augustine, *Contra Faustum*, 22.27.
14. Augustine, *De libero arbitrio*, 2.53.
15. Augustine, *The City of God*, 14.28.
16. Bonaventure, *Brevil.*, III, 8 (V, 237b). Bonaventure cites Augustine's *De Trinitate*, Bk 12:17f for support.
17. Bonaventure, *Brevil.*, III, 8 (V, 237a).
18. Bonaventure, *Brevil.*, III, 8 (V, 237a).
19. Bonaventure, *In II Sent.* d. 44, a. 2, q. 2 ad 4 (II, 1009b). See also Matthew De Benedictis, *The Social Thought of Saint Bonaventure: A Study in Social Philosophy*, Philosophical Studies, vol. 93 (Washington, D.C.: The Catholic University of America Press, 1946).
20. Bonaventure, *In II Sent.* d. 44, a. 3, q. 1 (II, 1011a).
21. Bonaventure, *In II Sent.* d. 44, a. 2, q. 2 ad 4.
22. Bonaventure, *In II Sent.*, d. 44, a. 2, q. 1.
23. Bonaventure, *In II Sent.* d. 44, a. 2, q. 1 ad 3.

Chapter 9

1. Bonaventure, *In III Sent.*, d. 1, a. 2, q. 1 resp. (III, 20b).
2. Bonaventure, *Brevil.*, IV, 1, 2 (V, 240a).
3. Bonaventure, *In III Sent.*, d. 1, a. 1, q. 4 con. (III, 17b).
4. Bonaventure, *Brevil.*, IV, 2 (V, 242b).
5. Bonaventure, *In II Sent.*, d. 6, a. 2, qq. 1–2 (II, 164–166).
6. Bonaventure, *Brevil.*, IV, 6 (V, 246b).
7. Bonaventure, *Brevil.*, IV, 7 (V, 248b).
8. Bonaventure, *Brevil.*, IV, 8 (V, 248b); cf. Bonaventure, *In III Sent.*, d. 15, aa.1–2 (III).

9. Bonaventure, *Brevil.*, IV, 8 (V, 249b); cf. Hugh of St. Victor, *De quauor voluntatibus in Christo.*

10. Anselm, *Cur Deus Homo*, ch. 2 and 20.

11. Bonaventure, *Brevil.*, IV, 9, 8 (V, 250b); cf. Bonaventure, *In III Sent.*

12. Bonaventure, *In IV Sent.*, d. 45, a. 1, q. 1 con. (940a).

13. Bonaventure, *In III Sent.*, d. 22, a. 1, q. 5 ad 1 (III, 462a).

14. Bonaventure, *In III Sent.*, d. 22, a. 1, q. 4 resp. (III, 459a).

15. Bonaventure, *In III Sent.*, d. 22, a. 1, q. 5 resp. (III, 461b).

16. Bonaventure, *In III Sent.*, d. 22, a. 1, q. 6 resp. (III, 433b).

17. Bonaventure, *The Tree of Life* (*Lignum vitae*), in *Bonaventure*, trans. Ewert Cousins, The Classics of Western Spirituality (New York: Paulist Press, 1978), ch. 9, par. 33, p. 159 (VIII, 80b–81a).

18. Bonaventure, *Brevil.*, IV, 5 (V, 246a).

19. Bonaventure, *Brevil.*, IV, 5 (V, 246a).

20. Bonaventure, *Brevil.*, V, 8 (V, 262a).

21. Bonaventure, *Hexaem.* I, 2 (V).

22. Augustine, *The City of God*, IV, 4, p. 139.

23. Jean-Pierre Torrell, OP. *Saint Thomas Aquinas*, vol. 1: *The Person and His Work*, trans. Robert Royal (Washington, D.C.: The Catholic University of America Press, 1996), 13. For Aquinas, see I. T. Eschmann, "Saint Thomas Aquinas on the Two Powers," *Medieval Studies* 20 (1958): 177–205; L. E. Boyle, "The *De Regno* and the Two Powers," in *Essays in Honour of A. C. Pegis*, ed. J. R. O'Donnell, 237–247.

24. Bonaventure, *In IV Sent.*, dubitum 3.

25. Bonaventure, *In IV Sent.*, d. 18, p. 2, a. 1, q. 3 (IV, 489a).

26. Bonaventure, *Perf ev.*, q. 4 a. 3 (V, 189–198).

27. Bonaventure, *In II Sent.* d. 44, a. 2, q. 2 ad 4.

Chapter 10

1. Bonaventure, *Brevil.*, V, 2 (V, 253b).

2. Bonaventure, *Brevil.*, V, 2 (V, 254a).

3. Bonaventure, *Brevil.*, V, 1 (V, 252b).

4. Bonaventure, *Brevil.*, V, 2 (V, 253b); cf. *In II Sent.*, d. 4, a.1, q. 2 ad 3 (II, 134).

5. Bonaventure, *Brevil.*, V, 2 (V, 254a).

6. Bonaventure, *Brevil.*, V, 1 (V, 252b).

7. Bonaventure, *Brevil.*, V, 1 (V, 253a).

8. McGrath, 3.

9. McGrath, 48–49.

10. McGrath, 53.

11. Bonaventure, *In II Sent.*, d. 26, a. 1, q. 3 resp. (II, 638a).

12. Bonaventure, *In II Sent.*, d. 26, a. 1, q. 3 ad 1 (II, 638b).

13. Bonaventure, *In II Sent.*, d. 26, a. 1, q. 4 resp. (II, 640b).

14. Bonaventure, *Brevil.*, 5, 4, 4 (V, 256b).

15. Bonaventure, *Brevil.*, I, 9 (V, 218a).
16. Bonaventure, *Brevil.*, I, 9 (V, 218a).
17. Gilson, *Philosophy of Bonaventure*, 402.
18. Carpenter, 45ff.
19. Bonaventure, *Itin.*, 4, 4 (V, 307a).
20. Bonaventure, *Itin.*, 4, 4 (V, 307a, quoted in Carpenter, 4, "These things attained, our spirit, in as much as it is in conformity with the heavenly Jerusalem, is made hierarchic in order to mount upward."
21. Bonaventure, *Hexaemeron*, 22, 24 (V, 441a).
22. Bonaventure, *Brevil.*, V, 3 (V, 255b).
23. Bonaventure, *Brevil.*, V, 3 (V, 255b).
24. Bonaventure, *Brevil.*, V, 3 (V, 255b); cf. Augustine, *Sermones*, 169, 11:13.
25. Thomas Aquinas, *Summa theologiae* Ia Iiae, q. 70, a. 1. Torrell, *Spiritual Master*, 216, n. 50.
26. Bonaventure, *Brevil.*, V, 4 (V, 256b).
27. Bonaventure, *In III Sent.*, d. 33, a. 1, q. 5 resp. (III, 723a).
28. Bonaventure, *In III Sent.*, d. 33, a. 1, q. 5 ad 1 (III, 723b); cf. *In I Sent.*, d. 37, a. 1, q. 1.
29. Plotinus, quoted in Bonaventure, *Hexaemeron*, VI, 6 (V).
30. Bonaventure, *Hexaemeron*, VI, 9–10 (V, 361b).
31. Bonaventure, *Hexaemeron*, VI, 24 (V, 362a).
32. Bonaventure, *Hexaemeron*, VI, 32 (V, 364b).
33. Bonaventure, *Hexaemeron*, VI, 30 (V, 364b).
34. Bonaventure, *Hexaemeron*, VI, 30 (V, 364b).
35. Bonaventure, *Brevil.*, V, 1 (V, 252b) ; cf. Anselm, *De veritate*, 12.
36. Bonaventure, *Brevil.*, V, 5 (V, 258a).
37. Meritum congrui, meritum digni, and meritum condigni. Trans. (Congruous merit, deserving merit, and condign merit).
38. Bonaventure, *Brevil.*, V, 7 (V, 260b).
39. Bonaventure, *Brevil.*, V, 7 (V, 261a).
40. Bonaventure, *Brevil.*, V, 8 (V, 261b).
41. See, Quinn, "Moral Philosophy," 54.
42. Bonaventure, *In III Sent.*, d. 33, a. 1, q. 4 resp. (III, 720a).
43. Bonaventure, *Brevil.*, V, 8 (V, 262a).
44. Bonaventure, *Brevil.*, V, 8, (V, 262a).

Chapter 11

1. McGinn, *The Flowering of Mysticism*, 10.
2. Hugh of St. Victor, *Lib. I de Sacrum*, p. XII, ch. 4 in Bonaventure, *In IV Sent.*
3. Bonaventure, *In IV Sent.*, d. 1, p. 2, a. 1, q. 3 resp. (IV, 35b).
4. Cf. Augustine, *Contra Faustum*, IX, 13; also Hugh of St. Victor, *De sacramentis*, I, VII, 12 and XI, 6.
5. Bonaventure, *Brevil.*, VI, 2 (V, 267a).

6. Bonaventure, *Brevil.*, VI, 4 (V, 268a).

7. Bonaventure, *In IV Sent.*, d. 1, p. 1, a. 1, q. 2 resp. (IV, 14b).

8. Bonaventure, *In IV Sent.*, d. 1, p. 1, a. 1, q. 2, resp. (IV, 14b).

9. The signification of the sacrament is derived from its institution, specifically the element involved receives its signification from its institution (Bonaventure, *In IV Sent.*, IV, 14b, 64, 627b, 692).

10. Bonaventure, *In IV Sent.*, d. 1, p. 1, a. 1, q. 2 ad 4 (IV, 15b).

11. Bonaventure, *In IV Sent.*, d. 1, p. 1, a. 1, q. 2 resp. (IV 14b).

12. Bonaventure, *In IV Sent.*, d. 1, p. 1, a. 1 ad 1 (IV, 14b).

13. Bonaventure, *In IV Sent.*, d. 1, p. 1, a. 1, q. 2 ad 2 (IV, 15a).

14. Pierre Pourrat, *Theology of the Sacraments: A Study in Positive Theology* (St. Louis: B. Herder, 1910), 167.

15. Bonaventure, *Brevil.*, VI, 1 (V, 265b).

16. Bonaventure, *In IV Sent.*, d. 1, p. 1, a. 1, q. 3 resp. (IV, 17a).

17. Bonaventure, *Brevil.*, VI, 1 (V, 265b).

18. Bonaventure, *Brevil.*, VI, 5 (V, 270a).

19. Bonaventure, *Brevil.*, VI, 5 (V, 270a).

20. Bonaventure, *Brevil.*, VI, 5 (V, 270a).

21. Bonaventure, *Brevil.*, VI, 5 (V, 270a).

22. Bonaventure, *In IV Sent.*, d. 1, p. 1, a. 1, q. 1 ad 2 (IV, 12b).

23. Ott, 340.

24. Bonaventure, *In IV Sent.*, d. 1, p. 1, a. 1, q. 1 resp. (IV, 12b).

25. Bonaventure, *In IV Sent.*, d. 1, p. 1, a. 1, q. 1 resp. (IV, 12a).

26. Bonaventure, *In IV Sent.*, d. 1, p. 1, a. 1, q. 1 ad 2 (IV, 12b).

27. Bonaventure, *In IV Sent.*, d. 1, p. 1, a. 1, q. 1 ad 4 (IV, 13b).

28. Bonaventure, *Brevil.*, VI, 6 (V, 271a).

29. Bonaventure, *Brevil.*, III, 5 (V, 234b–235a).

30. R. W. Southern, *Saint Anselm: A Portrait in a Landscape* (Cambridge: Cambridge University Press, 1990), 44.

31. Southern, *Saint Anselm*, 45.

32. Southern, *Saint Anselm*, 45.

33. Gerald O'Collins and Silvio Farrugia, *Catholicism: The Story of Catholic Christianity* (New York: Oxford University Press, 2003), 260.

34. Bonaventure, *Brevil.*, VI, 9 (V, 273b).

35. Bonaventure, *Brevil.*, VI, 9 (V, 274b).

36. Bonaventure, *In IV Sent.*, d. 11, p. 2, a. 1, q. 1 (IV, 254b).

37. Bonaventure, *In IV Sent.*, d. 11, p. 1, a. 1, qq. 2–3 (IV, 256–259).

38. Bonaventure, *Brevil.*, VI, 9 (V, 274b).

39. Bonaventure, *Brevil.*, VI, 9 (V, 275a).

40. Bonaventure, *Brevil.*, VI, 9 (V, 274a).

41. Bonaventure, *Brevil.*, VI, 9 (V, 275a).

42. Bonaventure, *Brevil.*, VI, 9 (V, 275a).

43. Bonaventure, *Brevil.*, VI, 10 (V, 276b).

44. *Justinian Institutes* I, 9; *De patria potestate*. For a detailed study of Bonaventure's views of the sacrament of matrimony, see Sister Paula Jean Miller, FSE,

Marriage: The Sacrament of Divine-Human Communion (Quincy, IL: Franciscan Press, 1996).

45. Harrison, 160.
46. Bonaventure, *Brevil.*, VI, 13 (V, 279a).
47. Bonaventure, *Brevil.*, VI, 13 (V, 279a).
48. Augustine, *De Genesi ad litteram*, 7, 12.

Chapter 12

1. Ilia Delio, "From Prophecy to Mysticism: Bonaventure's Eschatology in Light of Joachim of Fiore," *Traditio* 52 (1997):153–177. For translated primary texts of Joachim and Franciscan Spirituals influenced by him, see *Apocalyptic Spirituality: Treatises and Letters of Lactantius, Adso of Montier-en-Der, Joachim of Fiore, The Spiritual Franciscans, Savonarola*, trans., Bernard McGinn The Classics of Western Spirituality (New York: Paulist Press, 1979), 97–181. See also, Bernard McGinn, *The Calabrian Abbot: Joachim of Fiore in the History of Western Thought* (New York: Macmillan Publishing Company, 1985); Marjorie Reeves, "The Originality and Influence of Joachim of Fiore," *Traditio* 36 (1980): 271–288; Marjorie Reeves, *Joachim of Fiore and the Prophetic Future* (London: SPCK, 1976); E. Randolph Daniel, "St. Bonaventure: Defender of Franciscan Eschatology" in *S. Bonaventura 1274–1974*, ed. by Jacques Bourgerol (Grottaferrata: 1974), 4: 797–798; Richard K. Emmerson and Ronald B. Herzman, *The Apocalyptic Imagination in Medieval Literature* (Philadelphia: University of Pennsylbania Press, 1992), 34–75.

2. Gerard of Borgo San Donnino seems to be one so influenced to believe that the Gospel would be superseded by the Age of the Spirit. Gerard sees the Franciscans as the spiritual men who would user in a new eternal testament (Delio, 168, n. 80). Daniel tends to reject the long-standing reading of Joachim as holding that the age of the Spirit would transplant the age of the Son (E. Randolph Daniel, "The Double Procession of the Holy Spirit in Joachim of Fiore's Understanding of History," *Speculum* 55 [1980]:472, cited in Delio, 170). See also, Morton Bloomfield, "Joachim of Flora: A Critical Survey of His Canon, Teachings, Sources, Biography, and Influences," in *Joachim of Fiore in Christian Thought*, ed. Delno C. West (New York: B. Franklin, 1975), 1:260–271.

3. Delio, 155.
4. Ratzinger, *The Theology of History in St. Bonaventure*.
5. S. Clasen, E. R. Daniel, David Burr.
6. Bonaventure, *In I Sent.*, d. 5, a. 2, q. 2, dub. 4 (I, 121), quoted in Delio, 153. Joachim seems to have attacked Lombard's Trinitarian theology for teaching a quaternity by separating the essence or unity of God from the three persons. However, we do not have Joachim's text containing his criticism of Lombard, *De unitate seu de essentia trinitatis* (Daniel, "The Double Procession," 469–470).

7. McGinn, *The Calabrian Abbot*, 207.
8. McGinn, *The Calabrian Abbot*, 213.
9. Ratzinger, *The Theology of History*, 117. McGinn agrees with this conclusion: "Bonaventure decisively rejected the Joachite conception of the abolition of

the Gospel in the coming Third Age of the Holy Spirit (McGinn, *The Calabrian Abbot*, 219).

10. Ratzinger, *The Theology of History* 118.

11. Gilson, 142.

12. Bonaventure, *In IV Sent.*, d. 48, a. 1, q. 4 con. (IV, 988b).

13. Bonaventure, *Brevil.*, VII, 1 (V, 281b); cf. Augustine, *De civitate Dei*, VII, 30.

14. Augustine *De civitate* Dei, XXI, 26:4, quoted in Bonaventure, *Breviloquium*, I, 9 (V, 218b).

15. Bonaventure, *Brevil.*, I, 9 (V, 218b).

16. Bonaventure, *Brevil.*, I, 9 (V, 218b).

17. Bonaventure, *Brevil.*, I, 9 (V, 218b).

18. Bonaventure, *Brevil.*, VII, 2 (V, 282b).

19. Bonaventure, *Brevil.*, VII, 2 (V, 282b); cf. Augustine, *De civitate Dei*, XXI, 26.

20. Bonaventure, *Brevil.*, VII, 5 (V, 287a).

21. Bonaventure, *In IV Sent.*, d. 44, p. 1, a. 2, q. 1, resp. (IV, 911).

22. Bonaventure, *Brevil.*, VII, 5 (V, 286a).

23. Bonaventure, *In IV Sent.*, q. 47, a. 2, qq. 1–4 (IV, 975–980).

24. Bonaventure, *In IV Sent.*, q. 47, a. 2, q. 4 (IV, 980a–b).

25. Bonaventure, *Brevil.*, VII, 4 (V, 285b).

26. Bonaventure, *Brevil.*, VII, 4 (V, 285b).

27. Bonaventure, *Brevil.*, VII, 4 (V, 285b).

28. Bonaventure, *Brevil.*, VII, 6 (V, 288a). Bonaventure thinks that all the damned will suffer a threefold punishment: the loss of beatific vision, the pain of material fire, and the pain of worms. He also thinks that hell involves real, material fire.

29. Bonaventure, *Brevil.*, VII, 7 (V, 289b).

30. Bonaventure, *Brevil.*, prologue, n. 1.

31. Francis is an example. H.-F. Dondaine, "Cognoscere de Deo quid est." *Recherches de théologie ancienne et médiévale* 22 (1955): 72–78, cited in Torrell, *Saint Thomas Aquinas*, vol. 2, *Spiritual Master*, trans. Robert Royal (Washington, D.C.: The Catholic University of America Press, 2003), 28.

32. Bonaventure, *In III Sent.*, d. 35, u. 1 (III, 774a–b).

33. Bonaventure, *Triplic. via*, 7 (VIII, 17a).

34. See McGinn's discussion of the relation between peace and order and their relation to the threefold way, *The Flowering of Mysticism*, 103–104.

35. Bonaventure, *Leg. Mai*, prologue (VIII,504b).

36. Bonaventure, *Brevil.*, 7, 7 (V, 290b).

37. As twentieth-century French philosopher Jacques Maritain puts this notion, "An intelligible mystery is not a contradiction in terms. On the contrary, it is the most exact description of reality. Mystery is not the implacable adversary of understanding" (Jacques Maritain, *A Preface to Metaphysics*, 12).

38. Bonaventure, *Brevil.*, V, 6 (V, 260a).

39. Bonaventure, *Brevil.*, V, 6 (V, 260a).
40. See especially McGinn, *The Flowering of Mysticism*, 101–112.
41. Bonaventure, *Brevil.*, V, 6 (V, 260a).
42. Bonaventure, *Itin.*, VII, 5 (V, 313a). We find similar ecstatic language in Bonaventure's *Breviloquium* (V, 6 [V, 259b]).

Bibliography

Primary Sources: Bonaventure

Bonaventure. *Collationes in hexaemeron*. Edited by Ferdinand Delorme, OFM. Bibliotheca Franciscana Scholastica Medii Aevi, vol. 8. Ad Claras Aquas (Florentia): Collegium S. Bonaventurae, 1934.

———. *Doctoris seraphici S. Bonaventurae opera omnia*. Vols. I–IV, *Commentaria in quatuor libros sententiarum*; vol. V, *Opuscula varia theologica*; vol. VI, *Commentarius in Sacrum Scripturam*; vol. VII, *Commentarius in evangelium. S. Lucae*; vol. VIII, *Opuscula varia ad theologicam mysticam et res Ordiniis Fratrum minorum spectantia*; vol. IX, *Sermones de tempore, de sanctis, de B. Virgine Maria et de diversis*; vol. X, *Operum omnium complementum*. Edited by the Fathers of the Collegium S. Bonaventurae. Ad Claras Aquas (Quaracchi): Ex typographia Collegii S. Bonaventurae, 1882–1902.

———. *Sancti Bonaventurae sermones dominicales*. Edited by Jacques Bougerol. Grottaferrata: Collegio S. Bonaventura, 1977.

Primary Sources: Bonaventure: English Translations (All translations are from the English translations listed below. Translations from texts not listed below are my own.)

Bonaventure. *Breviloquium*. Translated by Erwin Esse Nemmers. St. Louis, Mo.: B. Herder Book Co., 1946.

———. "Christ the One Teacher of All." In *What Manner of Man: Sermons on Christ by St. Bonaventure*. Translated by Zachary Hayes, OFM. Chicago: Franciscan Herald Press, 1989.

————. *Collations on the Six Days*. Translated by José de Vink. Vol. 5 of *Works of Saint Bonaventure*. Paterson, N.J.: St. Anthony Guild Press, 1970.

————. *Disputed Questions on the Knowledge of Christ*. Translated by Zachary Hayes, OFM. Vol. 4 of *Works of Saint Bonaventure*, ed. George Marcil, OFM. St. Bonaventure, N.Y.: The Franciscan Institute, 1992.

————. *Disputed Questions on the Mystery of the Trinity*. Translated by Zachary Hayes, OFM. Vol. 3 of *Works of Saint Bonaventure*, ed. George Marcil, OFM. St. Bonaventure, N.Y.: The Franciscan Institute, 1979.

————. *Itinerarium mentis in Deum*. Translated by Philotheus Boehner, OFM. Vol. 2 of *Works of Saint Bonaventure*, ed. Philotheus Boehner and Sr. M. Frances Laughlin, SMIC. St. Bonaventure, N.Y.: The Franciscan Institute, 1956.

————. *On the Reduction of the Arts to Theology*. Translated by Zachary Hayes, OFM. Vol. 1 of *Works of Saint Bonaventure*, ed. F. Edward Coughlin, OFM. St. Bonaventure, N.Y.: The Franciscan Institute, 1996.

————. *The Tree of Life*. In *Bonaventure*. Translated by Ewert Cousins. The Classics of Western Spirituality. New York: Paulist Press, 1978.

Other Sources

Abate, Guiseppe. "Per la storia e la cronologia de S. Bonaventura, O. Min." *Miscellanea francescana* 49 (1949): 534–568.

Aertsen, Jan A. *Medieval Philosophy and the Transcendentals: The Case of Thomas Aquinas*. Edited by Josef Koch. *Studien und Texte zur Geistesgeschichte des Mittelalters*, LII. Leiden: E. J. Brill, 1996.

Alexander of Hales. *Magistri Alexandri de Hales Glossa in quattuor libros sententiarum Petri Lombardi*. Bibliotheca Franciscana Scholastica Medii Aevi, vol. 12. Quaracchi (Florence): Collegium S. Bonaventura, 1951.

————. *Summa theologica*. 4 Vols. Quaracchi (Florence): Collegium S. Bonaventura, 1924–1948.

Allard, Guy-H. "La technique de la 'Reductio' chez Bonaventure." In *S. Bonaventura 1274–1974*. Vol. 2. Grottaferrata (Rome): Collegio S. Bonaventura, 1973.

Anselm. *Monologion*. Stuttgart: Frommann Verlag, 1964.

Aristotle. *Metaphysics*. In *The Complete Works of Aristotle*. Edited by Jonathan Barnes. Bollingen Series LXXI. rev. ed. New Jersey: Princeton University Press, 1984.

————. *On the Soul*. In *The Complete Works of Aristotle*. Edited by Jonathan Barnes. Bollingen Series LXXI. New Jersey: Princeton University Press, 1984.

Augustine. *The City of God*. Translated by Henry Bettenson. New York: Penguin Books, 1972.

————. *Confessions*. Translated by Henry Chadwick. New York: Oxford University Press, 1992.

————. *Teaching Christianity: De Doctrina Christiana*. Translated by Edmund Hill, OP. Part I, Vol. 11 of *The Works of Saint Augustine: A Translation for the 21st*

Century. Edited by John E. Rotelle, OSA. Hyde Park, N.Y.: New City Press, 1996.

———. *The Trinity.* Translated by Edmund Hill, OP. Part I, Vol. 5 of *The Works of Saint Augustine: A Translation for the 21st Century.* Edited by John E. Rotelle, OSA. Hyde Park, N.Y.: New City Press, 1991.

Avicebron (Ibn Gabirol). *Fons vitae: Ex Arabico in Latinum Translatus ab Johanne Hispano et Dominico Gundissalino.* Edited by Clemens Baeumker. Beiträge zur Geschichte der Philosophie und Theologie des Mittelsalters, vol. 1, pt. 2–4. Münster: Aschendorff, 1995.

Baldner, Stephen. "St. Bonaventure and the Demonstrability of a Temporal Beginning: A Reply to Richard Davis." *American Catholic Philosophical Quarterly* 71 (1997): 225–236.

———. "St. Bonaventure on the Temporal Beginning of the World." *New Scholasticism* 63 (1989): 206–228.

Balduinus ab Amsterdam, OFM. Cap. "De ordine chronologico IV librorum commentarii in sententias S. Bonaventurae." *Collectanea franciscana* 41 (1971): 288–314.

Beaumont-Maillet, Laure. *Le Grand Couvent des Cordeliers de Paris: Etude historique et archéologique du XIIIe siècle à nos jours.* Bibliothèque de l'École des Hautes Études, 4th sec., vol. 325. Paris: Librairie Honoré Champion, 1975.

Bérubé, Camille, OFM. Cap. "De la philosophie à la sagesse dans l'itinéraire bonaventurien." *Collectanea franciscana* 38 (1968): 257–307.

———. "De la théologie à l'écriture chez saint Bonaventure." *Collectanea franciscana* 40 (1970): 5–70.

———. "De la théologie de l'image à la philosophie de l'objet de l'intelligence chez saint Bonaventure." In *S. Bonaventura 1274–1974.* Vol. 3. Grottaferrata (Rome): Collegio S. Bonaventura, 1973.

———. "Regain d'intéret des études bonaventuriennes." *Collectanea franciscana* 42 (1972): 103–117.

———. "Symbolisme, image et coincidence des contraires chez saint Bonaventure." *Collectanea franciscana* 40 (1980): 235–251.

Bettoni, Efrem. "Il fondamento filosofico della dottrina esemplaristica di san Bonaventura." In *Contributi di spiritualità bonaventuriana: atti del simposio internazionale.* Padova: Padua, 1974–1975.

———. "Natura e soprannaturale nella scuola francescana." *Sophia* 18 (1950): 52–59.

———. *Saint Bonaventure.* Translated by Angelus Gambatese, OFM. Notre Dame, Ind.: University of Notre Dame Press, 1964.

Bihl, M. "The Constitutions of Narbonne." *Archivum Franciscanum Historicum* (1941).

Bissen, J. M. *L'exemplarisme divin selon saint Bonaventure.* Paris: J. Vrin, 1929.

Bloomfield, Morton. "Joachim of Flora: A Critical Survey of His Canon, Teachings, Sources, Biography, and Influences." In *Joachim of Fiore in Christian Thought,* ed. Delno C. West (New York: B. Franklin, 1975), 1:260–271.

Boehner, Philotheus, OFM. "Die natürlichen Werte der Ehe nach dem hl. Bon-aventura." *Franziskanische Studien* 24 (1937): 1–17.

———. *John of Rupella — Saint Bonaventure*, Part 2 of *The History of the Franciscan School*. St. Bonaventure, N.Y.: St. Bonaventure University, 1944.

———. Notes and Commentary to *Itinerarium mentis in Deum*. In vol. 2 of *Works of Saint Bonaventure*, ed. Philotheus Boehner and Sr. M. Frances Laughlin, SMIC. St. Bonaventure, N.Y.: The Franciscan Institute, 1956.

———. "The Spirit of Franciscan Philosophy." *Franciscan Studies* 2 (1942): 217–237.

Boland, Vivian, OP. *Ideas in the Mind of God according to Thomas Aquinas: Sources and Synthesis*. Leiden: Brill, 1996.

Bonasea, Bernardino M., OFM. *God and Atheism: A Philosophical Approach to the Existence of God*. Washington, D.C.: The Catholic University of America Press, 1979.

———. "The Question of an Eternal World in the Teaching of St. Bonaventure." *Franciscan Studies* 34 (1974): 7–33.

Bonnefoy, Jean François. "Une somme bonaventurienne de théologie mystique: Le *De triplici via*." *France franciscaine* 15 (1932): 77–86, 227–64, 311–59; 16 (1933): 259–326.

Bougerol, Jacques Guy, OFM. *Bibliographia Bonaventuriana (c. 1850–1973)*. Grottaferrata (Rome): Collegio S. Bonaventura, 1974.

———. "Dossier pour l'étude des rapports entre Bonaventure et se Aristote." *Archives d'histoire doctrinale et littéraire du moyen age* 31 (1974): 135–222.

———. *Introduction to the Works of Bonaventure*. Translated by José de Vinck. Paterson, N.J.: St. Anthony Guild Press, 1964.

———. *Lexique Saint Bonaventure*. Paris: Éditions Franciscaines, 1969.

———. *Saint Bonaventure: Études sur les sources de sa pensée*. Northampton.: Variorium Reprints, 1989.

Bowman, Leonard J. "Cosmic Exemplarism of Bonaventure." *The Journal of Religion* 55 (April, 1975): 181–198.

———. "A View of St. Bonaventure's Symbolic Theology." In *Thomas and Bonaventure*, ed. G. McLean. *American Catholic Philosophical Association* 4 (1974): 25–32.

Boyle, L. E. "The *De Regno* and the Two Powers." In *Essays in Honour of Anton Charles Pegis*, ed. J. Reginald O'Donnell. Toronto: Pontifical Institute of Medieval Studies, 1974, 237–247.

Brady, Ignatius, OFM. "Bonaventure." In *The New Catholic Encyclopedia*. Vol. 2. New York: McGraw-Hill Book Company, 1967.

———. "The Distinctions of Lombard's Book of Sentences and Alexander of Hales." *Franciscan Studies* 25 (1965): 90–116.

———. "The Edition of the 'Opera Omnia' of St. Bonaventure (1882–1902)" *Archivum Franciscanum Historicum* 70 (1977): 352–376.

———. "The *Opera Omnia* of Saint Bonaventure Revisited." *Proceedings of the American Catholic Philosophical Association* 48 (1974): 295–304.

———. "St. Bonaventure's Doctrine of Illumination: Reactions Medieval and Modern." In *Bonaventure and Aquinas: Enduring Philosophers*, ed. Robert W. Shahan and Francis J. Kovach. Norman, Okla.: University of Oklahoma Press, 1976.

Brooke, Rosalind B. *Early Franciscan Government: Elias to Bonaventure.* Cambridge: Cambridge University Press, 1959.

———. "St. Bonaventure as Minister General." In *S. Bonaventura Francescana: Convegni del Centro di Studi sulla Spiritualità Medievale XIV.* Todi: Presso L'Accademia Tudertina, 1974, 75–105.

Brown, Stephen. "The Eternity of the World Discussion in Early Oxford." In *Mensch und Natur im Mittelalter, Miscellanea Mediaevalia*, vol. 21. New York: Walter de Gruyter, 1991, 259–280.

Bougerol, J. Guy, OFM. *Introduction à Saint Bonaventure.* rev. ed. Paris: J. Vrin, 1988.

———. *Introduction to the Works of Bonaventure.* Translated by José de Vinck. Paterson, N.J.: St. Anthony Guild Press, 1964.

Burr, David. *Olivi and Franciscan Poverty: The Origins of the Usus Pauper Controversy.* Philadelphia: University of Pennsylvania Press, 1989.

Callus, Daniel, OP. "The Origins of the Problem of the Unity of Form," *The Thomist* 24 (1961): 257–285.

———. "The Philosophy of St. Bonaventure and St. Thomas." *Blackfriars* 21 (1940): 151–164; 249–267.

Capelle, G. C. *Autour du décret de 1210: III-Amaury de Bène: Étude sur son panthéisme formel.* Bibliothèque thomiste, ed. Pierre Mandonnet, OP. Paris: Librarie Philosophique J. Vrin, 1932.

Carpenter, Charles. *Theology as the Road to Holiness in St. Bonaventure.* New York: Paulist Press, 1999.

Chântillon, Paul. "Saint Bonaventure et la philosophie." In *San Bonaventura maestro di vita francescana e di sapienza cristiana: Atti del congresso internazionale per il VII centenario di san Bonaventura da Bagnoregio: Roma, 19–26 settembre.* Vol. 1. Rome: Pontificia Facoltà Teologica San Bonaventura, 1976.

Chenu, Marie-Dominique, OP. "Le dernier avatar de la théologie orientale." In *Mélanges Auguste Pelzer: Études d'histoire littéraire et doctrinale de la scholastique médiévale offertes à Auguste Pelzer à l'occasion de son soixante-dixiéme anniversaire.* Louvain: Bibliothèque de l'Université, 1947.

———. *Nature, Man and Society in the Twelfth Century: Essays on New Theological Perspectives in the Latin West.* Edited by Jerome Taylor. Medieval Academy Reprints for Teaching, 37. Toronto: University of Toronto Press, 1997; originally published as *Le théologie au douzième siècle, Études de philosophie médiévale.* Paris: J. Vrin, 1957, 45.

———. "Profanidad del mundo—sacramentalidad del mundo, santo Tomas de Aquino y san Buenaventura." *Ciencia tomista* 101 (1974): 183–189.

———. *La théologie comme science au XIIIe siècle.* Paris: Librairie philosophique J. Vrin, 1957.

————. *Toward Understanding Saint Thomas*. Translated by A. M. Landry, OP, and D. Hughes, OP. The Library of Living Catholic Thought. Chicago: Henry Regnery Company, 1964.

Clarke, Norris, SJ. *Explorations in Metaphysics: Being—God—Person*. Notre Dame: University of Notre Dame, 1994.

————. "The Problem of the Reality and Multiplicity of Divine Ideas in Christian Neoplatonism." In *Neoplatonism and Christian Thought*, ed. Dominic J. O'Meara. Studies in Neoplatonism: Ancient and Modern, vol. 3. Albany, N.Y.: State University of New York Press, 1982.

Clop, Eusèbe. *Saint Bonaventure (1221–1274)*. Les Saints, Paris: Librairie Victor Lecoffre, 1922.

Coccia, Antonius, OFM Conv. "De Aeternitate Mundi apud S. Bonaventuram et Recentiores." In *S. Bonaventura: 1274–1974*. Rome: Collegio S. Bonaventura, 1974, 279–306.

Colish, Marcia. *Medieval Foundations of the Western Intellectual Tradition 400–1400*. The Yale Intellectual History of the West, ed. John W. Burrow, William J. Bouwsma, and Frank M. Turner. New Haven, Conn.: Yale University Press, 1997.

————. *The Mirror of Language: A Study in the Medieval Theory of Knowledge*. Yale Historical Publications, Miscellany 88. New Haven, Conn.: Yale University Press, 1968.

————. *Peter Lombard*. Brill's Studies in Intellectual History, ed. A. J. Vanderjagt. Vol. 41. New York: E. J. Brill, 1994.

Condren, Conal. "Rhetoric, Historiography and Political Theory: Some Aspects of the Poverty Controversy Reconsidered." *Journal of Religious History* 13, no. 1 (1984): 15–34.

Cousins, Ewert. *Bonaventure and the Coincidence of Opposites*. Chicago: Franciscan Herald Press, 1978.

————. "Bonaventure's Mysticism of Language." In *Mysticism and Language*, ed. S. Katz. New York: Oxford University Press, 1992.

————. "Franciscan Roots of Ignatian Meditation." In *Ignatian Spirituality in a Secular Age*, ed. G. Schner. Waterloo, Ontario: Wilfrid Laurier University Press, 1984.

————. "Language as Metaphysics in Bonaventure." In *Sprache und Erkenntnis im Mittelalter: Akten des VI. internationalen Kongresses für mittelalterliche Philosophie der société internationale pour l' étude de la philosophie médiévale, 29 August–3 September 1977 in Bonn*, ed. J. Beckmann. Vol. 2. Berlin: de Gruyter, 1981.

Crowley, T. "St. Bonaventure Chronology Reappraisal," *Franziskanische Studien* (1974): 310–322.

Dady, Mary Rachel. *The Theory of Knowledge of St. Bonaventure*. Washington, D.C.: The Catholic University of America Press, 1939.

Daniel, E. Randolph. "The Double Procession of the Holy Spirit in Joachim of Fiore's Understanding of History," *Speculum* 55 (1980):469–483.

————. "St. Bonaventure: Defender of Franciscan Eschatology." In *S. Bonaventura 1274–1974*. Vol. 4. Grottagerrata: Collegio S. Bonaventura, 1974, 797–798.

Davis, Richard. "Bonaventure and the Arguments for the Impossibility of an Infinite Temporal Regression." *American Catholic Philosophical Quarterly* 70 (1996): 361–380.

Dawson, Christopher. "Medieval Theology." In *Medieval Essays: A Study of Christian Culture*. Garden City, N.Y.: Image Books, 1959.

De Armellada, Bernardino. "Simbolismo metafísico y espiritualidad en san Buenaventura." In *San Bonaventura maestro di vita francescana e di sapienza cristiana: Atti del congresso internazionale per il VII centenario di san Bonaventura da Bagnoregio: Roma, 19–26 settembre 1974*. Vol. 3. Rome: Pontificia Facoltà Telogica San Bonaventura, 1976.

De Benedictis, Matthew M., OFM. *The Social Thought of Saint Bonaventure: A Study in Social Philosophy*. Washington, D.C.: The Catholic University of America Press, 1946.

Dekkers, Eligius, OSB. "Le Corpus Christianorum." *Studi Medievali* 3 (1962): 341–349.

Delio, Ilia. "From Prophecy to Mysticism: Bonaventure's Eschatology in Light of Joachim of Fiore." *Traditio* 52 (1997):153–177.

Denifle, H. S., and A. Chatelain, eds. *Chartularium Universitatis Parisiensis*. 4 vols. Paris, Delalain, 1889–1897.

Denzinger, Heinrich, and Peter Hünermann, eds. *Enchiridion symbolorum definitionum et declarationum de rebus fidei et morum*. Edition XXXVII. Freiburg in Breisgau: Herder, 1991.

Dettloff, W. " 'Christus tenens medium in omnibus': Sinn und Funktion der Theologie bei Bonaventura." *Wissenschaft und Weisheit* 20 (1957): 28–42, 120–140.

Dewan, Lawrence, OP. "*Obiectum*: Notes on the Invention of a Word." *Archives d'histoire doctrinale et littéraire du moyen âge* 48 (1981): 37–96.

Dionysius. *The Works of Dionysius the Areopagite*. Translated by John Parker. London: James Parker & Co., 1897–1899; reprint, Merrick, N.Y.: Richwood Publishing Company, 1976.

Dondaine, H. J. *Le corpus Dionysien de l'université de Paris au XIII siècle*. Rome: Storia e letteratura, 1935, 44.

Doucet, Victorin. *Prolegomena ad Summam Hales*. Quaracchi: Collegium S. Bonaventura, 1948.

Doyle, J. P. "Saint Bonaventure and the Ontological Argument." *Modern Schoolman* 52 (1974): 27–48.

Duby, Georges. *The Three Orders: Feudal Society Imagined*. Translated by Arthur Goldhammer. Chicago: University of Chicago Press, 1980.

Duhem, Pierre. *Le Système du monde*. Paris: A. Hermann, 1917.

Dupré, Louis. *The Other Dimension*. New York: Doubleday and Company, Inc., 1972.

Ehrle, F. "Der heilige Bonaventura, seine Eigenart und seine drei Lebensaufgaben." *Franziskanische Studien* 8 (1921): 109–124.

Elders, Léon. "Les citations d'Aristote dans le *Commentaire sur les Sentences* de saint Bonaventure." In *San Bonaventura maestro de vita francescana e di sap-*

ienza cristiana: Atti del congresso internazionale per il VII centenario di san Bonaventura da Bagnoregio: Rome, 19–26 settembre 1974. Vol. 1. Rome: Pontificia Facoltà Teologica San Bonaventura, 1976.

Emery, Kent. "Reading the World Rightly and Squarely." *Traditio* 39 (1983): 183–218.

Emmerson, Richard K. and Ronald B. Herzman. *The Apocalyptic Imagination in Medieval Literature*. Philadelphia: University of Pennsylbania Press, 1992.

Eschmann, I. T. "Saint Thomas Aquinas on the Two Powers," *Medieval Studies* 20 (1958): 177–205.

Estevez, Antonio Perez. *La materia, de Avicena a la escuela Franciscana*. Zulia, Venezuela: Editorial de la Universidad del Zulia, 1998.

Eugène, Christian. "Saint Bonaventure et le grand couvent des cordeliers de Paris," *Études franciscaines* 18 (Supplément annuel, 1968): 167–182.

Evans, G. R. *Anselm*. Outstanding Christian Thinkers. Wilton, Conn.: Morehouse Publishing, 1989

———. *Philosophy and Theology in the Middle Ages*. New York, Routledge, 1993.

Fonck, A. "Ontologisme." *Dictionnaire de Théologie Catholique*. Paris: Letouzey et Ané, 1931.

Forest, Aimé. *La structure métaphysique du concret selon saint Thomas d'Aquin*. Études de philosophie médievale. Paris: Libraire philosophique J. Vrin, 1956.

Foshee, Charles N. "St. Bonaventure and the Augustinian Concept of *Mens*." *Franciscan Studies* 27 (1967): 163–175.

Francis of Assisi. "The Admonitions." In *The Saint*, vol. 1 of *Francis of Assisi: Early Documents*, ed. Regis J. Armstrong, OFM Cap., J. A. Wayne Hellman, OFM Conv., and William J. Short, OFM. New York: New City Press, 1999.

———. "A Letter to Brother Anthony of Padua." In *The Saint*, vol. 1 of *Francis of Assisi: Early Documents*, ed. Regis J. Armstrong, OFM Cap., J. A. Wayne Hellman, OFM Conv., and William J. Short, OFM. New York: New City Press, 1999.

Gál, Gedeon. "Alexander of Hales." *The Routledge Encyclopedia of Philosophy*, ed. Edward Craig. Vol. 1. New York: Routledge, 1998.

Gauthier, René. "Trois commentaires 'averroistes' sur l'*Éthique à Nicomaque*." *Archives d'histoire doctrinale et littéraire du Moyen age* 16 (1947–1948): 187–346.

Gendreau, Bernard. "The Quest for Certainty in Bonaventure." *Franciscan Studies* 21 (March–June 1961): 104–227.

Gerkin, Alexander. *Theologie des Wortes: Das Verhältnis von Schöpfung und Inkarnation bei Bonaventura*. Dusseldorf: Patmos-Verlag 1963.

Gersh, Stephen. "John Scottus Eriugena and Anselm of Canterbury." In *Medieval Philosophy*, ed. John Marenbon. Routledge History of Philosophy, vol. 3. New York: Routledge, 1998.

Gerson, Lloyd P. "Plotinus and the Rejection of Aristotelian Metaphysics." In *Aristotle in Late Antiquity*, ed. Lawrence P. Schrenk. Studies in Philosophy and the History of Philosophy, ed. Jude P. Dougherty, vol. 27. Washington, D.C.: The Catholic University of America Press, 1994.

Ghellinck, J., De. *Le mouvement théologique du XII siècle*. Bruges: Éditons de Tempel, 1948.

Gilson, Étienne. *The Christian Philosophy of St. Augustine*. Translated by L. Lynch. New York: Random House, Inc., 1960.

———. "The Future of Augustinian Metaphysics." Translated by Edward Bullough. In *A Monument to Saint Augustine: Essays on Some Aspects of His Thought Written in Commemoration of His 15th Centenary*. London: Sheed & Ward, 1945.

———. *God and Philosophy*. Powell Lectures on Philosophy at Indiana University. Edited by W. Harry Jellema. New Haven, Conn.: Yale University Press, 1941.

———. *A History of Christian Philosophy in the Middle Ages*. New York: Random House, 1955.

———. *The Philosophy of St. Bonaventure*. Translated by Dom Illtyd Trethowan and Frank J. Sheed. Paterson, N.J.: St. Anthony Guild Press, 1965.

———. "Pourquoi saint Thomas a critiqué saint Augustin." *Archives d'histoire doctrinale et littériare du moyen age* 1 (1926–1927): 5–127.

———. *The Spirit of Medieval Philosophy* (*Gifford Lectures 1931–1932*). Translated by A.H.C. Downes. New York: Charles Scribner's Sons, 1940.

Gioberti, Vicenzo. *Introduzione allo studio della filosofia*, 2d ed. Milan: Fratelli Bocca, 1939–40.

Glorieux, P. "Le date des collations de Saint Bonaventure." *Archivum franciscanum historicum* 22 (1929): 257–272.

Golitzin, Alexander. *Et Introibo ad Altare Dei: The Mystagogy of Dionysius Areopagita with Special Reference to Its Predecessors in the Eastern Christian Tradition*. Thessalonike: Analecta Vlatadon, 1994, 59.

Gonzalez, O. *Mistério Trinitário y existencia humana: Estudio histórico teológico en torno a san Buenaventura*. Madrid: Ediciones Rialp, 1966.

Grant, Edward. *The Foundations of Modern Science in the Middle Ages: Their Religious, Institutional, and Intellectual Contexts*. Cambridge History of Science. New York: Cambridge University Press, 1996.

———. *God & Reason in the Middle Ages*. New York: Cambridge University Press, 2001.

———. *Planets, Stars and Orbs: The Medieval Cosmos 1200–1684*. New York: Cambridge University Press, 1994.

———. *Science and Religion, 400 B.C.–A.D. 1550: From Aristotle to Copernicus*, Greenwood Guides to Science and Religion. Westport, CT: Greenwood Press, 2004.

Gratien, Badin, Mariano d'Alatri, and Servus Gieben. *Histoire de la fondation et de l'évolution de l'Ordre des Frères Mineurs aux XIII siècle*. Bibliotheca Seraphico—Cappuccina 29. Rome: Istituto Storico dei Cappuccini, 1982.

Harrison, Carol. *Augustine: Christian Truth and Fractured Humanity*. Christian Theology in Context. New York: Oxford University Press, 2000.

Hayes, Zachary, OFM. *Bonaventure: Mystical Writings*. The Crossroad Spiritual Legacy Series. New York: The Crossroad Publishing Co., 1999.

———. "Christology and Metaphysics in the Thought of Bonaventure." In *Celebrating the Medieval Heritage: A Colloquy on the Thought of Aquinas and Bonaventure*, ed. David Tracy. *Journal of Religion* 58 (supplement, 1978).

———. *The Hidden Center*. Theological Inquiries: Studied in Contemporary Biblical and Theological Problems. New York: Paulist Press, 1981.

———. Introduction to *Disputed Questions on the Knowledge of Christ*. Vol. IV of *The Works of Saint Bonaventure*. St. Bonaventure, N.Y.: The Franciscan Institute, 1992.

Hemmerle, Klaus. *Theologie als Nachfolge: Bonaventura, ein Weg fur heute*. Freiburg im Breisgau: Herder, 1975.

Hodgson, Leonard. *The Doctrine of the Trinity*. New York: Charles Scribner's Sons, 1944.

Hopkins, Jasper. *A Companion to the Study of St. Anselm*. Minneapolis: University of Minnesota Press, 1972.

Hugh of St. Victor. *Didascalicon*. Translated by Jerome Taylor. New York: Columbia University Press, 1961.

———. *Hugonis de S. Victore opera omnia*. Patrologia latina. Edited by J. Migne. Vols. 175–177. Paris: Garnier Fratres, 1879–1880.

Imle, F. "Die Gabe des Intellektes nach dem heiligen Bonaventura." *Franziskanische Studien* 20 (1933): 34–50.

Inwood, Brad, and L. P. Gerson, trans. *Hellenistic Philosophy: Introductory Readings*. Indianapolis, Ind.: Hackett Publishing Co., 1988.

Iriarte, Lazaro, OFM Cap. *Historia Franciscana*. Nueva Edicion. Valencia: Editorial Asis, 1979.

Kelly, J.N.D. *Early Christian Doctrines*. rev. ed. San Francisco: Harper, 1978.

Kent, Bonnie. *Virtues of the Will: The Transformation of Ethics in the Late Thirteenth Century*. Washington, D.C.: The Catholic University of America Press, 1995.

Kerferd, G. B. "Nous." In *Encyclopedia of Philosophy*, ed. Paul Edwards. New York: The Macmillan Co. & The Free Press, 1967.

Kinn. James W. *The Pre-eminence of the Eucharist among the Sacraments according to Alexander of Hales, St. Albert the Great, St. Bonaventure, and St. Thomas Aquinas*. Dissertationes ad Lauream, 31. Mundelein, Ill.: St. Mary of the Lake Seminary, 1960.

Kirk, G. S., J. E. Raven, and M. Schofield, eds. *The Presocratic Philosophers*. 2d ed. Cambridge: Cambridge University Press, 1983.

Kovach, Francis. "The Question of the Eternity of the World in St. Bonaventure and St. Thomas: A Critical Analysis." *Southwestern Journal of Philosophy* 5 (1974): 141–172.

Krause, J. *Die Lehre des Hl. Bonaventura über die Natur der Körperlichen und geistigen Wesen und ihr Verhältnis zum Thomismus*. Paderborn, Germany: Schöningh, 1888.

Lambert, M. D. *Franciscan Poverty: The Doctrine of the Absolute Poverty of Christ and the Apostles in the Franciscan Order 1210–1323*. London: Society for the Promotion of Christian Knowledge, 1961.

Leff, Gordon. *Medieval Thought: St. Augustine to Ockham*. Chicago: Quadrangle Books, 1958.

Lemmens, Leonhard. *Der heilige. Bonaventura, Kardinal und Kirchen Lehrer aus dem Franzikanerorden 1221–1274*. Kempten: Jus Köselschen, 1909.

Libera, Alain de. "The Oxford and Paris Traditions in Logic." In *The Cambridge History of Later Medieval Philosophy*, ed. Norman Kretzman, Anthony Kenny, and Jan Pinborg. Cambridge: Cambridge University Press, 1982.

————. *Penser au moyen âge*. Paris: Editions du Seuil, 1991.

Liebeschütz, H. "Anselm of Canterbury: The Philosophical Interpretation of Faith." In *The Cambridge History of Later Greek and Early Medieval Philosophy*, ed. A. H. Armstrong. Cambridge: Cambridge University Press, 1967.

Little, A. G. "Guide to Franciscan Studies." *Études franciscaines* 41 (1929): 64–78.

Longpré, Ephrem. "Bonaventure." In *Catholicisme: Hier—Aujourd'hui—Demain*, ed. F. Jacquemet. Paris: Letouzey et Ané, 1950.

————. "Bonaventure." In *Dictionnaire de spiritualité*, ed. Marcel Viller, SJ. Paris: G. Beauchesne et ses fils, 1937.

————. "Bonaventure." In *Dictionnaire d'histoire et de géographie ecclésiastique*, ed. R. Aubert and E. Van Cauwenbergh. Paris: Letouzey et Ané, 1937.

————. "Saint Augustin et la pensée franciscaine." *France franciscaine* 15 (1932): 5–76.

————. "La théologie mystique de Saint Bonaventure." *Archivium franciscanum historicum* 14 (1921): 36–108.

Lottin, O. "La composition hylémorphique des substances spirituelles. Les débuts de la controversie." *Revue neo-scholastique de philosophie* 33 (1932): 21–41.

Lubac, Henri de. *Medieval Exegesis: The Four Senses of Scripture*. Translated by Mark Ebanc. Retrieval & Renewal: Ressourcement in Catholic Thought. Grand Rapids, Mich.: William B. Eerdmans Pub. Co., 1998; originally published as *Exégèse médiévale: Les quatre sens de l'écriture*. Paris: Éditions Montaigne, 1959.

Luciani, Albino card. "San Bonaventura ai cristiani di oggi." In *San Bonaventura maestro di vita francescana e di sapienza cristiana: Atti del congresso internazionale per il VII centario di san Bonaventura da Bagnoregio: Roma 19–26 settembre 1974*. Vol. 1. Rome: Pontificia Facoltà Teologica San Bonaventura, 1976.

Lutz, Eduar. *Die Psychologie Bonaventuras*. Münster: Aschendorf, 1909.

Maccagnolo, Enzo. "David of Dinant and the Beginnings of Aristotelianism in Paris." In *A History of Twelfth-Century Western Philosophy*, ed. Peter Dronke. New York: Cambridge University Press, 1988.

Madec, Goulven. "*Christus, scientia et sapientia nostra*. Le principe de cohérence de la doctrine augustinienne." *Recherches augustiniennes* 10 (1985): 77–85.

Majchrzak, Colman, OFM. *A Brief History of Bonaventurianism*. Pulaski, WI: Franciscan Publishers, 1957.

Marcil, George, OFM. "The Franciscan School." In *The History of Franciscan Theology*, ed. Kenan Osborne, OFM. St. Bonaventure, N.Y.: The Franciscan Institute, 1994, 319–320.

Marenbon, John. *Later Medieval Philosophy (1150–1350): An Introduction*. New York: Routledge & Kegan Paul, 1987.

Marion, Jean-Luc. *God without Being*. Translated by Thomas A. Carlson. Religion and Postmodernism Series. Chicago: University of Chicago Press, 1991.

Maritian, Jacques. "Language and the Theory of the Sign." In *Frontiers in Semiotics*, ed. John Deely, Brooke Williams, and Felicia Kruse. Bloomington: Indiana University Press, 1986.

Marrone, Steven P. *The Light of Thy Countenance: Science and Knowledge of God in the Thirteenth Century*. Studies in the History of Christian Thought, vol. 98, ed. Heiko A. Oberman. Boston: Brill, 2001.

Matthews, Gareth. *The Augustinian Tradition*. Berkeley: University of California Press, 1998.

Maurer, Armand, CSB. *Medieval Philosophy*. The Étienne Gilson Series, 4. Toronto: Pontifical Institute of Medieval Studies, 1982.

McCool, Gerald. *The Neo-Thomists*. Milwaukee, Wis.: Marquette University Press, 1994.

McEvoy, James. "Microcosm and Macrocosm in the Writings of St. Bonaventure." In *S. Bonaventura 1274–1974*. Vol. 2. Grottaferrata (Rome): Collegio S. Bonaventura, 1973, 309–343.

———. *Robert Grosseteste*. Great Medieval Thinkers. New York: Oxford University Press, 2000.

McGinn, Bernard, trans. *Apocalyptic Spirituality: Treatises and Letters of Lactantius, Adso of Montier-en-Der, Joachim of Fiore, The Spiritual Franciscans, Savonarola*. Classics of Western Spirituality. New York: Paulist Press, 1979.

———. *The Calabrian Abbot: Joachim of Fiore in the History of Western Thought*. New York: Macmillan Publishing Company, 1985.

———. *The Flowering of Mysticism: Men and Women in the New Mysticism (1200–1350)*. Vol. 3 of *The Presence of God: A History of Western Christian Mysticism*. New York: Crossroad, 1998.

McGrath, Alister E. *Iustitia Dei: A History of the Christian Doctrine of Justification*. 2d ed. New York: Cambridge University Press, 1998.

Miller, Sister Paula Jean, FSE, *Marriage: The Sacrament of Divine-Human Communion*. Quincy, IL: Franciscan Press, 1996.

Mistretta, Giambatista Ortoleva da. *L'Ontologismo e la Questione già inedita del serafico Dottore San Bonaventura su la cognizione certitudinale della verità* (Acireale: V. Strano, 1876), ed. Kenan B. Osborne. *The History of Franciscan Theology*. St. Bonaventure, N.Y.: The Franciscan Institute, 1994.

Monti, Dominic, OFM. Introduction to Vol. 5 of *The Works of Bonaventure: Saint Bonaventure's Writings Concerning the Franciscan Order*. St. Bonaventure, N.Y.: Franciscan Institute, 1994.

Moorman, John. *A History of the Franciscan Order: From Its Origins to the Year 1517*. Oxford: Clarendon Press, 1968.

———. *Medieval Franciscan Houses*. Franciscan Institute Publications, History Series, 4, ed. George Marcil, OFM. St. Bonaventure, N.Y.: Franciscan Institute, 1983.

———. *The Sources for the Life of St. Francis of Assisi*. Manchester: University Press, 1940.

Muckle, J. T. "Robert Grosseteste's Use of Greek Sources." *Medievalia et Humanistica* 3 (1945).

Murphy, Anthony. "Bonaventure." In *Medieval Philosophers*, ed. Jeremiah Hackett. Dictionary of Literary Biography, vol. 115. Detroit, Mich.: Bruccoli Clark Layman, 1992.

Noone, Timothy B. "Amalric of Bène." In *Dictionary of the Middle Ages*, ed. Joseph Strayer. Vol. 1. New York: Charles Scribner's Sons, 1982.

Nuchelmanns, Gabriel. *Theories of the Proposition: Ancient and Medieval Conceptions of the Bearers of Truth and Falsity*. Amsterdam: North-Holland Pub. Co., 1973.

O'Collins, Gerald, and Silvio Farrugia. *Catholicism: The Story of Catholic Christianity*. New York: Oxford University Press, 2003.

O'Donnell, Clement, OFM Conv. *The Psychology of St. Bonaventure and St. Thomas Aquinas*. Doctoral Dissertation for The Catholic University of America, 1937.

O'Leary, Conrad, OFM. *The Substantial Composition of Man According to Saint Bonaventure*. Doctoral Dissertation for The Catholic University of America, 1931.

O'Meara, John, J. "Augustine and Neoplatonism." *Recherches augustiniennes* 1 (1958): 91–111.

———. "The Neoplatonism of Saint Augustine." In *Neoplatonism and Christian Thought*, ed. Dominic J. O'Meara. Studies in Neoplatonism: Ancient and Modern, vol. 3. Albany, N.Y.: State University of New York Press, 1982.

———. *The Young Augustine: The Growth of St. Augustine's Mind Up to Conversion*. New York: Longmans, Green, and Company, 1954.

Oromi, Miguel, OFM. "Ejemplarismo metafísico." Introduction to *Colaciones sobre el Hexaémeron o Iluminaciones de la Iglesia*, ed. Leon Aboros, OFM, Bernardo Aperribay, OFM, and Miguel Oromi, OFM. In vol. 3 of *Obras de San Buenaventura*. 2d ed. *Biblioteca Autores Cristianos*, vol. 19. Madrid: Biblioteca de Autores Cristianos, 1957.

Oroz-Reta, José. "Aristotelismo y Agustinismo en la doctrina de san Buenaventura." In *San Bonaventura maestro di vita francescana e di sapienza cristiana: Atti del congresso internazionale per il VII centenario di san Bonaventura da Bagnoregio: Roma, 19–26 settembre 1974*. Vol. 1. Rome: Pontificia Facoltà Telogica San Bonaventura, 1976.

Osborne, Thomas, Jr., "*Unibilitas*: The Key to Bonaventure's Understanding of Human Nature." *Journal of the History of Philosophy* 37 (1999): 227–251.

Ott, Ludwig. *Fundamentals of Catholic Dogma*. Translated by Patrick Lynch. St. Louis, Mo.: B. Herder Book Co., 1954.

Pattin, Adrian, OMI, ed., "Le *Liber de causis* Édition établie à l'aide de 90 manuscripts avec introduction et notes." *Tijdschrift voor Filosofie* 28 (1966): 90–203.

Pegis, Anton. "The Dilemma of Being and Unity." In *Essays in Thomism*, ed. Robert E. Brennan, OP. New York: Sheed and Ward, 1942.

———. "St. Bonaventure, St. Francis, and Philosophy." *Medieval Studies* 15 (1953): 1–13.

―――. "St. Bonaventure Revisited." In S. Bonaventura 1224–1974. Vol. 2. Grottaferrata (Rome): Collegio S. Bonaventura, 1973.

―――. St. Thomas and the Problem of the Soul in the Thirteenth Century. Toronto:
Pontifical Mediaeval Studies, 1978.

Peifer, John Frederick. The Concept in Thomism. New York: Bookman Associates,
Inc., 1952.

Philo. De opificio mundi. In The Works of Philo. Translated by C. D. Yonge. Pea-
body, Mass.: Hendrickson Publishers, 1994.

Pieper, Josef. Scholasticism. New York: Pantheon Books, 1967.

Polidori, Maria Luisi. Cività and Bagnoregio. Florence: Bonechi, 1999.

Portalié, Eugène, SJ. A Guide to the Thought of Saint Augustine. Chicago: Henry
Regnery Company, 1960.

Pourrat, Pierre. Theology of the Sacraments: A Study in Positive Theology. St. Louis:
B. Herder, 1910.

Quaracchi Editors. "Disertatio de eius vita." In vol. 10 of Doctoris seraphici S.
Bonaventurae opera omnia: operum omnium complementum. Ad. Claras Aquas
(Quarracchi): Collegium S. Bonaventurae, 1891.

Quinn, John F. "Certitude of Reason and Faith in St. Bonaventure and St. Thomas." In St. Thomas Aquinas 1274–1974, Commemorative Studies. Vol. 2. Toronto: Pontifical Institute of Medieval Studies, 1974, 105–140.

―――. "The Chronology of St. Bonaventure (1217–1257)." Franciscan Studies
32 (1972): 168–186.

―――. The Historical Constitution of Saint Bonaventure's Philosophy. Toronto: Pontifical Institute of Mediaeval Studies, 1973.

―――. "The Moral Philosophy of St. Bonaventure." Southwestern Journal of Philosophy 5 (1974): 39–70.

Ratzinger, Joseph. Milestones: Memoirs 1927–1977. Trans. Erasmo Leiva-Merikakis.
San Francisco: Ignatius Press, 1998.

―――. The Theology of History in St. Bonaventure. Chicago: Franciscan Herald
Press, 1989.

Reeves, Marjorie. Joachim of Fiore and the Prophetic Future. London: Society for
the Promotion of Christian Knowledge, 1976.

―――. "The Originality and Influence of Joachim of Fiore." Traditio 36 (1980):
271–288.

Régnon, Théodore de, SJ. Études de théologie positive sur la sainte Trinité, 3 vols.
Paris: Victor Retaux et Fils, 1892–1898.

Reynolds, Philip L. "Analogy of Names in Bonaventure." Medieval Studies 65
(2003): 117–162.

―――. "Bonaventure's Theory of Resemblance." Traditio 49 (2003): 219–255.

―――. "Threefold Existence and Illumination in St. Bonaventure." Franciscan
Studies 17 (1982): 206–229.

Richard of St. Victor. Richard of St. Victor: Selections. Translated by Grover Zinn.
Classics of Western Spirituality. New York: Paulist Press, 1979.

Robert, Patrice. "Le problème de la philosophique bonaventureienne: Discipline autonome ou heteronome?" *Laval théologique et philosophique* 7 (1951): 36–43.

Robinson, Pascal. "Bonaventure," *Catholic Encyclopedia*. New York: Robert Appleton Company, 1907.

Robson, Michael, OFM Conv. "Saint Anselm and the Franciscan Tradition." In *Robert Grosseteste: New Perspectives on His Thought and Scholarship*, ed. James McEvoy. Instrumenta Patristica XXVII. Turnhout, Belgium: Brepols Publishers, 1995, 223–256.

——— *St. Francis of Assisi: The Legend and the Life*. London: Geoffrey Chapman, 1997.

Roch, Robert, SJ. "The Philosophy of St. Bonaventure—A Controversy." *Franciscan Studies* 19 (1959): 209–226.

Roest, Bert. *A History of Franciscan Education (c. 1210–1517)*. Education and Society in the Middle Ages and Renaissance, vol. 11. Boston: Brill, 2000.

Russell, R. P. "Augustinianism." *New Catholic Encyclopedia*. Vol. 1. New York: McGraw-Hill Book Company, 1967, 1065–1066.

Russo, Renato. *La metodologia del sapere nel sermone di S. Bonaventura "Unus est magister vester Christus."* Grottaferrata: Editiones Collegii S. Bonaventurae, 1982.

S. Bonaventura 1274–1974. Vol. 1, *Dottore Serafico: nelle rafigurazione degli artisti*; Vol. 2, *Studia: de vita, mente, fontibus et operibus*; Vol. 3, *Philosophica*; Vol. 4, *Theologica*; Vol. 5, *Bibliographica Bonaventuriana*. Grottaferrata (Rome): Collegio S. Bonaventura, 1974.

Sabatier, Paul. *Vie de Saint François d'Assise*. Paris: Fischbacker, 1894.

Scheffczyk, Leo. *Creation and Providence*. Translated by Richard Strachan. The Herder History of Dogma. New York: Herder and Herder, 1970.

Schufeider, Gregory. *Confessions of a Rational Mystic*. Purdue University Series in the History of Philosophy. West Lafayette, Ind.: Purdue University Press, 1994.

Schwendinger, F. "Die Erkenntnis in den ewigen Ideen nach der Lehre des hl. Bonaventura." *Franziskanische Studien* 15 (1928): 69–95, 193–244; 16 (1929): 29–64.

Shahan, Robert W., and Francis J. Kovach, eds. *Bonaventure and Aquinas: Enduring Philosophers*. Norman: University of Oklahoma Press, 1976.

Sharp. D. E., "The Philosophy of Richard Fishacre." *The New Scholasticism* 7 (October 1933): 281–282.

Smalley, Beryl. *The Study of the Bible in the Middle Ages*. 2d ed. Notre Dame, Ind.: University of Notre Dame Press, 1964.

Smeets, E. "Bonaventure." In *Dictionnaire de théologie catholique*, ed. A. Vacant, E. Mangenot, and É. Amann. Paris: Libraire Letouzey et Ané, 1932.

Sokolowski, Robert. "Matter, Elements and Substance in Aristotle." *Journal of the History of Philosophy* 8 (July 1970): 263–288.

Sorabji, Richard. "Infinity and the Creation." In *Philoponus and the Rejection of*

Aristotelian Science. Ed. Richard Sorabji. Ithaca, NY: Cornell University Press, 1987, 164–178.

Sorrell, Roger D. *St. Francis of Assisi and Nature: Tradition and Innovation in Western Christian Attitudes toward the Environment.* New York: Oxford University Press, 1988.

Southern, R. W. *Saint Anselm: A Portrait in a Landscape.* Cambridge: Cambridge University Press, 1990.

————. *Scholastic Humanism and the Unification of Europe.* Vol. 2. *The Heroic Age.* Malden, Mass.: Blackwell Publishers, 2001.

————. *St. Anselm and His Biographer.* Cambridge: Cambridge University Press, 1966.

Spade, Paul Vincent. "Late Medieval Logic." In *Medieval Philosophy*, ed. John Marenbon. *Routledge History of Philosophy*, vol. 3. New York: Routledge, 1997, 402–425.

Speer, Andreas. "Bonaventure and the Question of a Medieval Philosophy." *Medieval Philosophy and Theology* 6 (March 1997): 25–46.

————. Commentary on *Quaestiones disputatae de scientia Christi.* Hamburg: Meiner, 1992.

————. "The Discovery of Nature: The Contribution of the Chartrians to Twelfth Century Attempts to Found a *Scientia Naturalis.*" *Traditio* 52 (1997):135–151.

————. "*Metaphysica reducens*: Metaphysik als erste Wissenschaft im Verständnis Bonaventuras." *Wissenschaft und Weisheit* 49 (1986): 169ff.

————. *Triplex Veritas: Wahrheitsverständnis und philosophische Denkform Bonaventuras.* Franziskanische Forschunge 32. Werl in Westfalen: Dietrich Coelde, 1987.

Stiebing, Hans. "Bonaventura's Einteilung der Wissenschaften als Beleg fur universalkategoriales Vorgehen in der Wissenschaftstheorie des Mittelalters." In *Sprache und Erkenntnis im Mittelalter: Akten des VI. internationalen Kongresses fur mittelalterliche Philosophie der société internationale pour l étude de la philosophie médiévale, 29 August–3 September 1977 in Bonn*, ed. J. Beckmann. Vol. 2. Berlin: de Gruyter, 1981.

Stohr, A. *Die Trinitätslehre des hl. Bonaventura: Eine systematische Darstellung und historiche Würdigung* (Münster: Aschendorf, 1923.

Studer, B. "*Sacramentum et exemplum* chez saint Augustin." In *Studia Patristica*, ed. E. Livingstone. Vol. 16, Part 2.

Szabo, Titus. *De SS. Trinitate in creaturis refulgente.* Rome: Orbis Catholicus, 1955.

Tavard, G. H. "The Coincidence of Opposites: A Recent Interpretation of Bonaventure." *Theological Studies* 41 (1980): 576–584.

Théry, G., OP. *Autour du décret 1210: I-David de Dinant: Étude sur son panthéisme matérialiste.* Bibliothèque thomiste, ed. Pierre Mandonnet, OP. Kain, Belgium: Le Saulchoir, 1925.

Thomas of Celano, *The Remembrance of the Desire of a Soul.* In *The Founder*, vol. 2 of *Francis of Assisi: The Early Documents*, ed. Regis J. Armstrong, OFM Cap. et al. New York: New City Press, 2000.

Thomson, Williell R. *Friars in the Cathedral: The First Franciscan Bishops 1226–1261*. Toronto: Pontifical Institute of Medieval Studies, 1975.

Todisco, Orlando. "Interpretazione simbolica del pensiero di S. Bonaventura." *Studie ricerche francescane* 4 (1975): 199–226.

Torrell, Jean-Pierre, OP. *Saint Thomas Aquinas*. 2 vols. Translated by Robert Royal. Washington, D.C.: The Catholic University of America Press, 1996.

Ubaghs, Gérard Casimir. *De mente S. Bonaventurae circa modum quo Deus ab homine cognoscitur*. Louvain: Typographie de Vanlinthout, 1859.

————. *Essai d'idéologie ontologique ou considérations philosophiques sur la nature de nos idées et sur l'ontologisme en général*. Louvain: Typographie de Vanlinthout, 1860.

Van Caenegem, R. C. *Guide to the Sources of Medieval History*. Europe in the Middle Ages Series. Vol. 2. New York: North-Holland Publishing Company, 1978.

Van Fleteren, Frederick. "The Ascent of the Soul in the Augustinian Tradition." In *Paradigms in Medieval Thought Applications in Medieval Disciplines: A Symposium*, ed. Nancy Van Deusen and Alvin E. Ford. Lewiston, New York: Edwin Mellon Press, 1990.

Van Steenberghen, Fernand. *Aristotle in the West: The Origins of Latin Aristotelianism*. Louvain: E. Nauwelaerts, Publisher, 1955.

————. *The Philosophical Movement in the Thirteenth Century*. Edinburgh: Nelson, 1955.

————. *La philosophie au XIII siècle*. 2d ed. Paris: Institut supérieur de philosophie, 1991.

————. "Saint Bonaventure contre l'éternité du monde." In *S. Bonaventura: 1224–1974*. Rome: Collegio S. Bonaventura, 1974, 259–278.

————. *Siger de Brabant d'après ses oevres inédites*. Louvain: Édtions de l'Institute supérieur de philosophie, 1931.

Van Winden, J.C.M., OFM. *Chalcidius on Matter: His Doctrine and Sources: A Chapter in the History of Platonism*. Philosophia Antiqua, vol. 9. Leiden: E. J. Brill, 1959.

Veuthey, Léon. "Les divers courants de la philosophie augustino-franciscaine au moyen age." In *Scholastica ratione historico-critica instauranda*, Acta Congressus Scholastici Internationalis Rome, 1950. Rome: Pontificium Athenaeum Antonianum, 1951.

————. *S. Bonaventurae philosophia christiana*. Rome: Officium Libri Catholici, 1943.

Vinck, José de. "Two Aspects of the Theory of the *Rationes Seminales* in the Writings of Bonaventure." In *S. Bonaventura 1274–1974*. Vol. 3. Grottaferrata (Rome): Collegio S. Bonaventura, 1973.

Von Balthasar, Hans Urs. "Bonaventure." In *Studies in Theological Style: Clerical Styles*. Vol. 2 of *The Glory of the Lord*. Translated by Andrew Louth, Francis McDonagh, and Brian McNeil. San Francisco: Ignatius Press, 1984, 260–362.

————. "Denys." In *Studies in Theological Style: Clerical Styles*. Vol. 2 of *The Glory of the Lord.* Translated by Andrew Louth, Francis McDonagh, and Brian McNeil. San Francisco: Ignatius Press, 1984, 260–362.

Wallace, William, OP. *The Modeling of Nature.* Washington, D.C.: The Catholic University of America Press, 1998.

Walz, Matthew D. "Theological and Philosophical Dependences in St. Bonaventure's Argument against an Eternal World and a Brief Thomistic Reply." *American Catholic Philosophical Quarterly* 72 (1998): 75–98.

Wéber, Édouard-Henri, OP. *Dialogue et dissensions entre Saint Bonaventure et St. Thomas d'Aquin à Paris (1252–1273).* Bibliothèque Thomiste XLI, ed. M. D. Chenu. Paris: Librairie Philosophique J. Vrin, 1974.

Weisheipl, James, OP. "Albertus Magnus and Universal Hylomorphism: Avicebron: A Note on Thirteenth-Century Augustinianism." *The Southwestern Journal of Philosophy* 10 (Fall 1979): 239–260.

Wenin, Christian. *Thesaurus Bonaventurianus.* Louvain: Université catholique de Louvain, 1972.

Wolter, Hans. "The Papacy at the Height of Its Power, 1198 to 1216." In *Handbook of Church History: From the High Middle Ages to the Eve of the Reformation,* ed. Hubert Jedin and John Dolan; trans. Anselm Biggs. New York: Herder and Herder, 1970, v. 4.

Woo, Esther. "Theophanic Cosmic Order in St. Bonaventure." *Franciscan Studies* 32 (1973): 306–330.

Wulf, Maurice de. "Augustinisme et aristotélisme au XIII siècle." *Revue néoscolastique* (1901).

Zinn, Grover A. "Book and Word: The Victorine Background of Bonaventure's Use of Symbols." In *S. Bonaventura 1224–1974.* Vol. 2. Grottaferrata (Rome): Collegio S. Bonaventura, 1973.

———. "Hugh of St. Victor." In *Dictionary of the Middle Ages,* ed. Joseph R. Strayer. Vol. 6. New York: Charles Scribner's Sons, 1985.

Index

Abate, Giuseppe, 189n25
Abelard, Peter, 5
Abraham, 115, 147, 166
abstraction, 57–58
accident(s), 174
act, 45
  pure, 61, 70
actuality (*entelechy*), 52, 61
Adam, 115, 138, 144, 176
Aertsen, Jan, xii
Aeterni Patris, 32
affection, social, 108
Albert the Great, 34, 35, 40, 41
Alexander of Alexandria, 21
Alexander of Hales, xiii, 10, 20, 49,
    61, 77, 89, 121–22
  Summa fratris Alexandri, 20, 155,
    193n71
Alexandrines, 79
Al-Ghazali, 143
alterity, principle of, 45
Amaury of Bene, 41
Ambrose of Milan, St., 174
analogy, 66
  analogical names, 67
  analogical resemblance, 67

anamnesis, 63
Anaxagoras, 47
angel(s), 45, 54, 109, 131–32, 135
Anselm of Canterbury, St., 8, 68, 74,
    99, 122, 137, 142, 146–47, 161,
    193n71
  ontological proof, 65
  satisfaction theory of, 147
  truth, notion of, 86
Anselm of Canterbury, works of
  *De conceptu virginali et originali
    peccato*, 211n2
  De veritate, 161
  Monologion, 122
Anselm of Laon, 4
Anthony of Padua, St., xiii, 7
apophatic tradition, 26, 185
Apostles' Creed, 146–47, 180
Appenine Mountains, 9
appetite, 99, 106, 182
  concupiscible, 95, 99, 136
  irascible, 99, 101, 136
Aquinas. *See* Thomas Aquinas, St.
arguments
  from authority, 29, 35
  from reason, 29, 35

and trinitarian theology, 118
Scholastics, 59, 86, 99, 182
Schwendinger, F., 204n86
science, modern, 39–40
scripture, sacred, 7, 29, 31, 89, 114,
    162
  allegorical interpretation of, 114,
    116, 117
  anagogical, 116, 117
  interpretation, 114
  literal interpretation, 114, 116
  moral interpretation, 116
  and theology, 209nn1–2
scripture, sacred, books of. *See
  individual books*
self-knowledge, 95
self-transcendence, 186
seminal reasons (*rationes seminales*),
    47, 51, 198n41
semiotics, 25–26. *See also* metaphysics:
  semiotic
sense(s)
  external, 31, 55
  internal, 55
separationism, 187n1, 195n30
Sermon on the Mount, 162
serpent, 135–36
sexual intercourse, 176
sign, 84, 166–70, 172, 174
  demonstrative, 169
  external, 176
  intentional (*signa data*), 25
  and signified, 76
  and Truth, 84
  world as, 106, 108
signification, 169
  allegorical, 169
  proper, 169
Silic, Rufin, 12
sin, 104–5, 135–39, 158–59, 171
  mortal, 138–39, 175, 181
  venial, 138–39
  See also original sin
Sirach, book of, 138
sloth, 96

social animal, 109, 139
social orders (conjugal, domestic, and
    civil), 108
society, 109
sola scriptura, 114
Son of God, 75
soteriology, 141
soul
  Aristotle's definition of, 52
  and body, 46
  capacity for God (*capax Dei*), 93
  creation of, 132
  diseases of, 98
  greatness of (magnanimity), 103
  image of trinity, 129
  mover (*motor*) of body, 54
  passions of, 98
  powers of, 51, 54–56
  rational, 51, 132
  and unitability, 53–54
species (sensible likeness), 57, 67, 130,
    174–75
spiritual theology, 19
Stoics, 31, 42, 183
studia generalia, 7
subordinationism, 143
substance, 44–45, 174
  composite (*hoc aliquid*), 54
  and plurality of substantial forms,
    50
  as sign, 25
  universal, 72
Supreme Being. *See* Being, Supreme
synderesis, 105–6, 135

temperance, 99, 100
theology, 23, 25, 114
  and philosophy, xii, 27, 28, 29, 32
  as practical science, 184
  and sacred scripture, 209nn1–2
  as sapiential habit, 23
  as way of life, 23
Thomas Aquinas, St., 18, 33, 34, 35,
    40, 41, 49, 58, 62, 86, 99, 113,
    150, 159, 205n113

LaVergne, TN USA
09 January 2010
169451LV00002B/2/P